PAULINE MYSTICISM

PAULINE MYSTICISM

CHRIST IN THE MYSTICAL TEACHING OF ST. PAUL

ALFRED WIKENHAUSER

HERDER
FREIBURG

NELSON
EDINBURGH-LONDON

This translation by Joseph Cunningham

is based on the second German edition of "Die Christusmystik des Apostels Paulus",

published by Herder, Freiburg, 1956

First edition published 1960 by Herder, Freiburg, West Germany

and Nelson, Edinburgh-London

Library of Congress Catalog Card Number: 60-8091

© 1960 by Herder KG

Made and printed by Herder Druck, Freiburg, West Germany

Contents

Preface

THE mystical union between the faithful and Christ has been described as the heart of St. Paul's piety. The Apostle was a profound thinker who traced the foundations of Christian Theology. But in texts like Gal. 2:20, Phil. 1:21, and Col. 3:4, he appears above all as fervent disciple of the crucified and risen Christ, the Apostle whose very life after his conversion was Christ. St. Paul makes it quite clear that this mystical union with Christ was not a personal privilege reserved for himself or for a chosen few. It is a precious gift which God gives to every Christian, and it carries with it serious obligations.

The present work was the first study of St. Paul's mysticism to appear from a Catholic source. It is the author's hope that the present revised and expanded edition will meet a need at the present day when there is an increased interest in Biblical Theology.

Freiburg im Breisgau,
November, 1955.

Translator's Note

For the citations from Scripture I have used the Challoner revision of the Rheims-Douay version. There are occasions when it does not interpret certain texts in exactly the same way as the author of this book. But such disagreements cause no real difficulty, and they are, I believe, inevitable, no matter which version is used.

Most of the quotations from pagan sources have been checked against the originals.

Some of the books mentioned in the bibliography have appeared in English, for example, Rhode's *Psyche,* and Nilsson's *A History of Greek Religion.* However, I have retained Professor Wikenhauser's references, except in the case of Prat's *Théologie de S. Paul,* the English version of which appears in many priests' bookcases.

I would like to express here my gratitude to those who in various ways assisted me in this work.

St. Malachy's College, Belfast,
March 1959.

Abbreviations

PhilolWschr	=	Philologische Wochenschrift
ThStKr	=	Theologische Studien und Kritiken
ThWb	=	Theologisches Wörterbuch zum Neuen Testament, edited by G. Kittel and G. Friedrich
ZntW	=	Zeitschrift für die neutestamentliche Wissenschaft
ZsystTh	=	Zeitschrift für systematische Theologie

Introduction

Is there a mystical element in the theology and spirituality of St. Paul? Was St. Paul influenced by the mysticism of his time? These two questions have provoked lively discussion among modern scholars.[1] The interest in these problems is partly due to a growing appreciation of mysticism in our time even outside the Catholic Church; another factor is the popularity of studies of the Oriental and Hellenistic religions and their spirituality.

There is no agreement among scholars concerning the exact nature of mysticism, and this is an obstacle to any study of St. Paul's mysticism. It is more than eighty years since Heinrich Denifle, who had an extensive knowledge of the medieval mystics, complained that the concept of mysticism is the most ill-defined and fluid concept in all theology,[2] and this judgement

Note: Where the titles of works or articles are abbreviated in these footnotes, the full title will be found in the Bibliography at the end of the book.

[1] See Deissmann, *Paulus* ([2]1925), p. 111, note 1, and the two articles by M. Dibelius mentioned in the Bibliography. But Catholic studies of St. Paul's mysticism have been sporadic and not very detailed: the principal Catholic studies are: Bartmann, *Paulus,* pp. 74–113; Meinertz, "Mystik und Mission bei Paulus" in *Zeitschrift für Miss.-Wiss.,* xiii (1923), pp. 1–12; Soiron, "Die Christusmystik des hl. Paulus" in *Akad. Bonif.-Korresp.,* xxxix (1923–4), pp. 27–37; J. B. Colon (see Bibliography); J. Huby (ibid.); and W. Grossouw, *In Christ* (Westminster, Maryland, 1952).

[2] *Hist.-pol. Blätter* (1875), p. 685.

applies with even greater force to present-day studies in Comparative Religion. It is no great exaggeration to say that each scholar has his own idea: some restrict the term mysticism to a small number of phenomena in the spiritual life, while others apply it to a wider field. That is why theologians do not agree about whether there is a mystical element at all in St. Paul's spirituality. Some deny it entirely, while others say that he was steeped in Hellenistic mysticism. Others again concede that there are strong mystical elements in his spirituality.

The antipathy of most Protestants towards mysticism has contributed to this state of affairs. The theory that Christian mysticism is an offshoot from Neo-platonism, and that it is a debased form of Christian piety, was fathered by Albrecht Ritschl (1822–1889). Since his time Protestant students of Theology and Comparative Religion have confined the term mysticism to the ecstatic union with God which Plotinus († A.D. 270) described.[3] In recent years, however, there has been a tendency to return to the older use of the term mysticism, and to reject this restricted meaning as an unwarranted innovation.[4]

The present study takes the word mysticism in its wider sense as meaning – not only in Christian theology, but also in Comparative Religion generally – *that form of spirituality which strives after (or experiences) an immediate contact (or union) of the soul with God.* This "union" appears in a number of modes, and the term mysticism cannot be restricted to any one of them; there are diverse forms of mysticism, though some are superior to others.

[3] See E. Peterson, "Zur Methode der Mystik", in *ZsystTh,* ii (1924), p. 146 et seq.

[4] See Deissmann, *Paulus,* p. 117 et seq.

The present work deals with union with Christ in the mysticism of St. Paul. We intend first to examine the nature of this
union and the terms by which Paul describes it. This is to be
followed by an investigation of how the union is brought
about. Finally we will show where it differs from other types
of mysticism, and contrast it with the Oriental and Hellenistic
mysticism of St. Paul's time. St. Paul's idea of the Mystical
Body of Christ would be relevant here, but as we have dealt
with it elsewhere it will not be treated at length.[5]

[5] A. Wikenhauser, *Die Kirche als der mystische Leib Christi nach dem
Apostel Paulus* (Münster, ²1940).

I

The Forms in which St. Paul expresses his Doctrine

NONE of St. Paul's epistles contains a set exposition of his doctrine of union with Christ. To reach a definition – or rather a description – of what he meant by mystical union with Christ, we must therefore investigate his numerous statements and allusions concerning the interior religious relationship which exists between himself – and Christians generally – on the one hand, and Christ, the Triumphant Lord, on the other. This task is difficult, but not impossible.

The ancients had no noun for mysticism.[1] There was an adjective μυστικός meaning "occult", and particularly "the initiated" or "concerning the Mysteries"; there was also a verb μυεῖσθαι which meant "to be initiated". The adjective occurs neither in Paul nor in any other New Testament writer.[2] The verb is used once by Paul, in Phil. 4:12; but it is impossible to determine whether this carries the connotation of initiation into the Mysteries ("everywhere and in all things I am instruct-

---

[1] See Leisegang, *PhilolWschr* (1924), p. 137 et seq.

[2] τὰ μυστικά = The Mysteries, e.g., Thucydides, vi, 28.

ed"), or if it simply means in a general way that he is "familiar" with all.[3]

The noun "mysterium" occurs twenty-one times in Paul.[4] But his use of the word does not shed any light on his mysticism. In the language of the pagan Mystery Religions the word "mysterium" meant a ceremony or a truth which must be kept secret. This is not its meaning in St. Paul; he uses it to refer to the mysterious divine decree, decided from eternity and hidden in God, concerning the work of human salvation which was manifested, carried out, and completed in Christ.

This meaning of the word is clearly expressed in 1 Cor. 2:6 et seq.: "Howbeit we speak wisdom among the perfect: yet not the wisdom of this world, neither of the princes of this world that come to nought. But we speak the wisdom of God in a mystery, a wisdom which is hidden, which God ordained before the world unto our glory: which none of the princes of this world knew. For if they had known it, they would never have crucified the Lord of glory."

It is only at the end of time that the divine decree shall be fully revealed and brought to completion: hence a special eschatological significance often attaches to the word "mysterium" in Paul, as for example in 1 Cor. 15:51: "Behold, I tell you a mystery. We shall all indeed rise again: but we shall not all be changed"; and Rom. 11:25: "For I would not have you

---

[3] See G. Bornkamm, *ThWb*, iv, 834: "The concrete problems and gifts of everyday life are the place where Paul suffers the 'mysteries', i.e., experiences the power of Christ." See also Windisch, *Paulus und Christus*, p. 217 et seq.

[4] G. Bornkamm, Art. μυστήριον in *ThWb*, iv, 809–34 (825–8: *The Mystery of Christ*).

ignorant, brethren, of this mystery" (i.e., of the final conversion of Israel).

Whatever the precise shade of meaning, the word "mysterium" always refers to truths which of themselves are unattainable by men, and which can be revealed only by God.

The question of what St. Paul meant by mystical union with Christ must therefore be approached from another angle. The problem should be posed in this form: What expressions does St. Paul use concerning the mysterious union between himself – and indeed all Christians – and the person of Christ Triumphant? How exactly does he describe this union? What does he say about its nature and character?

All mysticism may be reduced to two fundamentals: the entry of man into the Divinity and the entry of the Divinity into man.[5] Either man rises to God, or God descends to man. These two kinds of mystical union with God may appear together, or one may appear without the other. The latter kind, the indwelling of the Divinity in man, is usually found in primitive religions; when it occurs in higher forms of religion, the emphasis is generally on drawing the divine Spirit into the human soul.

For Paul also, fellowship with Christ is marked by the fact that man is in Christ and Christ is in man. Paul uses both expressions: "in Christ" and "Christ in us". But "in Christ" is much the more common of the two.

There are some texts where both ideas are closely linked. A particularly clear example is Rom. 8:8 et seq.: "And they who are in the flesh cannot please God. But you are not in the

---

[5] See Reitzenstein, *Hellenist. Mysterienreligionen,* pp. 73, 381.

19

flesh, but in the spirit, if so be that the Spirit of God dwell in you." The following words show that this "Spirit of God" is also the Spirit of Christ: "Now if any man have not the Spirit of Christ he is none of his. And if Christ be in you, the body indeed is dead, because of sin: but the spirit liveth, because of justification." There is a link between being in Christ and possessing Christ – or the Spirit of Christ; anyone who is "in Christ" – i.e., who belongs to his Body – also possesses the Spirit of Christ. The phrase "Christ in us" is not so frequent (see below II, 3), because it is through the Spirit that Christ dwells and works in us (see II, 2 and 3).

The same thought is probably expressed in 1 Cor. 12:12 et seq., where Paul compares the members of the Mystical Body of Christ to the limbs of a human body. The relation between Christ and those who are his is like the relation between the limbs and the body; although there are many limbs, yet they form the unity of one body: "For in *one* Spirit were we all baptized into *one* body . . . and in *one* Spirit we have all been made to drink." The Apostle's meaning is that by Baptism the Christians have been incorporated into Christ and have all received the Spirit of Christ. They are all surrounded and permeated by the one spiritual Christ, and so are joined into a unit.[6]

The same truth is expressed more briefly and more simply

[6] There are two ways of translating and understanding 1 Cor. 12:13 a: 1. The *one* Spirit, which all receive in Baptism, makes the *one* Body: εἰς (ἐν σῶμα) denotes the purpose or the effect. This is the exegesis of Joh. Weiß, Lietzmann, and Allo of this text; also Oepke in *ThWb,* ii, 537, and Schlier, *Galaterbrief,* p. 62, note 3: "What arises or appears by means of Baptism is the Body of Christ as the Church." 2. The other interpretation of this text is that by Baptism one is incorporated into the Body of Christ – a spiritual Body – which already exists. This is the

in Col. 2:6: "As therefore you have received Jesus Christ the Lord, walk ye in him: rooted and built up in him." Phil. 3:8–9 differs from this only by referring to the future: "I count them" (i.e., all things) "but as dung, that I may gain Christ and may be found in him."[7] "Being found in Christ" is something which takes place in this life, not merely in the life to come. The goal of Paul's endeavour is to appear even outwardly as one who truly "is in Christ" (see the expression in 1 Cor. 2:4).

These texts show that "to be in Christ" and "to have Christ in oneself" are simply the two aspects of one and the same idea: the Christian is in a mysterious vital union with Christ, and all his actions are performed under Christ's influence.

We will now examine each of these facets of union with Christ more closely.

1. "IN CHRIST"

The Christian abides in Christ. This is one aspect of union with Christ. St. Paul expresses it in various ways, but his favourite phrase is "in Christ (Jesus)" or "in the Lord".

Adolf Deissmann of Berlin, although a Protestant, was a vig–

view of Percy, *Der Leib Christi in den paulinischen Homologumena* (Lund, 1942), p. 15 et seq., and of O. Casel, *Archiv f. Liturgiewissenschaft,* i (1950), p. 302, and of Kümmel in Lietzmann (4th ed.), ad loc. Probably verse 13b ("in one Spirit we have all been made to drink") also refers to Baptism, and not to the Eucharist or Confirmation (this is also Allo's view, ad loc.). There is correspondence between βαπτισθῆναι (baptized) and ποτισθῆναι (made to drink). There is a remarkable parallel in Mark 10:38: "Can you drink (πιεῖν) of the chalice that I drink of, or be baptized with the baptism (βαπτισθῆναι) wherewith I am baptized?"

[7] See L. Brun, *Symbolae Arctoae,* i, 23; Dibelius, ad loc.

orous champion of St. Paul's mysticism. In 1892 he published a study of the phrase "in Christ",[8] where he showed that this phrase – and "in the Lord" – occurs in 164 places in the Pauline writings, including the Pastoral Epistles. He considers that Paul uses this phrase to express the closest conceivable union between the Christian and Christ the triumphant spiritual Lord, and he finds this meaning in every single case where the phrase occurs: "This favourite phrase of Paul's had for him a malleable mystical significance."[9] He does not claim that the phrase has always precisely the same full significance, and he admits that in some passages it has already become a congealed term.

Deissmann's thesis has been vigorously assailed. There are some scholars who deny absolutely that the phrase "in Christ" has any mystical content; indeed they do not agree that the doctrine of mystical union with Christ is to be found in Paul at all.[10] However, most scholars content themselves with saying that Deissmann's interpretation cannot be upheld in all 164 cases,[11] and it is true that Deissmann goes too far, for a number of these texts cannot be construed as expressions of this doctrine, as they cannot refer to the interior permanent vital union between the Christian and his exalted Lord.

---

[8] *Die neutestamentliche Formel "in Christo Jesu"* (Marburg, 1892).

[9] Deissmann, *Paulus*, p. 111: "Dieses urpaulinische Losungswort 'in Christus' ist plastisch mystisch empfunden."

[10] See E. v. Dobschütz in *ThStKr*, xcv (1923–4), p. 326 et seq.; idem, *Der Apostel Paulus*, i, p. 42 et seq.; J. Bang in *Norsk Theologisk Tidskrift* (1920), pp. 35–88; pp. 97–128.

[11] Joh. Weiss in *ThStKr* (1896), pp. 1–33; *Urchristentum*, p. 359 et seq.; H. Böhlig in *Neutest. Studien* for G. Heinrici (Leipzig, 1914), p. 170 et seq.; F. Prat, *Theology of St. Paul*, ii, p. 391 et seq., note M.; L. Brun in *Symbolae Arctoae*, i, p. 19 et seq.; H. E. Weber in *Neue kirchl. Zeitschr.*

There are two groups of such texts:

1. Those in which the phrase is due to the influence of the LXX on St. Paul's language, or where Hellenistic usage provides an explanation. In such cases the words "in Christ" do not form a phrase, for the preposition is really attached to the preceding verb. There are not many passages of this kind:

(a) To boast[12] "in Christ" in 1 Cor. 1:31; 2 Cor. 10:17; Phil. 3:3. In these three cases the preposition ἐν (in) goes with the verb, for Paul elsewhere uses the preposition ἐν (in) after the verb "to boast" where English uses "of" – thus, "makest thy boast of God" Rom. 2:17; "we glory in God" Rom. 5:11; "glory in men" 1 Cor. 3:21; 2 Thess. 1:4; "boast of the law" Rom. 2:23; "in tribulations" Rom. 5:3; "in other men's labours" 2 Cor. 10:15; "in my infirmities" 2 Cor. 12:9; "in the cross" Gal. 6:14.

On the other hand, there are three passages – Rom. 15:17; 1 Cor. 15:31; and Phil. 1:26 – where "in Christ" denotes the sphere in which the activity takes place.

(b) To hope: 1 Cor. 15:19, "If in this life (i.e., for this life) only we have hope in Christ, we are of all men most miserable". In this text Christ is the object of our hope; the construction is an imitation of the LXX. See Psalm 55:5; Judges 9:26; 4 Kings 18:5.

(1920), p. 215 et seq.; P. Feine, *Der Apostel Paulus,* p. 559 et seq.; F. Büchsel, *Der Geist Gottes im N.T.,* p. 292, note 3, and "'In Christus' bei Paulus" in *ZntW,* xlii (1949), pp. 141–58; H. Lietzmann on Rom. 6:11 (in *Handbuch zum N.T.*); Bertrams, *Das Wesen des Geistes,* p. 96 et seq.; Posselt in *PhilolWschr* (1918), p. 887; Dibelius on 1 Thess. 3:8; 4:2, also the two works named in note 1; Windisch, *Der 2. Korintherbrief,* p. 40 et seq.; Sommerlath, *Ursprung des neuen Lebens,* pp. 65–8; Oepke in *ThWb,* ii, 537 et seq.; Meinertz, *Theologie des N.T.,* ii, p. 135 et seq.

[12] Bultmann in *ThWb,* iii, 646–54.

2. There are texts containing the phrase "in Christ" where he is speaking of Christ as the vehicle of God's work, or of the presence in Christ of heavenly things.[13] Paul uses the phrase "in Christ" to denote the union of being and life between the Christian and his exalted Lord. But this is not its only use; it sometimes refers to God's actual completion of the Redemption. Hence there is no mystical meaning in passages which deal with God's work for the Redemption of mankind as revealed in history. There are of course cases where it is impossible to determine whether or not a passage has a mystical meaning, for Paul himself did not draw a hard and fast line between the historical act of Redemption and the continuing work of the Mediator.

There is no mystical reference in the following texts: 1 Thess. 5:18: "In all things give thanks: for this is the will of God in Christ Jesus concerning you all."

2 Cor. 5:19: "For God indeed was in Christ, reconciling the world to himself." The same idea is expressed with the preposition διά (= through) in Rom. 5:11: "Jesus Christ by whom we have now received reconciliation", and in 2 Cor. 5:18: "who hath reconciled us to himself by Christ".

Rom. 3:24: "Being justified freely by his grace, through the redemption that is in Christ Jesus." The Redemption is not repeated each time a newly converted Christian is incorporated: it was completed once and for all by an act of Christ, namely by his sacrificial death.[14]

---

[13] See H. E. Weber, op. cit., p. 220 et seq.; J. Weiss, *Urchristentum,* p. 360; Chr. Maurer in *Ev. Theologie,* xi (1951–2), p. 159 et seq.

[14] Lietzmann, *Röm.,* ad loc., is very good on this point; see Rom. 5:8 et seq.

Col. 1:16: "In him were all things created." Here the preposition is either instrumental (= by) or else locative (= in and with).

Col. 1:13 et seq.: "Who ... hath translated us into the kingdom of the Son of his love in whom we have redemption through his blood, the remission of sins." Here "in whom" means "by whom".

Col. 2:15: God has triumphed over the principalities and powers "in himself", i.e., by his Resurrection and Exaltation.

Eph. 2:13: "But now in Christ Jesus, you, who some time were afar off, are made nigh by the blood of Christ." Here "by the blood of Christ" refers back to "in Christ Jesus", and so the reference is probably to a single act – either the death of Christ or baptism in Christ's death.

This is not an exhaustive list of the texts where there is no mystical thought. It could be expanded by the addition of Gal. 3:13 et seq.; Rom. 8:39; Phil. 3:14; Col. 2:3, 9, 15; and Eph. 1:20; 2:13 and 4:32. The same probably applies to other passages from Ephesians where there is stress on the historical redemptive act of God. In addition there are texts which are disputed.

Nevertheless it is significant that Paul so often wrote "in Christ" in places where we would have expected to read "by Christ". Evidently he wished to bring out the point that to some extent Christ was the abode of God's gracious presence, the place where God willed and worked the salvation of men.

But in the overwhelming majority of cases the phrase "in Christ" denotes a mystical relationship between the Christian and Christ Triumphant. The phrase occurs in the most diverse contexts, but in every case it refers to being in Christ, to a mysterious vital union with him, to things and powers which derive from this union or which presuppose it. These passages appear in very different contexts, and so they may be divided into categories only to a limited degree.[15]

"To be in Christ" denotes the possession of a new life of an utterly different kind: "If then any be in Christ a new creature" (2 Cor. 5:17). That is why St. Paul can say of himself: "The things that were gain to me ... I ... count them but as dung, that I may gain Christ and may be found in him" (Phil. 3:7–9). Because of their union with Christ, Christians are sons of God (Gal. 3:26), alive unto God (Rom. 6:11), saints (Phil. 1:1; 4:21), sanctified (1 Cor. 1:2), light (Eph. 5:8); they have access to the Father (Eph. 3:12), and need not fear condemnation (Rom. 8:1: "There is now therefore no condemnation to them that are in Christ Jesus"); they have liberty from the Law which previously enslaved men (Gal. 2:4); each Christian should be perfect in Christ (Col. 1:28); being in Christ assures them of the resurrection (1 Thess. 4:16; 1 Cor. 15:22).

"In Christ" justification takes place: "If, while we seek to be justified in Christ, we ourselves also are found sinners, is Christ then the minister of sin? God forbid" (Gal. 2:17). "Him, who knew no sin, he (God) hath made sin for us: that we might be made the justice of God in him" (2 Cor. 5:21).

---

[15] See the attempts of H. E. Weber, op. cit., p. 222 et seq.; L. Brun, op. cit., p. 19 et seq.; Sommerlath, *Ursprung des neuen Lebens,* p. 93 et seq.; Mittring, *Heilswirklichkeit,* pp. 135–44; Oepke in *ThWb,* ii, 537 et seq.; Büchsel in *ZntW,* xlii, pp. 141–58 (not convincing, see M. Zerwick in *Verbum Domini,* xxix [1951], p. 184 et seq.). W. Schmauch, *In Christus, Eine Untersuchung zur Sprache und Theologie des Paulus* (Gütersloh, 1935), tries to attach different meanings to the various forms of the phrase (i.e., in Christ, in Christ Jesus, in the Lord); but he is unsuccessful, see *Theol. Rev.,* xxxv (1936), pp. 137–40.

Being in Christ the Christian has special power, strength, joy, gladness, and confidence. Paul declares: "I can do all things in him who strengthens me" (Phil. 4:13). In Eph. 6:10 he can say "Be strengthened in the Lord and in the might of his power."

Christians are men of joy; their vital union with Christ continually makes them joyful. Paul declares his own joy (Phil. 4:10: "I rejoice in the Lord exceedingly"), and he encourages gladness among his communities ("Rejoice in the Lord", Phil. 3:1; 4:4).

From his union with Christ he draws courage and confidence in all situations ("I have much confidence in Christ Jesus to command thee that which is to the purpose", Philemon 8), particularly during his imprisonment (Phil. 2:19: "I hope in the Lord Jesus to send Timothy unto you shortly", and even: "I trust in the Lord that I myself also shall come to you shortly" 2:24). His union with Christ is also at the root of his confidence in the communities: "I have confidence in you in the Lord that you will not be of another mind" (Gal. 5:10), and "We have confidence concerning you in the Lord that the things which we command, you both do and will do" (2 Thess. 3:4). Full of joy he can tell the Philippians that many of the brethren, having confidence in the Lord because of his imprisonment, are speaking the word of God more fearlessly (Phil. 1:14).

Paul is convinced that union with Christ is beyond all price. That is why he can say "Stand fast in the Lord" (Phil. 4:1), and "Walk ye in him" (Col. 2:6), and he can make the glad declaration: "We live, if you stand in the Lord" (1 Thess. 3:8).

Service or work "in Christ" is often mentioned by Paul.[16]

---

[16] See Böhlig, op. cit., p. 173 et seq.; H. E. Weber, op. cit., p. 219.

H. E. Weber has drawn notice to the fact that the phrase "in the Lord" is particularly common in this context.

Aquila and Priscilla are called his "helpers in Christ Jesus" (Rom. 16:3), a description which he also applies to Urbanus in Rom. 16:9. He declares that Tryphaena and Tryphosa "labour in the Lord", and that Persis "hath much laboured in the Lord" (Rom. 16:12). He describes Apelles as "approved in Christ" (Rom. 16:10), which must refer to his services to Christianity. It is not clear what exactly he means when he calls Rufus "elect in the Lord" (Rom. 16:13). The labour of which he speaks in 1 Cor. 15:58 is not the work of the Gospel, but the work of individual perfection: "knowing that your labour is not vain in the Lord"; he means that success is guaranteed by their union with Christ. The work of the Gospel is mentioned in 1 Cor. 9:1 et seq.: "Are not you my work in the Lord? . . . You are the seal of my apostleship in the Lord", and again in 2 Cor. 2:12: "When I was come to Troas for the Gospel of Christ and a door was opened unto me in the Lord." The message which he preaches to his communities springs from his inmost soul which is united with Christ: "Before God, in Christ we speak" (2 Cor. 2:17; 12:19).

Paul calls his helper Tychicus "our dearest brother and faithful minister and fellow servant in the Lord" in Col. 4:7; see Eph. 6:21. In 1 Thess. 5:12 he speaks of those who "are over you in the Lord". There is a kindred use of the phrase in 1 Cor. 4:15: "If you have ten thousand instructors in Christ, yet not many fathers." He is referring to some special office or task in Col. 4:17: "Take heed to the ministry which thou hast received in the Lord, that thou fulfil it."

St. Paul has the same idea in mind when he describes himself in Eph. 4:1 as "a prisoner in the Lord", and when he speaks of his "bands in Christ" in Phil. 1:13, or calls Epaphras his "fellow prisoner in Jesus Christ" (Philemon 23). He is imprisoned as Christ's herald whom God leads as a captive in his triumphal procession in Christ (2 Cor. 2:14).

H. E. Weber[17] would say that the texts which speak of service in Christ are not mystical in the narrower sense, though they shade off into a mystical meaning. The fact is that the phrase "in Christ" means that the work or the imprisonment is something which is withdrawn from the natural sphere; it does not belong to the merely natural plane, for the persons concerned are mystically united to Christ Triumphant and work for him, for his glory and for the advancement of his work. The activity in question takes place entirely in the sphere of Christ, or as modern theology would say "on the supernatural plane". Paul and his fellow workers are not ordinary workers, servants or prisoners; they are ministers of Christ (Col. 1:7) and ministers of the Gospel (see 1 Thess. 3:2: "Timothy . . . the minister of God in the Gospel of Christ").

So there is no doubt that the texts which speak of service in Christ have a mystical meaning.

Another category of mystical texts is made up of those which describe membership of the Christian Church as belonging to the Body of Christ. Johann Weiss[18] says that there is nothing specially mystical in these texts. But, even if Weiss is right in his assertion, the fact remains that these passages can be understood only in the light of Paul's doctrine that every Christian on conversion enters into a mysterious permanent

[17] Ibid.   [18] *Urchristentum*, p. 360.

29

union of life and being with Christ. It has been pointed out that the adjective "Christian" will usually be an adequate rendering in these passages, and that we are dealing with a conventional phrase. Perhaps the phrase ἐν Χριστῷ soon crystallized as a set form; nevertheless it is much more pregnant with meaning than our word "Christian"[19].

In the following texts the expression "in Christ" is simply a crystallized phrase: "The churches of Judea which were in Christ" (Gal. 1:22) means the Christian churches; "The churches of God which are in Judea in Christ Jesus" (1 Thess. 2:14) means the Christian churches; "Them that are of Narcissus' household, who are in the Lord" (Rom. 16:11) means the Christian members of the household of Narcissus. Other similar cases are: "them that are in Christ Jesus" (Rom. 8:1), "brethren in Christ Jesus" (Col. 1:2), "brethren in the Lord" (Phil. 1:14), "little ones in Christ" (1 Cor. 3:1), "wise in Christ" (1 Cor. 4:10), "the dead who are in Christ" (1 Thess. 4:16), and "they that are fallen asleep in Christ" (1 Cor. 15:18). In all these cases the word "Christian" renders the meaning. Similarly Paul calls himself "a man in Christ", meaning a Christian (2 Cor. 12:2).

Yet even these texts have some reference to mystical union with Christ Triumphant, as we see from Rom. 16:7: "Andronicus and Junias . . . who also were in Christ before me". It would be correct, but not adequate, to translate the clause "who were Christians before me": Paul's meaning is that they were in a mystical vital union with Christ before him. Again in Gal.

---

[19] Dibelius, *Glaube und Mystik*, p. 696: "Evidently being a Christian immediately entailed being aware that one was in Christ." See also Mundle, *Glaubensbegriff*, pp. 150–2.

3:28: "You are all one in Christ", there is a reference to the Body of Christ; yet it is significant that the preceding verse says: "As many of you as have been baptized in Christ have put on Christ."

There are texts which say that the mutual relations between Christians should be genuinely Christian, that is, they should be the relations which are fitting among persons who are in an intimate vital union with Christ and belong to his Mystical Body. Examples of such texts are: Rom. 16:1: "I commend to you Phoebe . . . that you receive her in the Lord as becometh saints"; Phil. 2:29: "Receive him therefore with all joy in the Lord"; Phil. 4:21: "Salute ye every saint in Christ Jesus" (as a brother in Christ, as a Christian brother); 1 Cor. 16:19: "Aquila and Priscilla salute you much in the Lord, with the church that is in their house." Even greetings must reflect the sacred sphere in which Christians live; they should breathe the spirit of Christ. In Rom. 16:8 Paul describes Ampliatus as "most beloved to me in the Lord". He means that his love for Ampliatus is not simply human affection; it is rooted in the vital union with Christ.

This survey is by no means exhaustive. But it is sufficient to demonstrate the variety with which Paul uses the phrase "in Christ". In spite of their diversity these texts all agree that Christ is the vital principle of Christians. Their new life depends on this mystical union with him. We would be justified in using the analogy of a fish whose vital element is water, and which can live only in water. In the same way the Christian lives in Christ, draws all vital power from him, and indeed is a Christian only as long as he lives in this union with Christ.

There are other phrases besides "in Christ" which express the idea of being in Christ.

Twice Paul speaks of "putting on Christ". The underlying idea is expressed most clearly in Gal. 3:26–9: "For you are all the children of God by faith in Christ Jesus. For as many of you as have been baptized in Christ have put on Christ. There is neither Jew nor Greek: there is neither bond nor free: there is neither male nor female. For you are all *one* in Christ Jesus. And if you be Christ's (in this manner), then are you (like him) the seed of Abraham, heirs according to the promise." It is evident from the development of St. Paul's thought that "in Christ" is equated to "put on Christ", which in turn means the same as "being Christ's". The means for reaching this state is Baptism.

The expression "to put on Christ" is a metaphor in which Christ is compared to a heavenly robe which is ready for all men; by putting on this robe men enter into a new world and are enveloped in this new world. The new relationship to Christ is not merely ethical, it is ontological. It is not simply a fresh rule of conduct. The man who "puts on Christ" gains a share in Christ's being, and this participation produces "Christ in us", the "new man".[20] And since Christ is the seed of Abraham (Gal. 3:16), it follows that Christians also are the seed of Abraham and heirs of the promise which was given to him.

This interpretation of Gal. 3:27 is not incompatible with the injunction of Rom. 13:14: "Put ye on the Lord Jesus Christ." By their conduct Christians must manifest the effect which the sacrament has wrought objectively (see Rom. 6:11, 13). This injunction of Rom. 13:14 is closely related to the command of Col. 3:9 et seq., and Eph. 4:22 et seq., where the readers are

[20] H. Schlier, *Galaterbrief*, p. 128 et seq. The phrase "to be Christ's" also has not a merely ethical meaning; it denotes membership of the Body of Christ or possession of the Spirit (Rom. 8:9).

told to put off the old man and his works, and to put on the new man, who is according to the image of his Creator. These are cases of the use of mystical terms in an ethical context (see below III, 3).

2. "OF CHRIST"

Does Paul also use the genitive case of Christ to express his doctrine of mystical union with Christ? Deissmann [21], Reitzenstein[22] and Schmitz[23] think that he does, and they say that in the writings of St. Paul the phrase "of Christ" is parallel to "in Christ". E. von Dobschütz, on the other hand, regards this as an "attempt to increase the evidence in favour of St. Paul's mysticism", and he has criticized it strongly.[24] According to him this genitive denotes dependence, and is used by Paul to denote possession (as in "the slave of Christ"); he points out that Paul was a pupil of the Rabbis, and that his thought is cast in a legal mould. "The worst possible way of distorting Paul's thought is to suppress these legal concepts and to replace them with mystical ideas."

It is beyond doubt that of itself the genitive need not necessarily express the mystical union between the faithful and their Lord. Yet in some of the texts where Paul speaks of Christ in the genitive it is possible to discern in the relationship with Christ a mystical element as well as the purely legal concept.[25] As the

---

[21] *Paulus*, p. 126.

[22] *Hellenist. Mysterienreligionen*, p. 334.

[23] *Die Christusgemeinschaft des Paulus im Lichte seines Genitivgebrauchs* (1924).

[24] *ThStKr*, xcv (1923–4), p. 326 et seq.

[25] See Schmitz, *Lebensgefühl des Paulus*, p. 127.

frequency of the phrase "in Christ" shows, mystical ideas play quite as large a part in Paul's thought as do legal concepts; indeed when he is speaking of belonging to Christ, mystical ideas are the more prominent. There are a number of texts where phrases with the genitive of "Christ" obviously have a mystical element, for example: Gal. 3:29 (see above p. 32); 5:24: "They that are Christ's have crucified their flesh", where the echo of Rom. 6:6 shows that Paul is here thinking of "being in Christ"; 1 Cor. 1:12: The cry "I indeed am of Paul etc.", is dismissed by asking "Was Paul then crucified for you? Or were you baptized in the name of Paul?" In 1 Cor. 15:23 "they that are of Christ" are "those that are in Christ" and "they that are fallen asleep in Christ" (verse 18; see 1 Thess. 4:15: "the dead who are in Christ"); Rom. 8:9 et seq.: ". . . he is none of his (i.e., Christ's). And if Christ be in you . . ." Perhaps 2 Cor. 10:7 also can be cited here: "If any man trust to himself, that he is Christ's, let him think this again with himself, that as he is Christ's, so are we also."

But this does not settle the matter. The Pauline epistles have no less than sixty-one nouns followed by the genitive of "Christ", "Jesus Christ" or "The Lord", and these texts all deal with basic theological ideas. Deissmann[26] suggested the name "mystical genitive" for these cases, for he claimed that they express in the same way as the phrase "in Christ" the mystical union between Christians and Christ. His pupil Otto Schmitz[27] investigated the matter thoroughly; he preferred to speak of a "general characterizing genitive", but otherwise he agreed with Deissmann's thesis.

[26] *Paulus* ([1]1911), p. 94 et seq.
[27] See above, note 23.

We need not argue about terminology. But what of the facts? There are two important points which emerge from these studies:[28]

1. The grammarians distinguish a number of uses of the genitive – objective genitive, subjective genitive, genitive of the agent, and possessive genitive. Schmitz has demonstrated that at least some of the uses of the phrase "of Christ" cannot be brought under any of these categories. He has also shown that the conventional categories do not cover all the uses of the genitive which are found in the LXX and Jewish writers of Greek, and even in inscriptions from Greek-speaking lands.

2. It is clear that the Pauline doctrine of union with Christ is expressed in a number of these cases. The following examples – only a small selection – prove this point:

The charity of Christ: In 2 Cor. 5:14 Paul says: "The charity of Christ presseth us: judging this, that if one died for all, then all are dead." This is not an objective genitive, for when the object of love is a person Paul uses the preposition εἰς (= towards); this is illustrated in Col. 1:4: "Hearing your faith in Christ Jesus and the love which you have towards all the saints."

It seems more plausible and more apt, to take this as a subjective genitive, and to construe it as "The love which Christ has for us". But the context is against such an interpretation. Paul is thinking primarily of a present power, not of the past act of love which Christ accomplished for us upon the Cross.

Paul is here defending himself. He says: "I am not commending myself, for I do not do anything for myself; if I am in ecstasy, that is for God; if I speak when not in ecstasy, I do so for you;

---

[28] See also Meinertz, *Theologie,* ii, p. 136 et seq.

35

for I am moved by the love of Christ, and the love of Christ wishes Christians to live for him, not for themselves." So the meaning of verse 14 is that Paul's actions do not spring from selfish motives; he is moved by the mysterious power of the love of Christ, which alone shapes his conduct. This power derives from an actual situation at the present moment – namely that "the many" participate in the death of the one Christ. Of course he is thinking of the past event of Christ's death on the Cross, but this past event is here and now producing its effect on his soul. Paul is moved and governed by a *present* power which is described as the "charity of Christ". This power derives from his mystical union with Christ.

The same applies to Eph. 3:14–19: "For this cause I bow my knees to the Father . . . that he would grant you according to the riches of his glory, 1. to be strengthened by his Spirit with might unto the inward man, 2. that Christ may dwell by faith in your hearts that, being rooted and founded in charity you may be able (a) to comprehend with all the saints what is the breadth and length and height and depth (of the heavenly structure of salvation, that is, of the heavenly inheritance in the sense of 1:18 et seq.) – the four dimensions were originally a description of the entirety of the astral world – (b) to know also the charity of Christ which surpasseth all knowledge."

This cannot be an objective genitive, for Paul would never have said that our love for Christ surpasses all knowledge. Undoubtedly it may be a subjective genitive, meaning the love of Christ for us. However, there is a strong mystical strain throughout the passage, as we see from the clause "That Christ may dwell in your hearts". It is more natural therefore to take the phrase "charity of Christ" as a unit, and to understand by it the living stream of "Christ-charity" which flows through those who are "in Christ", a stream whose depths can never be sounded, however often they are tested.

In any event it is beyond dispute that Paul is not here referring to the past deed in which the love of Christ was manifested before all men's eyes; he is thinking of a power which at the present operates in Christians.

The patience of Christ (2 Thess. 3:5): "The Lord direct your hearts, in the charity of God and the patience *of Christ.*" Paul is not thinking of the patience which Christ practised in his life. The context does not favour such an interpretation; and moreover, he never used this Greek expression when referring to the Passion in which Christ's patience was so wonderfully displayed. The meaning is rather that Paul desires for his readers the patience which must be in them because Christ abides and works in them (= "Christ-patience").

The work of Christ: Epaphroditus brought Paul a gift from the Philippians, and in Phil. 2:30 Paul praises him "because for the work of Christ he came to the point of death". Naturally this does not mean an action performed by Christ. Neither does it mean a work performed for Christ. "Work of faith" (1 Thess. 1:3) or "work of the ministry" (Eph. 4:12) are the terms by which Paul describes the preaching of the Gospel and kindred matters such as, in this case, the bringing of help. The genitive indicates the nature of the work – it belongs to the sphere of Christ.

There is a clearer example in 1 Cor. 15:58: "Therefore, my beloved brethren, be ye steadfast and unmovable: always abounding in the work of the Lord, knowing that your labour is not vain in ($\dot{\epsilon}\nu$) the Lord." The phrase "labour in the Lord" indicates that "the work of the Lord" also is something mystical. Paul is not speaking here of the preaching of the Gospel, but simply of the Christian life. His meaning is: Be perfect Christians and let no labour discourage you, for this work will bring a rich reward.

The same idea recurs in 1 Cor. 16:10, where he says that Timothy "worketh the work of the Lord, as I also do". The Lord is not engaged in the work which Timothy does. The expression "work of the Lord" is to be understood as a unit meaning "Lord's work". The work is done in the Lord (cf. "fellow servant in the Lord"), it is intimately connected with him. It is not profane and worldly, but belongs to the sphere of Christ. It is like Paul's longing for the Philippians, which is not an ordinary human longing for other people, but is a longing "in the bowels of Jesus Christ" (Phil. 1:8).

Prisoner of Christ: "For this cause, I Paul, the prisoner of Jesus Christ, for you Gentiles" (Eph. 3:1; also Philemon 9; see 2 Tim. 1:8). This is not a subjective genitive, which would mean that Christ had made Paul a prisoner. Moreover, he does not mean that he is suffering imprisonment for Christ; he says explicitly that he is suffering it for the Gentiles. Paul calls himself the prisoner of Christ because he is aware of his mystical fellowship with Christ, and therefore his imprisonment also lies in this supernatural sphere. That is why he can describe himself in Eph. 4:1 as "a prisoner in the Lord" (see Philemon 23: "Epaphras, my fellow prisoner in Christ Jesus").

Further examples could be cited. However, these texts seem sufficient to establish with certainty the following three points:

1. It is remarkable how often Paul uses the genitive of "Christ" in this way. In many cases the genitive may be ignored, for it

38

sounds superfluous to us, just as is often the case with the phrase "in Christ": the sentence would run more smoothly without it. This suggests that the same psychological process underlies his use of both phrases, "in Christ" and "of Christ".

2. It is certain that the conventional grammatical categories are often inadequate. But we cannot simply group together the cases which do not fit into the usual categories, and make one new category – this is the great weakness of Schmitz' thesis. Dibelius[29] has summed up the position by saying that we must distinguish two types of case: (a) special constructions which are due to rhetorical considerations, e.g., 1 Cor. 7:22 "the freeman of the Lord", and 1 Cor. 9:21; and (b) conventional phrases with the genitive, which were not invented by Paul, but were taken over and adapted by him, such as "Faith of Christ" and "Gospel of Christ".

3. When Paul uses the genitive of "Christ" he prefers to attach it to nouns which represent important concepts in his theology, such as Gospel, Faith, Charity, Blood, Truth, Might, Peace, Life, Coming, Spirit, Body. What psychological reason induced the Apostle to adopt these singular expressions? Anyone who admits that the phrase "in Christ" denotes a mystical relationship will have no doubt about the answer: the phrases with the genitive of "Christ" reflect Paul's doctrine of the interior mystical relation between the Christian and his Lord Triumphant. In other words, both phrases, "in Christ" and "of Christ", have the same psychological explanation. We need not assume that Paul was always clearly conscious of

[29] *Theol. Blätter,* iii (1924), p. 282 et seq. Although he agrees otherwise with Schmitz, he does not wish to abandon the usual grammatical terms.

this as he was speaking and writing; but we may say that these phrases came to his tongue as an expression of his subconscious thought.

We could not say *a priori* that this use of the genitive must necessarily convey a mystical meaning. But in the light which other texts shed on his doctrine of union with Christ, it is clear that this genitive is often used in a mystical sense.

3. "CHRIST IN US"

Christ is in Christians, he abides in them. This is the other aspect of the mystical relationship between Christ and man. References to this aspect are comparatively scanty in St. Paul's epistles, but there are texts which demonstrate that he was familiar with the idea of the indwelling of Christ – as distinct from the indwelling of the Spirit. However, he does not use a special phrase to express this, as he uses "in Christ" (ἐν Χριστῷ) for the other aspect.

The mystical relationship is thus described in Rom. 8:9–10: "But you are not in the flesh, but in the spirit, if so be that the *Spirit* of God *dwell in you*. Now if any man have not the Spirit of Christ, he is none of his. And if *Christ be in you,* the body indeed is dead, because of sin: but the spirit liveth because of justification."[30] It is clear from this text that the doctrine of the indwelling of Christ himself in Christians – indeed in each

---

[30] See Dibelius, *Paulus und die Mystik,* p. 69: This text shows "that Paul can describe the new life as the indwelling of either Christ or of the Spirit. So the mystical fellowship with Christ – using the word 'mystical' with all due reservations – can also be described in terms of the Spirit: there is no difference."

individual Christian – was accepted by the Romans as much as by Paul himself.

Another important passage is 2 Cor. 13:2–5. On his second visit to Corinth – the "intermediate journey" – Paul had shown gentleness and forbearance towards the sinful members of the community (12:21). His action had been misinterpreted, and doubt had been cast on his apostolic authority from which he derived special power; indeed his standing as an Apostle had been denied, and his opponents had not hesitated to say: "His epistles indeed are weighty and strong; but his bodily presence is weak and his speech contemptible" (10:10). In other words, they alleged that during his time in Corinth he had given no evidence to show that he was speaking in virtue of a special authority received from the Lord. Paul expresses this accusation by asking "Do you seek a proof of *Christ that speaketh in me?*" (13:3).

Reitzenstein has correctly pointed out [31] that Paul could not have used a stronger expression. He does not mean simply that Christ dwells in him as in other Christians. His point is that Christ speaks through him, and so Paul's injunctions are to be received as the instructions of Christ.

Paul is compelled to defend and assert his apostolic office, and to do so he undertakes to revisit Corinth (13:1), and threatens that if there is no improvement (13:7 et seq.) he will give them the proof they asked for (13:3a) by mercilessly condemning the unrepentant sinners (13:2). Then they shall realize that Christ who dwells in Paul and works through him is not weak in regard to them, but that he is unmistakably strong (13:3b).[32]

---

[31] *Hellenist. Mysterienreligionen,* p. 370.

[32] This is paraphrased in 13:10: "That, being present, I may not

Hitherto they have seen only weakness in him. He explains why this is so: because of his mystical union with Christ ("in him" 13:4) Paul must undergo the same experience as Christ, who was crucified in weakness but was afterwards raised up by God's power. So, he continues, they should rather examine themselves: "Know you not your own selves (that is, you know very well) that *Christ Jesus is in you,* unless perhaps you be reprobates?"(13:5). This is an injunction to the Corinthians not to query Paul's standing as an Apostle, but rather to examine seriously whether their own standing as Christians still exists. He expresses "their standing as Christians" by the phrase "Christ in you".

It has been pointed out that it is the community and not the individual members, who are being addressed here. But Christ dwells in the community by dwelling in its individual members; that is why Paul can describe as a "temple of God" both the community (1 Cor. 3:16; 2 Cor. 6:16) and individual Christians (1 Cor. 6:19: "your body").

From this difficult section of the epistle we learn that Christ dwells in everyone who is a Christian. But in the case of his Apostles he produces effects in word and work which he does not produce in the ordinary Christians who do not possess such a charism.

Another text which refers to all Christians is Eph. 3:16 et seq., which has already been cited on page 36. This passage teaches that Christ can abide in us more or less perfectly, that there are degrees of Christ's indwelling. Paul is here repeating what he often says: when men become Christians an objective and

deal more severely, according to the power which the Lord hath given me unto edification, and not unto destruction."

sacramental effect is wrought on their being: this effect must be manifested and expressed in their conduct.[33] The indwelling of Christ and the strengthening of the interior man go together. It follows that the indwelling of Christ should affect their conduct. In this case the effect of his indwelling is a deeper knowledge of God and of the great inheritance which is prepared for us (see Eph. 1:18), as well as of the charity of Christ which surpasses all knowledge. In Paul's eyes the soul's ultimate goal is to "be filled unto all the fulness of God" (3:19), that is, to attain the stage of being a perfect Christian in piety and conduct.

The Epistle to the Galatians contains a fine expression of the thought that Christ dwells in the faithful, and that the purpose of this indwelling is to produce ever greater and more profound effects in their piety and conduct. The epistle is an appeal to the Galatians whom Paul's adversaries were trying to estrange from him: "My little children, of whom I am in labour again, *until Christ be formed in you.* And I would willingly be present with you now and change my voice[34] because I am ashamed for you" (4:19 et seq.). Paul had once already been in labour when he converted the Galatians to Christ. Now he is in labour again, and this labour will come to an end only when Christ is formed in them, that is, when Christ has become a new self (Gal. 2:20) in them, vital and powerful, and when each of them shows a complete image of Christ both in their being and in their acts.

[33] See below, chap. III, 3. In his study of Christ's presence in us through faith according to Eph. 3:17, G. Söhngen rather considers the dogmatic side of the question in his collected volume, *Die Einheit in der Theologie* (Munich, 1952), pp. 324–41.

[34] According to Schlier *(Galaterbrief)* Paul means that he would wish to speak with "the voice of an angel", that is, in heavenly language.

Paul certainly does not mean that the Galatians are cut off from Christ and that Christ no longer abides in them. But there is a very serious risk that they may lose Christ, for they possess only a faint imprint of his image, and it may be altogether obliterated. Paul is most anxious that the form of Christ should again be imprinted upon them with increased clarity and effect, for this is the goal of the Christian life. Each one should become "perfect in Christ Jesus" (Col. 1:28) and attain "the measure of the age of the fulness of Christ" (Eph. 4:13).

We have here a particularly clear statement of the religious and moral aspect of union with Christ. Along with Christ a new vital power enters into men, and, unless it is impeded, this power gives Christians the form of Christ.

Schlier suggests that Gal. 4:19 should be translated "until Christ be formed among you". His argument is that Paul is here thinking not of individuals in whose souls Christ dwells, but of the Galatian community as a whole. However, this does not affect the point at issue, for the community is born through the growth of Christ in individuals (see below, page 148, note 42).

Another text which may be considered here is Col. 1:27. In the preceding two verses Paul speaks of the divine office which was entrusted to him, to announce to the Gentiles the word of God, the mystery which was hidden from ages and generations but is now revealed to the saints: "To whom (i.e., to you) God would make known the riches of the glory of this mystery among the Gentiles, *which is Christ, in you* the hope of glory." The fact of preaching to the Gentiles is not the mystery. The mystery is the material which is preached: the glory of the incarnate Son of God, whose indwelling guarantees that we shall see the glory of the world to come. The words "in you" should not be construed to mean "(preached) among you". Immediately before this point, in verse 24, Paul speaks of union with the Passion of Christ; and in verse 28 the phrase "perfect in Christ Jesus" is also mystical. This indicates that the phrase "in you" of verse 24 should be construed as an expression of the spiritual indwelling of Christ.[35]

In Col. 3:9 et seq., Paul calls upon his readers to put off the old man with his (bad) works and to put on the new man, the image of his Creator. There are two passages which are exact parallels to this text: Rom. 13:14 and Gal. 3:27. The former passage: "Put ye on the Lord Jesus Christ", is mystical and refers to conduct, as the passage from Colossians also does. The passage from Galatians: "As many of you as have been baptized in Christ have put on Christ" is also mystical, but it is sacramental rather than moral. So in Col. 3:10, Paul says that his readers should become "Christ-men", striving to reproduce the image of Christ in their interior man and to receive Christ himself into themselves. This is followed by verse 11: "Where (that is, if you live in the sphere of Christ) there is neither Gentile nor Jew, circumcision nor uncircumcision, Barbarian nor Scythian, bond nor free. But Christ is all and in all (ἐν πᾶσιν)". In other words, Christ makes them all a unity, he *is* this unity (this is the idea of the Body of Christ), and at the same time he is present in each individual man (as in a member).[36] There is a fairly close parallel to this in Eph. 4:22-4.

---

[35] This is the view of Schmitz, *Christusgemeinschaft,* p. 90; Dibelius, ad loc.

[36] See Dibelius, ad loc.; Tr. Schmidt, *Leib Christi,* p. 150.

A similar meaning attaches to the "inward man" (ὁ ἔσω ἄνθρωπος) of 2 Cor. 4:16: "For which cause we faint not: but though our outward man is corrupted, yet the inward man is renewed day by day." This "inward man" is identical with "Christ in us", our new life (Gal. 2:20; Col. 3:4). The expression recurs in Eph. 3:16, where Paul prays that God may grant them "to be strengthened by his Spirit with might unto the inward man"; this prayer is obviously paraphrased in the following verse: "that Christ may dwell by faith in your hearts". The "inward man" corresponds to the "new man" of Col. 3:9 and Eph. 4:23: "Put on the new man."

These two expressions do not directly denote Christ, but human nature renewed by Christ who is the New Man (1 Cor. 15:45, 47). Then by metonymy he says "Christ" for the "new man" in Gal. 3:27: "have put on Christ", and Rom. 13:14: "Put ye on the Lord Jesus Christ."

Finally there is one passage of supreme importance[37] whose mystical character is denied by no one[38]: "For I, through the law, am dead to the law, that I may live to God: with Christ I am nailed to the cross. And I live, now not I: *but Christ liveth in me.* And that I live now in the flesh: I live in the faith of the Son of God, who loved me and delivered himself for me." (Gal. 2:19 et seq.)

[37] On this passage see Schauf, *Sarx,* p. 142 et seq.; Casel in *Theol. Revue* (1925), p. 377; Schmitz, *Christusgemeinschaft,* p. 130 et seq.; p. 247 et seq.

[38] For example, Clemen, *Mystik* (1923), p. 19: "the most impressive mystical statement, from which all our knowledge of Paul's mysticism is derived". v. Dobschütz (*ThStKr,* xcv [1923–4] 397), admits that this passage can be put forward in favour of St. Paul's mysticism with at least an appearance of justice.

46

Like Christ, and with Christ, Paul has died. When he says this, he is thinking of Baptism – as Rom. 2:6 et seq. shows – which symbolizes and also brings about death. Since Christ's death took place on the Cross, Paul can say in Rom. 6:6 that he is crucified with Christ. This crucifixion with Christ annihilates his previous life, the life of the flesh, which he describes in Rom. 7:24 as "the body of this death"; his self, his old Adam (Rom. 7:14 et seq.), which was under the domination of sin, has perished. In place of this vanished life there is a new life which springs from Christ; indeed it is identical with Christ's life, so that he can say: "Christ liveth in me", that is, Christ lives in the shell of the old man which still survives. Christ is drawn into him, his self is now the state of Christ-life, or, as he says in Phil. 1:21: "For to me, to live is Christ."

Nevertheless Paul was well aware that he had not yet discarded the body of the flesh and that his natural earthly life, the life "in the flesh" (Phil. 1:22; 2 Cor. 10:3) was not destroyed by this new Christ-life. It will be fully shed only at the Resurrection, when the new life shall appear full and untramelled (Col. 3:4). That is the explanation of Gal. 2:20: "And that I live in the flesh: I live in the faith of the Son of God, who loved me and delivered himself for me." Paul must continue his natural human life for the time being, but his life is now on a new level, "in faith" in the Lord who died for him, faith which preserves and develops the new life.

It is clear from this passage that Christ himself dwells in Paul, and in Paul's eyes this indwelling of Christ is identical with his new life. His life is "Christ-life". Yet he does not consider that his self is annihilated; the second part of verse 20 makes this quite clear, and rules out any interpretation of the first part of the verse which would suggest otherwise. As Lehmann says: "Paul has approached the verge of mysticism", – Lehmann uses the word in its narrowest sense – "but he has not taken the final step into it. His self is not annihilated; now only Christ lives and reigns in it."[39] Johann Weiss also realizes this: "In the second part of verse 20, instead of the mystical formula he gives a description which presents Christ in his full personality, and which assigns a different role to the human person concerned: he does not speak of the self entering into Christ and being absorbed by him in a passive manner; the mystical formula is replaced by the language of active piety, where he looks gratefully on Christ's act of love, grasps Christ's grace, and co-operates with his good and holy Will."[40]

[39] *Mystik im Heidentum und Christentum* (Leipzig, 1923), p. 49 et seq.
[40] *ZntW* (1920), p. 140.

II

The Nature of Union with Christ

THE previous chapter surveyed the most important of St. Paul's utterances about the mystical union of life between the Christian and Christ Triumphant. We must now examine the nature of this mystical union, and attempt to elucidate it as far as possible, taking into account the personality and theology of the Apostle. In particular we shall have to investigate how these utterances are to be understood in relation to what he taught about the nature and operations of Christ Triumphant.

It is clear from what has already been said that St. Paul was convinced that every Christian is joined to Christ Triumphant in a deeply interior union of grace, and that this union may be described by saying that the Christian is in Christ and that Christ dwells and works in the Christian. Any attempt to elucidate this relationship, or even to describe it, immediately raises the question of how Paul conceived this union; did he regard it as a fusion of the two persons, or as the entry of the Christian into Christ?

To solve this problem we must investigate the meaning of the two phrases "in Christ" and "Christ in us".

1. THE MEANING OF THE PHRASE "IN CHRIST"

This is much the more common of the two phrases. How does Paul conceive of the Christian being in Christ?

It need hardly be said that he is not thinking of Christ in his earthly form. He has in mind Christ Triumphant who has risen from the dead and sits at the right hand of the Father; Christ who belongs to the next world.

Deissmann thinks that the phrase "in Christ" signifies that the spiritual Christ is the place where the Christian is.[1] He points out that it is not merely a graphic phrase to stress the idea of fellowship with Christ: Paul, he says, thought of Christ Triumphant as leading a spiritual existence, as we see from his interchanging of the phrases "in Christ" and "in the Spirit". If we admit that Paul thought of Christ Triumphant as a Spirit, then we need no longer apply the phrase to union with Christ in his earthly form. We cannot speak of "being in Plato" or "being in Moses", but this does not mean that we cannot speak of being in the living spiritual Christ.

This explanation of Deissmann's has been widely accepted. But it is based on the premise that we conceive of the spiritual Christ in a material manner, something like the wind or the air. Deissmann thinks that this was Paul's conception of the living Christ, although he did not give a clear philosophical definition of the concept "spiritual". "The Apostle formulated his ideas in a popular manner with the usual elasticity of the ancients; he probably had in mind a light etherial form of existence, such as he probably also applied to God."[2]

[1] Deissmann, *Formel "in Christo Jesu"*, p. 81 et seq.; p. 97 et seq.
[2] *Paulus*, p. 113.

50

Yet this corporeality is nothing earthly or material; for in Paul there is a deep cleavage between *Sarx* (Flesh) and Spirit *(pneuma)*. A number of authors have rejected Deissmann's explanation, and certainly it cannot be accepted without reservation.[3]

He is correct when he says that Paul can speak of being in Christ only because he considers Christ as having a spiritual form of existence. It is also true that the preposition "in" must be understood in its original locative sense,[4] as is shown clearly by the phrases in Gal. 3:26–9: "put on Christ", "Children of God . . . in Christ", and "one in Christ".

On the other hand, it is not correct to say that Paul was thinking of being in some element like the air, for, in spite of Deissmann's assertion, Paul does not interchange "in Christ" and "in the Spirit".

At this point we can only make a very general statement: when Paul uses the phrase "in Christ", he means that the Christian lives on a new level.[5] This becomes obvious when we notice that "being in Christ" is contrasted with "being in the flesh, in sin, in the law, in the world".

A few examples will illustrate this point:[6] Rom. 7:5: "When

---

[3] For example, H. E. Weber, p. 224 et seq.; Schmitz, *Christusgemeinschaft,* p. 240 et seq.; Feine, *Apostel Paulus,* p. 76 et seq.; Büchsel, *Geist Gottes,* p. 293.

[4] This is also the view of Oepke in *ThWb,* ii, p. 538; Percy, *Leib Christi,* p. 22; Maurer, *Ev.Theologie,* xi (1951–2), p. 159. Büchsel in *ZntW,* xlii, pp. 141–58, is incorrect.

[5] On what follows see Tr. Schmidt, *Leib Christi,* p. 85 et seq.; Bartmann, *Paulus,* p. 76 et seq.; Schmitz, op cit., p. 240 et seq.; Büchsel, *Geist Gottes,* p. 292 et seq.; Sommerlath, *Ursprung des neuen Lebens,* p. 96 et seq.

[6] See especially Deissmann, *Paulus,* p. 139 et seq.

we were in the flesh, the passions of sins, which were (awakened) by the law, did work in our members, to bring forth fruit unto death"; Rom. 8:8: "They who are in the flesh cannot please God." Speaking of the new life he says: Rom. 8:1: "There is now therefore no condemnation to them that are in Christ Jesus"; Col. 2:20: "If then you be dead with Christ from the elements of this world, why do you yet decree as though living in the world?"; Rom. 2:12: "Whosoever have sinned without the law shall perish without the law: and whosoever have sinned in the law (= being subjects of the Law, the Jews) shall be judged by the law"; Rom. 3:19: "We know that what things so ever the law speaketh, it speaketh to them that are in the law"; Rom. 6:2: "We that are dead to sin, how shall we live any longer therein?" In all these cases the preposition "in" could be replaced by the phrase "under the influence of".

In Paul's eyes his own life – and therefore the life of anyone who becomes a Christian in adult age – falls into two great periods which are sharply contrasted. In the past he lived on a level which is called "sin", "flesh", "the world", or "death"; now his life is on a plane which is most aptly described by the phrase "in Christ". In every passage where the phrase "in Christ" is used in its full sense, the reference is to the origin or the possession or the effects of the new life (see Rom. 6:4: "in newness of life") which the Christian possesses since he became a Christian.

So it is correct to say that the phrase "in Christ" expresses the new level of life and power on which the Christian has his being.[7]

---

[7] See Sommerlath, op. cit., p. 93.

"In the Spirit" is a phrase which Paul uses nineteen times, and he often makes exactly the same statement about the Spirit as he makes about Christ. Deissmann maintains that there are fifteen cases where the phrase "in the Spirit" carries with it the same Pauline concepts as are attached to "in Christ".[8] Here are some examples:

To be in the Spirit: Rom. 8:9: "You are not in the flesh but in the Spirit." Compare with this 1 Cor. 1:30: "Of him are you in Christ"; 2 Cor. 5:17: "If then any be in Christ a new creature"; Rom. 8:1: "There is now therefore no condemnation to them that are in Christ"; Rom. 16:11: "Salute them that are of Narcissus' household, who are in the Lord."

Stand fast: Phil. 1:27: "you stand fast in one spirit." Compare with this Phil. 4:1: "Stand fast in the Lord"; 1 Thess. 3:8: "Now we live, if you stand in the Lord."

Sanctified: Rom. 15:16: "Sanctified in the Holy Ghost". Compare 1 Cor. 1:2: "Sanctified in Christ Jesus".

Sealed: Eph. 4:30: "Grieve not the holy Spirit of God: whereby you are sealed unto the day of Redemption." Compare Eph. 1:13: "In whom (Christ) you also, after you had heard the word of truth, . . . were signed with the holy Spirit of promise."

Rejoice: Phil. 3:1; 4:4: "Rejoice in the Lord". Compare Rom. 14:17: "The kingdom of God is . . . justice and peace and joy in the Holy Ghost."

Speak: 2 Cor. 2:17; 12:19: "We speak before God in Christ";

---

[8] However, this is not true of all these passages, as is pointed out by Prat (*Theology of St. Paul,* ii, p. 395) and Percy (*Leib Christi,* p. 20, note 52). According to Percy there is no real parallel in 1 Cor. 12:9; Phil. 1:27; Col. 1:8; Eph. 4:17 (?23), 30; 5:18; Rom. 14:17. "In one spirit" in Phil. 1:27 simply means "unanimously" as in 1 Cor. 1:10.

Rom. 9:1: "I speak the truth in Christ." Compare Rom. 8:15: "You have received the spirit of adoption of sons, whereby we cry: Abba (Father)"; 1 Cor. 12:3: "No man, speaking by the Spirit of God, saith Anathema to Jesus. And no man can say The Lord Jesus, but by the Holy Ghost."

Bear witness: Rom. 9:1: "I speak the truth in Christ: I lie not, my conscience bearing me witness in the Holy Ghost." Compare Eph. 4:17: "I say and testify in the Lord."

Moreover in 1 Cor. 1:9 Paul speaks of the "fellowship of his (God's) Son", while in 2 Cor. 13:13 and Phil. 2:1 he mentions the "communication of the Holy Ghost". Again in Rom. 8:34 et seq. he says that Christ intercedes with the Father for us, while in 8:26 et seq. he had spoken of the Spirit helping our prayer.

Deissmann maintains that the same interchange of terms occurs in regard to the indwelling of Christ in Christians. Paul says "the Spirit in us" as well as "Christ in us" (see below II, 2).

Closer examination of the cases where Paul uses these two phrases with the same ideas reveals an interesting fact: Paul always uses the phrase "in Christ" when he is speaking of salvation as such, while he reserves the phrase "in the Spirit" for the conduct of the faithful as contrasted with the life of the natural man, and especially for the new sphere of life as contrasted with the life of "the flesh" (σάρξ), or when he is dealing with the effects of the Spirit on the interior life of the believer.[9]

This difference in usage may be illustrated by considering the passages where he speaks of being in Christ or in the Spirit.

[9] Thus Percy, *Leib Christi,* pp. 20–22.

Texts like Rom. 8:1; 1 Cor. 1:30; 2 Cor. 5:17; and Phil. 3:9, which speak of being in Christ, mean that objectively the believer is on the plane of salvation. On the other hand, a passage like Rom. 8:9: "You are not in the flesh but in the spirit", refers to the nature of this plane of life in contrast to the life of "the flesh", the life of the natural man; the Spirit is the vital influence which gives the new life its quality.

Again, the injunction of Col. 2:6: "Walk ye in him (in Christ)" is an exhortation to remain loyal to their faith in Christ, as we see from the following verse. This is different from Gal. 5:16 where the stress falls on conduct: "Walk in the spirit: and you shall not fulfil the lusts of the flesh." Operations of the Holy Ghost are described as speaking by the Holy Ghost in 1 Cor. 12:3 and joy in the Holy Ghost in Rom. 14:17.

What has been said about the phrase "in the Spirit" applies generally to what Paul says of the Spirit. The Spirit stands in contrast to the flesh (Rom. 8:4 et seq.; Gal. 5:16 et seq.; 6:8) and to the letter (of the Law: Rom. 7:6; 2 Cor. 3:16–18). Time and again Paul reminds his readers that they should "walk in the Spirit and not in the flesh" (Rom. 8:4, 12 et seq.; 1 Cor. 3:3; Gal. 5:16), and that their conduct must be influenced by the Spirit of God (Rom. 8:14). Before conversion they had walked in all kinds of sin and iniquity (Gal. 5:19–22; Rom. 7:5; Eph. 2:2, 10; 4:17–19; Col. 3:7), but now they must walk in "newness of life", that is, in a new life (Rom. 6:4; see Rom. 14:15; Gal. 5:11; Eph. 5:2, 8; Col. 4:5). They must "walk worthy of God" (Col. 1:10; 1 Thess. 2:12).

The contrast between the Spirit and the flesh is paralleled by the antithesis of the Spirit and the letter, meaning the Jewish Law. Christians are free from the Law, and they serve God in the new way of the Spirit, not in the old way of the letter (Rom. 7:6). The New Testament is not a testament of the letter; it is a testament of the spirit, for "the letter killeth, but the spirit quickeneth" (2 Cor. 3:6).

Above all Paul regards the Spirit as a divine power,[10] as we see clearly from those texts where the word for power (δύναμις) is used as an equivalent for spirit. Thus the resurrection is due to the power of God according to 1 Cor. 6:14 and 2 Cor. 13:4, while it is attributed to the Spirit in Rom. 8:11. Paul prays in Eph. 3:16 that God may grant his readers "to be strengthened by his Spirit with might into the inward man". Paul tells us that the Spirit dwells in men; he says the same of the power of Christ: "Your members are the temple of the Holy Ghost, who is in you" (1 Cor. 6:19); "Gladly therefore will I glory in my infirmities, that the power of Christ may dwell in me" (2 Cor. 12:9); "To him who is able to do all things more abundantly than we desire or understand, according to the power that worketh in us: to him be glory" (Eph. 3:20). Elsewhere Paul speaks of "the power of the Holy Ghost", as in Rom. 15:13, 19: "in the power of the Holy Ghost"; 1 Cor. 2:4: "in shewing of the Spirit and power"; and Gal. 3:5: "He therefore who giveth to you the Spirit and worketh miracles among you".

It is clear from these examples that Paul does not think of the Spirit as a kind of fluid element. The Spirit is rather a power, a divine power which is not at man's free disposal,

---

[10] See especially Bertrams, *Wesen des Geistes,* p. 28 et seq.; Bartmann, *Paulus,* p. 77, p. 92 et seq.; O. Schmitz in *Festgabe f. Deissmann* (1927), p. 160 et seq.

but is a gratuitous gift from God to man. Through the Spirit God works in men.

This was the meaning of Spirit in the Old Testament and in writings before Paul. They almost always ascribed to the Spirit prophecy, ecstasy, and other extraordinary spiritual phenomena. It is most unusual for these writings to regard the Spirit as the effective influence on conduct. Being "in the Spirit" meant being in an ecstasy, just as it still does in the Apocalypse (1:10; 4:2; 17:3). The Spirit was understood as a supernatural divine power which could suddenly and irresistably take possession of a man.

Paul also attributes such phenomena to the Spirit: we have only to think of what he says about charisms in 1 Cor. chap. 12–14. In those chapters he insists that all the different gifts are given by one and the same Spirit. Indeed he uses the phrase "in the Spirit" in 1 Cor. 12:3: "No man, speaking by (ἐν) the Spirit of God, saith Anathema to Jesus."

But more often Paul speaks of the Spirit as the power which influences conduct (Rom. 5:5; 8:15 et seq.; 15:13; Gal. 4:6; 5:5; Eph. 3:16; Phil. 1:19). Bertrams[11] and Bartmann[12] rightly stress this point. In Paul's eyes the Spirit is primarily a divine power which operates in man. And when he speaks of being in the Spirit, he is not thinking of being at rest in a certain element: one who is "in the Spirit" is under the influence of a divine power, from which he derives strength and might.

For Paul, therefore, the divine Spirit was a power and an influence which he had experienced; this power had intervened

[11] Op. cit., pp. 46–70.
[12] Op. cit., p. 92.

profoundly in his life, and thereafter influenced it decisively.[13] In Rom. 15:18 et seq., he juxtaposes "Christ" and "the Spirit": "I dare not to speak of any of those things which *Christ* worketh not by me, for the obedience of the Gentiles, by word and deed, by the virtue of signs and wonders, in the power of the *Holy Ghost*." This text shows the relationship which exists between Christ and the Spirit: In the Apostle – and therefore in every Christian – Christ works through the Holy Spirit.

However, there is still a problem inherent in Paul's use of the phrase "in Christ": the difficulty is that he equates the level of salvation with a Person. His use of the phrase "in the Spirit" helps us to understand the nature of the new life; but it does not explain how he can say that the Christian is in the spiritual Christ when he conceives of Christ as a Person. Moreover, "in Christ" is a much more common phrase in St. Paul's writings than "in the Spirit". From the preponderance of this phrase we must assume that when Paul used the expression "in Christ" or "in the Lord" he was thinking not so much of the soul receiving power; his idea was rather that a concrete personality was in contact with the soul.

Some scholars have approached this problem by enquiring into the history of the phrase "in Christ". Paul is the first New Testament writer to use it, and there is no evidence that it was in the Christian vocabulary before his time.[14]

It is possible that the phrase was inspired by some other

---

[13] Paul is well aware that the Spirit is a Person as well as a divine power. This is true to an even greater degree of Christ Triumphant, who is always a distinctive Person in Paul and is never represented as an impersonal power. This matter is discussed in II, 3.

[14] The phrase "in Christ" occurs three times in 1 Peter – 3:16; 5:10,

similar expressions in the Greek Old Testament, and Deissmann has tried to show[15] that it was suggested by the Old Testament phrase "in God" and "in the Lord", and that it is modelled on these expressions. He says that in Hab. 3:18: "I will rejoice in the Lord" a mystical meaning attaches to "in the Lord", and he finds an echo of this verse in Phil. 3:1; 4:4. The Septuagint version of Psalms often uses the phrase "in God" – an expression which he says was also a favourite of Paul's – and he claims that this phrase also had a mystical significance.

But it must be remembered that we have here a literal translation of a Hebrew preposition, and we cannot assert dogmatically that the translator gave the phrase a mystical turn.[16] Moreover, the phrase "in God" – which Deissmann calls a favourite of Paul's – occurs altogether seven times in the Epistles, and of these seven cases two (Rom. 2:17 and 5:11) may be discounted, for the preposition in these passages depends on the verb;[17] probably this applies also to 1 Thess. 2:2. There is a strange expression in the introductory verse of each of the Epistles to the Thessalonians: "the church of the Thessalonians in God the Father and in the Lord Jesus Christ" (1 Thess. 1:1; 2 Thess. 1:1). But this expression is not paralleled elsewhere, and probably it means no more than "beloved of God" in Rom. 1:7 or "the Church of God" in 1 Cor. 1:2 and 2 Cor. 1:1. It resembles the phrase "in Christ", and presumably is modelled

14. But Bernhard Weiss' suggestion that 1 Peter was written before the Pauline Epistles has rightly received little support.

[15] *Paulus,* p. 116 et seq.

[16] See Böhlig in *ZntW,* xiv (1913), pp. 30–2, who says that the phrase "in the Lord" occurs only sixteen times, and all these cases are translations of the Hebrew original. See also H. E. Weber, op. cit., p. 253.

[17] See also Schmidt, *Leib Christi,* p. 98.

on it, but it does not carry the deep mystical significance of that phrase.[18] This leaves only two passages of the seven: Col. 3:3: "Your life is hid with Christ in God" and Eph. 3:9: "The mystery (of the conversion of the Gentiles to Christianity) which hath been hidden from eternity in God, who created all things". In both cases the preposition has a locative sense, meaning "with God". The text from Colossians is strongly reminiscent of 2 Cor. 5:1: "We know, if our earthly house of this habitation be dissolved, that we have a building of God, a house not made with hands, eternal in heaven." Both passages mean that the new life of Christians – of which the glorified body is a part – will not be fully manifested until the appearance of Christ, who is now out of sight with God (in Heaven). In other words "in God" means "in Heaven", just as in Wisdom 5:15: "The just shall live for evermore and their reward is with the Lord." The Jews believed that the reward of the just is stored in Heaven (see Matt. 5:12). The original text of the Wisdom passage reads "in the Lord"; this means "with God", for the Jews avoided using the divine Name.

These three texts speak of a thing – as distinct from a person – being in God, and I do not believe that they shed any worthwhile light on the meaning or even the history of the phrase "in Christ". The two phrases deal with different ideas.

Lohmeyer[19] suggests that the phrase "in the Law", which Paul sometimes uses, is the model for the expression "in Christ". The Law was the economy of salvation for the Jews. But there

---

[18] See Dibelius on 1 Thess. 1:1; Wissmann, Πίστις und Christus-frömmigkeit, p. 103 et seq.

[19] Die Grundlagen der paulinischen Theologie (Tübingen, 1929), pp. 139–46.

are not more than five places where the phrase "in the Law" may refer to the realm of salvation in which the pious Jew has his life; in these five cases (Rom. 2:12; 3:19; Phil. 3:6; Gal. 3:11; 5:4) the Law may be regarded as a counterpart of the level of salvation on which the Christian lives. However, the Jews never spoke of "being in the Law", so it is likely that the influence was rather the other way – the phrase "in Christ" suggested "in the Law".[20]

We need not consider the celebrated sentence of the Areopagus discourse: "He (God) be not far from every one of us. For in him we live and move and are" (Acts 17:27 et seq.). If this sentence expresses the theology of the Stoics and the pantheism of the Greeks, then it cannot be regarded as Paul's own belief: it must be looked upon as a clever exploitation by the missionary of those ideas of his hearers which were known to him.[21]

The meaning of the phrase "in Christ" cannot be explained by the history of the expression, for such an approach to the problem presupposes that the phrase came first and that the idea sprang from it. The case is exactly the reverse: it was the idea that produced the phrase. The obvious assumption is that Paul invented this phrase in order to express the relationship which becoming a Christian creates between the Christian and Christ Triumphant. It is of course possible that the Apostle

[20] See Percy, *Leib Christi*, p. 22, note 55.

[21] The Stoic origin of this sentence is defended by M. Pohlenz in *ZntW*, xlii (1949), pp. 101–4. It is denied by B. Gärtner, *The Areopagus Speech and Natural Revelation* (Upsala, 1955), pp. 179–98, who says that this sentence simply conveys the entire dependence of man on (the one personal) God in all respects (life, movement, existence). See A. Wikenhauser, *Apostelgeschichte* (Regensburg, ³1956), ad loc.

used a phrase which already existed as a vehicle for his thought –
to that extent the history of the phrase may be of value – but
even if this is true, the meaning of the phrase will depend on
Paul's intentions and not on the ideas of whoever first used it.
In fact no evidence has been adduced to show that the phrase
did exist before Paul used it; all the indications are that it was
Paul's own creation. In that case it must be interpreted in the
light of Paul's theology and spirituality.

Two points are clear concerning this relationship with Christ,
and they are of importance for the understanding of the phrase
"in Christ". The relationship begins when one becomes a
Christian, namely by receiving Baptism (see below III, 1),
and it comes to an end when one passes into the more perfect
state of "being with Christ".

In Baptism the faithful have put on Christ and thereby have
become "one in Christ" (Gal. 3:27). That is why both individuals
and the Christian churches can be described as "in Christ" (Rom.
16:7, 11; 1 Cor. 1:30; Gal. 1:22; 1 Thess. 2:14).

Regarding the end of this relationship Lohmeyer aptly says:
"When Paul speaks of being in Christ or living in Christ, he is
referring to life in this present world."[22] He never uses the phrase
"in Christ" when speaking of his profound hope that he will be
clothed in a spiritual body and will be for ever with his heavenly
Lord; in such cases his phrase is "with Christ" (σὺν Χριστῷ). It is

---

[22] In *Festgabe f. A. Deissmann*, p. 220. Being "with Christ" between
death and the Resurrection, and also after the Resurrection, is discussed
now by J. Jeremias in *ThWb*, v, 769; J. Dupont, *Syn Christo. L'union
avec le Christ suivant S. Paul*, i: "*Avec le Christ*"*dans la vie future* (Louvain,
1952). See the review of this by P. Benoit in *Rev. biblique,* lxi (1954), pp.
120–4.

only at the resurrection, when Christ shall appear in majesty, that we shall begin to "be with Christ" (see Col. 3:4). To be with Christ is the final goal and the supreme aim of the Christian. It is also Paul's deepest desire, as he reveals in Phil. 1:23: "I am straitened between two: having a desire to be dissolved and to be with Christ, a thing by far the better. But to abide still in the flesh is needful for you." At the Second Coming of Christ "the dead who are in Christ shall rise first. Then we who are alive, who are left, shall be taken up together with them in the clouds to meet Christ, into the air: and so shall we be always with the Lord" (1 Thess. 4:15 et seq.). "Being in Christ" comes to an end when it attains its purpose and we are "with Christ".

Being in Christ is brought about by the sacramental act of dying with and rising with Christ in Baptism. Baptism has not merely a passing significance; its effect endures, for it causes us to "be in Christ". Although Paul never says this in set terms, it is clearly his teaching, particularly in Rom. 6:4 et seq.: "We are buried together with him by Baptism unto death: that as Christ is risen from the dead by the glory of the Father, so we also may walk *in newness of life* (= in a new life). . . . So do you also reckon that you are dead to sin, but alive unto God in Christ Jesus our Lord." Moreover, this is not the sole significance of our sacramental dying with Christ and rising with him. Baptism is also a pledge that we shall be "with Christ", which is the consummation of being "in Christ", and it gives us access to him: "If we be dead with Christ, we believe that we shall live also together with Christ" (Rom. 6:8).

To sum up what has been established at this point, Paul uses the phrase "in Christ" to express his conviction that the Christian lives on a plane where his entire life is profoundly influenced by a divine power, and where to some degree the very quality of his life has been changed (see especially 2 Cor. 5:17). This plane is confined to life before death, as we see by examining the Apostle's use of the other phrase "with Christ".

But this does not solve the problem, for the special character-istic of this plane of life is that it is equated to the spiritual Christ. When Paul uses the expression "in Christ", he is not thinking of physical location in Christ nor of being under the influence of an impersonal power. This fact cannot be sufficiently emphasized. The phrase "in the Spirit" emphasizes the idea of an influencing power; it occurs only nineteen times, while "in Christ" is used one hundred and sixty-four times. In Paul's mind, to be in Christ means being under the power and influence of the personal Christ.

An instructive parallel is found in 1 Cor. 7:14: "The unbeliev-ing husband is sanctified by (=ἐν) the believing wife: and the unbelieving wife is sanctified by the believing husband."[23] Here Paul thinks of the Christian husband or wife as a person. It is clear how he envisages the sanctification of the pagan by the Christian partner: the Christian exercises a sanctifying influence on the pagan, and the pagan partner is under this influence; in other words, he is within the sphere of a personal power which affects him strongly. There is no question here of any idea of spatial presence. Similarly we must conceive of the spiritual Christ as a spiritual and personal power which continually influences all who have entered a vital union with him.

Investigation of the phrase "in the Spirit" does not solve the problem of how Paul conceived of Christians being in a person.

[23] See Büchsel, *Geist Gottes,* p. 293.

The question must be approached from another angle. But first the other mystical phrase calls for examination.

2. THE MEANING OF THE PHRASE "CHRIST IN US"

The phrase "in Christ", as has already been said, occurs one hundred and sixty-four times in St. Paul's epistles, and generally has a mystical meaning. It is therefore at first glance surprising that only a few passages mention the indwelling of Christ in Christians. It has already been shown that the idea of Christ dwelling in men must play an important part in St. Paul's mysticism. Yet the fewness of the references to this doctrine need cause no surprise when we realize how frequently Paul refers to the indwelling of the Spirit of Christ, of the Spirit of God, or simply of the Spirit. An examination of these references will help to elucidate what seems strange to us – the idea of a Person, Christ, dwelling in a man.

The indwelling of the Spirit of Christ is mentioned in a number of passages. In Rom. 8:9, Paul says: "If any man have not the Spirit of Christ, he is none of his", and he adds immediately "and if Christ be in you": obviously the two phrases are identical in meaning. In Gal. 4:6 he says: "Because you are sons, God hath sent the Spirit of his Son into your hearts, crying: Abba, Father" (cf. Rom. 8:15). This prayerful cry is raised by the Spirit of God's Son in our hearts. Speaking of himself Paul says in 1 Cor. 2:16: "We have the νοῦς of Christ". The word νοῦς literally means "mind", but it obviously means "Spirit" here. He uses νοῦς here instead of πνεῦμα, the usual word for Spirit, because the word νοῦς occurs in the Isaias passage which he had cited as a proof immediately before: "Who

65

hath known the mind (νοῦς) of the Lord, that he may instruct him?" The whole passage 1 Cor. 2:6–16 deals with the Spirit of God in men (2:12). So the Spirit of God, or the Spirit from God is identical with the Spirit of Christ. In 2 Cor. 3:17 he speaks of the Spirit of the Lord: "Where the Spirit of the Lord is, there is liberty." The Spirit of Christ is mentioned in Phil. 1:19: "the supply of the Spirit of Jesus Christ".

The "power of Christ"[24] is a kindred notion, and sometimes Paul speaks of it dwelling in men. According to Col. 1:29 Paul labours to make all men perfect Christians "according to his (Christ's) working which he worketh in me in power" – the idea here is the same as in Phil. 4:13: "I can do all things in him who strengtheneth me", that is, in Christ; see 1 Tim. 1:12; 2 Tim. 4:17. He says that he prefers to glory in his infirmities rather than in the charismatic favours which he has received "that the power of Christ may dwell in me" (2 Cor. 12:9). In this passage Paul speaks of the power of Christ almost as if it were a substance or an independent being[25]; see also 1 Cor. 5:4[26].

As a rule Paul speaks simply of the Spirit or the Spirit of God.

The Spirit dwells in Christians: Rom. 8:9: "the Spirit of God dwell in you"; 8:11: "if the Spirit of him that raised up Jesus

---

[24] See O. Schmitz, "Der Begriff δύναμις bei Paulus" in *Festgabe f. A. Deissmann* (1927), p. 146 et seq.

[25] See Windisch, *Der 2. Korintherbrief*, p. 392.

[26] The Rabbinical Commentary *Sifrê* uses similar language about the majesty *(Kabod)* of God: "The name (or the majesty) of God rests on him upon whom suffering comes" (*Sifrê* on Deut. 6:5; Kittel, p. 57). The same commentary on Deut. 1:24 says that "the Holy Spirit rested upon Rahab". The same idea appears in Eccles. 24:13 (Wisdom is to dwell in Jacob) and John 1:14 (the Word dwelt amongst us); see also John 1:32 et seq.

Christ from the dead dwell in you"; 1 Cor. 3:16: "the Spirit of God dwelleth in you"; 6:19: "the Holy Ghost, who is in you, whom you have from God"; 2 Tim. 1:14: "the Holy Ghost who dwelleth in us".

The Spirit works in Christians: Rom. 8:16: "The Spirit himself giveth testimony to our spirit"; 8:26: "the Spirit helpeth our infirmity", "the Spirit himself asketh for us with unspeakable groanings"; 8:14: "Whosoever are led by the Spirit of God" – who, the next verse tells us, dwells in them. In 1 Cor. 14:14 he says "My spirit prayeth". Eph. 2:2 tells us that the evil spirit "now worketh on the children of unbelief".

God gives the Spirit: Rom. 5:5: "The charity of God is poured forth in our hearts by the Holy Ghost who is given to us"; 2 Cor. 1:22 and 5:5: "God who hath given us the pledge of the Spirit"; Gal. 3:5: "He therefore who giveth to you the Spirit"; 1 Thess. 4:8: "God, who also hath given his holy Spirit in us".

The Christians have received the Spirit: Rom. 8:15: "You have received the spirit of adoption of sons"; 1 Cor. 2:12: "We have received . . . the Spirit that is of God"; 12:13b: "In one Spirit we have all been made to drink"; 2 Cor. 11:4: "if you receive another Spirit, whom you have not received"; Gal. 3:2: "Did you receive the Spirit by the works of the law or by the hearing of faith?"

They have the Spirit: Rom. 8:23: "ourselves also who have the first fruits of the Spirit"; 1 Cor. 7:40: "I think that I also have the Spirit of God."

It is significant that there are only two texts where Paul says that God – as distinct from the Spirit of God – dwells in men: both texts are Old Testament citations.

To begin with the more important text, 2 Cor. 6:16 says: "You are the temple of the living God; as God saith: *I will dwell in them* and walk among them. And I will be their God, and they shall be my people."[27]

This quotation is from Lev. 26:12, but the original does not contain the sentence: "I will dwell in them". This idea of God's indwelling does not appear anywhere in the Old Testament, not even in the Septuagint.

But Philo the philosopher refers to this passage in Leviticus and speaks of God dwelling in the pious man; indeed, like Paul[28] he calls the pious man a temple of God.[29] In his work "On rewards and punishments" Philo says (§ 123): "Of such a spirit the prophet (Moses) says that God walks in him as in a royal palace, for the spirit of the wise man is really the palace and dwelling of God." Elsewhere Philo explains that the invisible Lord of All walks silently alone in the souls of those who are entirely pure, while angels or divine Logoi dwell in those who are not yet thoroughly purified, so that by learning virtue they may become entirely pure. "It is evident how many crowds of wicked dwellers must withdraw in order that the One may enter. Strive therefore, O soul, to become a house of God, a holy temple, a majestic dwelling."[30] Seneca also (Ep. 31:11) speaks of God dwelling in the body of a man. Paul's idea is paralleled in John 14:23: "We

---

[27] See Windisch, op. cit., p. 216.

[28] In this passage it is the body of Christians, and not individuals, which Paul calls a temple of God. But elsewhere he applies the description "temple" both to the community (1 Cor. 3:16; 2 Cor. 6:16) and to individuals (1 Cor. 6:19).

[29] See Reitzenstein, *Hellenist. Mysterienreligionen,* p. 310.

[30] *De somniis,* i, § 148 et seq. See also *ThWb,* iv, 580, 585 note 14, 15.

(i.e., Christ and the Father) will come to him and will make our abode with him." It was a familiar notion among the Hellenistic Jews.[31] The words "I will dwell in them" are probably suggested by Ez. 37:27: "And my tabernacle (κατασκήνωσις) shall be with (ἐν) them"; but this Ezechiel passage does not refer to dwelling in men.

The other passage where Paul speaks of God being in men is 1 Cor. 14:25; there he tells how the infidel is impressed by the fact that the Christian prophets can read his heart: "And so, falling down on his face, he will adore God, affirming that God is among (ἐν) you indeed." This is a citation from the Septuagint version of Isaias 45:15. Paul intended to convey that God is "in you" – not "among you" – for his point is that the infidel recognizes a higher Power speaking from the Christian prophet. The Septuagint version of the original Isaias passage reads: "In thee is God"; it refers to the foreign peoples being convinced that Jahweh is the only God and wishing to join his people among whom alone he dwells. Paul has accommodated the text to suit his purpose.

These are the only Pauline texts which speak of God dwelling in men. Presumably if he had not been citing from the Old Testament here, he would have spoken of the indwelling of the Spirit of God, or simply of the indwelling of the Spirit. This assumption is reasonable in view of his language in two passages which are parallels to the first of these texts: 1 Cor. 3:16: "Know you not that you are the temple of God and that the Spirit of God dwelleth in you?" and 6:19: "Know you not that your members are the temple of the Holy Ghost, who is in you?" Paul

[31] Reitzenstein, op. cit., p. 310, deals with the spread of this idea.

must have understood the Old Testament passages to mean that God dwells in men through his Spirit.

Schmidt[32] alleges that the idea of God dwelling in men occurs elsewhere in Paul. He points to Eph. 2:21 et seq., and 4:6. But this interpretation cannot be upheld. Eph. 2:22 speaks of "an habitation of God in the Spirit", and the context here is the spiritual structure of the Church. The expression in Eph. 4:6 has hardly any relevance to the present theme, even if we merely consider it as a form of expression; in fact it is simply a description of unity modelled on Hellenistic patterns.

Paul speaks of the Spirit of Christ as well as of the Spirit of God. This is a natural expression to use, when we recall that by the Redemption Christ has won from the Father the gift of the Spirit (see Acts 2:33), and so the Holy Ghost can be called the gift of Christ. Paul says that the possession of the Spirit is a gift which all who are baptized receive in virtue of their vital union with Christ; he speaks of the Spirit dwelling in such men. So it is quite obvious why he calls Christ, or his Spirit, their new vital principle (Gal. 2:20). It is true that he also speaks of the Spirit of God; indeed he mentions the Spirit of God more often than the Spirit of Christ. This is partly due to his Jewish upbringing; it also reflects the fact that in the last analysis the Spirit is a gift from God.

The frequency with which Paul speaks of the Spirit of God, the Spirit, or the Holy Ghost, does not prove that he had a doctrine of mystical union with the Spirit which can be set alongside his doctrine of union with Christ, as though there were several forms of union with God. Paul speaks only of

[32] *Leib Christi,* p. 96.

being "in Christ" or "in the Lord": he never uses the phrase "in God", except for the two texts which have already been examined, and which have not a mystical meaning (II, 1). The phrase "in the Spirit" is not really parallel with "in Christ". St. Paul's writings do not contain a specific doctrine of mystical union with God (see below IV, 3).

Christ, or the Spirit of Christ, dwells in Christians. How does Paul conceive of this indwelling? That is the problem which must now be faced.

It has been suggested[33] that Paul is using figurative language in these passages: these expressions, it is alleged, do not envisage the Lord or his Spirit being alive and present in the faithful; they simply mean that the historical figure of Jesus and the motives for conduct which he inspired live on in men. This is an entirely false picture of Paul's thought. If the Apostle had meant merely that men should imitate the life of Christ on earth, he would not have insisted so strongly on the resurrection precisely in those places where he speaks of indwelling. What dwells in the faithful is not the image of Christ on earth, but the Lord who was raised up by God. Moreover, this interpretation of Paul's thought takes no account of his statements that the Spirit of Christ dwells in Christians; for by the Spirit of Christ he does not mean simply Christ's ideas; he means a living spiritual Being. As Büchsel[34] rightly says, for Paul, Christ was not merely a unique and profoundly spiritual man of high moral calibre who was, and still is, an inspiration to us; in Paul's eyes Christ is he who died for Paul and for all men (Gal. 2:20), was raised up

[33] This suggestion is discussed in Büchsel, *Geist Gottes,* p. 295.
[34] Ibid.

by God, and now sits triumphantly at the right hand of God, clothed in a spiritual body. There is a fundamental gulf between Paul's idea of Christ's indwelling and the inspiration provided by the memory of a man long dead. "Christ is not merely an ideal which stands before Paul's eyes: he is a reality which operates in Paul."[35]

Paul is certainly not using metaphor. His words mean that Christ who died and who rose again from the dead, is present as a living person in those who believe in him. He does not simply mean that Christ is the power of his new moral and religious life. It is certainly true that Paul considered the new life of the Christian as an operation of the Spirit of Christ;[36] that applies to the charisms as well as to conduct. In spite of their diversity the charisms all derive from the one Spirit: "All these things, one and the same Spirit worketh, dividing to everyone according as he will" (1 Cor. 12:11). The moral and religious life also is not merely a human operation, it too is a "fruit" of the Spirit: "The fruit of the Spirit is, charity, joy, peace, patience, benignity, goodness, longanimity, mildness, faith, modesty, continency, chastity" (Gal. 5:22). That is why "power" and "Spirit" are closely related as in 1 Thess. 1:5 and 1 Cor. 2:4; indeed they can be interchanged – compare Rom. 8:11 with 1 Cor. 6:14; 2 Cor. 13:4. In Rom. 15:13,19 Paul speaks of "the power of the Holy Ghost".

It would, however, be a perversion of Paul's thought to interpret his words about the indwelling of Christ or of his Spirit as meaning that he conceives of an impersonal power operating

---

[35] Ibid.
[36] See Bertrams, *Wesen des Geistes,* p. 28 et seq.; Sommerlath, *Ursprung des neuen Lebens,* p. 60; Schmidt, *Leib Christi,* p. 75 et seq.

in Christians. Just as with the phrase "in Christ", Paul is speaking literally. He means that the spiritual Christ, a living Person, is present in the just and operates in them; and in this statement the emphatic word is "Person".

It is quite true that some passages could be interpreted otherwise. But there are other texts where there is no possible doubt that Paul conceives of the Spirit as a spiritual being, like angels and demons;[37] and when he speaks of his indwelling or operation in men he is thinking of a personal presence. Johannes Weiss has summed up the point accurately if somewhat crudely: "The form of the idea is entirely archaic – animistic – primitive: it is a second spiritual being which dwells in Christians."[38]

There are passages where the Spirit who is communicated to men is described as something objective, independent of the spirit of man, and in no way confused with man's inner life: Rom. 8:16: "The Spirit himself giveth testimony to our spirit that we are the sons of God"; Gal. 4:6: "Because you are sons (of God), God hath sent the Spirit of his son into your hearts, crying: Abba, Father". These verses can be understood only if Paul conceived of man and the Spirit who dwells in him as two distincts persons; man is represented as a hearer of the cry "Abba, Father", the testimony of the Spirit. A similar expression occurs in 1 Cor. 14:14: "If I pray in a tongue, my spirit prayeth: but my understanding is without fruit." In 1 Cor. 2:10 et seq. the spirit of man is distinct from the "Spirit that is of God", who searches "the deep things of God".

This picture is not changed by passages like 1 Cor. 6:16

---

[37] Büchsel, op. cit., p. 397.
[38] ZntW, xix (1920), p. 131; see also Büchsel, op. cit., p. 431 et seq.

et seq.: "Know you not that he who is joined to a harlot is made one body? For they shall be, saith he (that is, the Old Testament), two in one flesh. But he who is joined to the Lord is one spirit (with him)." Clement of Alexandria explains correctly that "spirit" here means the spiritual body (σῶμα πνευματικόν), a union of the glorified (spiritual) Lord and his members; this union, which is of a higher degree and more full of grace, is what we call the Mystical Body of Christ.[39] Paul here says that the Christian enters upon an interior fellowship with the Lord. But just as there is no fusion of personality between the first mentioned pair, so we have no right to postulate such a fusion between Christ and the Christian.

The matter is even clearer in those passages where Paul speaks of Christ himself – not of his Spirit – dwelling in men. He always thinks of Christ as a Person, and when he says that Christ dwells in him, he is thinking of Christ who died on the Cross, was raised up by God, and now sits at the right hand of the Father interceding for us (Rom. 8:34). As Büchsel says: "Christ who is present in Paul is not merely a power or some kind of principle; he is the historical Person with his individual character and his own experiences. When Paul says that Christ is in him he means that this individual Person is present in him."[40] We could sum up Paul's teaching by saying that the Person who died on the Cross for me, is now raised from the dead and continues his life in me. As Gloël[41] aptly says: In Paul's eyes

---

[39] *Stromata,* vii, 87, 3 – 88, 2. See *Archiv f. Liturgiewissenschaft,* i (1950), p. 302.

[40] Op. cit., p. 294 et seq.

[41] J. Gloël, *Der Heilige Geist in der Heilsverkündigung des Paulus* (Halle, 1888), p. 174.

there is an intimate connection between the two phrases of Gal. 2:20: "for me" and "in me".

So, according to Paul, when Christ dwells and works in the just man he does so as a Person, and not merely as a power or as an impersonal force; and nevertheless each retains his own personality and they are not fused by one person absorbing the other. This idea sounds unfamiliar to us, and the question arises how Paul conceives of one person dwelling in another. We can take as our starting point the fact that Christ who dwells in men is a spiritual being, the spiritual Christ: that is why Paul speaks simply of the Spirit or of the Spirit of Christ.

The indwelling and operation of a demon in a man must have been a familiar idea to the ancients, and it provides an analogy which helps to elucidate the present problem.

Both the New Testament and classical literature provide abundant evidence that a demon – a spiritual being hostile to God – can enter a man, control his whole physical and spiritual being, and take possession of him.[42] He dominates the man's body: he can cause illness, for example, lameness, deformity (Luke 13:11, 16), dumbness (Matt. 9:32 et seq.) and blindness (Matt. 12:22); he can toss the man about, and make him foam at the mouth and gnash his teeth, and can render him numb (Mark 9:18); he can cast him into fire and water (Mark 9:22), and can give him enormous strength (Mark 5:3 et seq.). Moreover the demon can dominate the man's spirit: the possessed man must obey him, the demon speaks through him, and for a time renders him unconscious (Mark 1:24; 5:6 et seq. etc.).

---

[42] See Rohde, *Psyche*, ii (1921), p. 14 et seq.; Bousset–Gressmann, *Religion des Judentums* (³1926), p. 336 et seq.; Foerster, Art. Δαίμων in *ThWb*, ii, 1–20.

These phenomena can happen repeatedly (Mark 9:17 et seq.; Matt. 17:15).

Diabolical possession provides us with an analogy, but it is only an analogy. It is not a true parallel. In both cases a personal spiritual being dwells in a man and operates in him. But there the resemblance ceases. The demon enters the man whom he possesses, as an enemy; he overpowers him, enslaves him, and injures him both in body and in spirit. The Holy Spirit is present in order to help the man; he gives him higher powers and capabilities and awakens in him a new glorious life. The demons are numerous, and are under one head (Mark 3:22); only one man can be possessed by one – or several (Mark 5:9; Luke 8:2) – of them. The Spirit of Jesus is one, and he dwells simultaneously in a number of men, in all Christians.

The effect upon a man of a prophetic spirit is another analogy. The pagan authors frequently mention such cases[43]. We have only to think of the expression ἔνθεος (literally "full of God"), and the corresponding noun ἐνθουσιασμός, as well as the Latin phrase *plenus Deo*. Speaking of the divinely inspired poet[44] Plato applies to him what was originally said of the worshippers of Bacchus; "He becomes full of the god and loses his senses, and his spirit is no longer in him" (Ion 534b). Sophocles in "Antigone" (line 963) called the ecstatic worshippers of Dionysus "women filled with God". The poet Lucan described the ecstasy of the Pythia as follows: "The God enters into her,

---

[43] Rohde, op. cit., p. 19 et seq.; Reitzenstein, *Hellenist. Mysterienreligionen*, p. 73 et seq.; p. 105, note 2; pp. 237, 322 et seq.

[44] The "inspiration" of a poet was regarded as analogous to the inspiration of prophets: hence *vates,* which originally meant a seer, came to mean a poet (see Reitzenstein, op. cit., p. 322).

drives out her soul, and orders the man (that is, her spirit) to
withdraw completely from her breast."[45] And Philo said of
prophets: "Whoever is really inspired and full of God cannot
grasp with his understanding what he is saying";[46] and again:
"When he is inspired he falls into unconsciousness, for his thought
wanes and leaves the tower of the soul, but the divine spirit has
entered and made his dwelling there."[47]

A more familiar comparison is the operation of the Spirit upon
the ancient prophets of Israel. The idea of the Spirit of God
operating on men and in men appears in the Old Testament,
though it is not one of the predominant themes.[48] Occasionally it is said that the Spirit of Jahweh influences human conduct.
But more often he produces ecstasy and charisms; he is the author
of the gifts of prophecy, of reading hearts, of working miracles
and of speaking in ecstasy. This is true of the New Testament also: see 1 Cor. chap. 12–14; Acts 2:1 et seq.; 10:14 et
seq.; 19:6.

---

[45] *Pharsalia,* v, 166 et seq.

"Non unquam plenior artus
Phoebados inrupit Paean mentemque priorem
Expulit atque hominem toto sibi cedere iussit
Pectore."

[46] *De spec. leg.,* i, § 65. See Leisegang, *Der Heilige Geist,* i (1919), p. 145 et seq.

[47] *De spec. leg.,* iv, § 49. It is interesting to note the verbal resemblance (ἐνῳκηκότος τοῦ θείου πνεύματος) to Rom. 8:11; Col. 3:16; 2 Tim. 1:14.

[48] P. Volz, *Der Geist Gottes* (Tübingen, 1911); H. Gunkel, *Die Propheten* (Göttingen, 1917); Büchsel, *Geist Gottes,* pp. 1–36; Bousset, *Kyrios Christos,* pp. 110–13; P. van Imschoot, "L'action de l'Esprit de Jahvé dans l'AT" in *Rev. des sciences philos. et théol.,* xxiii (1934), pp. 553–87.

But all these charismatic [49] operations of the Spirit of God are given only to particular individuals, and are not permanent gifts which the person in question can use as and when he wishes. When a man becomes an organ of the Spirit he feels possessed by a spiritual divine power from outside himself, which overpowers him, transcending his own strength of will and spirit – and sometimes his physical capabilities, as in the case of Elias: 3 Kings 18:46 – and compelling him irresistibly to make use of these new faculties. Ezechiel tells us (3:22): "The hand of the Lord was upon me, and he said to me: Rise and go forth into the plain, and there I will speak to thee", and Isaias (8:11) says: "Thus saith the Lord to me: As he hath taught me, with a strong arm, that I should not walk in the way of this people." The inner compulsion with which the prophets are seized by God is clearly depicted especially by Amos and Jeremias. Amos says (3:8): "The lion shall roar: Who will not fear? The Lord hath spoken: Who shall not prophesy?" In other words, if God chooses a man as his instrument, the man has no choice but to obey and speak. There is an interesting parallel in 1 Cor. 9:16: "A necessity lieth upon me. For woe is unto me if I preach not the Gospel." Jeremias tells of his unsuccessful effort to ignore God's call: "Thou hast deceived me, O Lord, and I am deceived: thou hast been stronger than I, and thou hast prevailed." He tried to avoid the heavy burden of prophesying, which God laid upon his shoulders, but he could not escape it: "Then I said: I will not make mention of him nor speak any more in his name. And there came in my heart as a burning fire, shut up in my bones: and I was wearied, not being able to bear it" (20:7 et seq.).

[49] J. Brosch, *Charismen und Ämter in der Urkirche* (Bonn, 1951).

There are also similar instances recorded in the New Testament: Acts tells of Agabus (11:28; 21:10), of people speaking in ecstasy (10:44 et seq.; 19:6), and above all of the events at Pentecost (2:4 et seq.). Paul also knew of these extraordinary gifts of the Spirit, and he deals explicitly with them in 1 Cor. chap. 12–14. But he insists that they must not be over-estimated, for charity is superior to any of them (chap. 13).

Evidently these operations of the Spirit were all out of the ordinary, and really should be classed with miracles. Under the Old Testament not every Israelite was granted these charisms; and though they seem to have been very numerous in the Corinthian community, nevertheless not every Christian receives them. Paul himself enjoyed such gifts of the Spirit, as he declares in 1 Cor. 14:18: "I thank my God I speak with all your tongues." But he makes it perfectly plain that no Christian has any claim to these charisms, and that no charismatic should wish to have all, or even the highest, charisms at his disposal: "All these things one and the same Spirit worketh, dividing to every one according as he will" (1 Cor. 12:11).

When Paul mentions the indwelling of Christ or of his Spirit, he is not thinking of charisms, for he declares quite clearly that Christ dwells in all Christians without exception. It is true of all Christians that Christ dwells in them (Rom. 8:10; 2 Cor. 13:5; Eph. 3:17; Col. 1:27), that Christ must be (perfectly) formed in them (Gal. 4:19), and that they are the temple of God and the Spirit of God dwells in them (1 Cor. 3:16; 6:19; 2 Cor. 6:16; see also Gal. 5:16–25). The indwelling of which Paul speaks is lasting, and its purpose is not the production of extraordinary effects. Christ abides in Christians as the principle of the new Christian life, in order to influence their

79

conduct. Surprising though it may seem, Paul was almost the first to realize that this moral influence of the Spirit of God or of Christ is a normal feature in the life of every Christian; indeed he equates it with being a Christian. As H. Bertrams points out, there is little evidence that the authors of the Synoptic Gospels and of Acts connected the conduct of Christians with the Spirit. Paul was the first to give a thorough statement of the sanctifying power of the Spirit, and he did so in a masterly fashion.[50]

So when we speak of Paul's doctrine of union with Christ we are not referring to his – or other people's – extraordinary charismatic experiences such as speaking in tongues, prophesying and being transported to the third Heaven; we mean the mysterious and lasting union with the spiritual Christ Triumphant which Paul expresses by the phrases "in Christ" and "Christ in us". The effect of this union is the creation and development of the true Christian life.

It is true that charisms also are the work of the same Spirit as is the principle of the new life in Christians. But charisms are merely special and unusual phenomena in the Christian life, they are not an essential part of it. All Christians possess the Spirit of Christ as a vital force in the conduct of their lives; but the Spirit does not produce charisms in all Christians.

3. CHRIST AND THE SPIRIT

How does Paul conceive of Christ who dwells in us and in whom we dwell? This question has been posed a number of

[50] Bertrams, *Wesen des Geistes,* p. 46. See also Bousset, *Kyrios Christos,* p. 112.

times during the preceding sections. We must now return to it again and try to reach a definite conclusion.

The principal question at issue is whether Christ with whom we are united is a Person or an impersonal force. In other words, is the spiritual Christ, the Lord Triumphant, identical with the divine Spirit? Johannes Weiss and some others answer this question in the affirmative.

In his exegesis of 1 Cor. 12:13[51] Weiss says that an almost insoluble problem arises from the fact that the clearly defined Person of Christ Triumphant is simultaneously the formless divine power of the Spirit which is diffused in many beings; he concludes that such difficulty is inseparable from mystical piety: "Christ is said to be not merely in one person but in all the faithful, and at the same time all the faithful are in Christ. This is possible only if the idea of Christ becomes vague and if his personality is dissolved in a pantheistic manner. This is expressed by describing Christ as the Spirit." A posthumously published article contains the same theory: "in Paul's writings 'to be in Christ' means to be fully absorbed in a mystical union with the heavenly Lord; in this union the personality loses its individuality, and the thought of Christ penetrating all (2 Cor. 3:17) takes its place. In Paul's eyes Christ the Person is metaphysically identical with the impersonal Spirit. He was able to make this equation because he was trained in the thought of his time which drew no hard and fast line between an abstract idea and personality; moreover, the picture which the Gospel tradition presents had not the strong influence on him which it has on us."[52]

[51] *Der 1. Korintherbrief* (1910), p. 303.
[52] *ZntW* (1920), p. 139 et seq.

Nevertheless Weiss himself is not quite convinced of this theory, for he wonders, in view of Gal. 2:20, whether Paul really did have a pantheistic conception of Christ, and he doubts if total absorption was what he meant by the mystical union of Christians with Christ.[53] In fact he does not give an accurate picture of Paul's thought.

It is, of course, correct to say that there is a far-reaching parallelism between "Christ" and "Spirit" and the ideas associated with these two words. We have already seen the relationship which exists between the phrase "in Christ" and "in the Spirit", and between "Christ in us" and the "Spirit in us". The parallels are not confined to these phrases, as may be seen from the following examples:[54]

1. Justified in the name of our Lord Jesus Christ and the Spirit of our God (1 Cor. 6:11), and in Christ (Gal. 2:17).

   Circumcision of the heart in the Spirit (Rom. 2:29), and in Christ (Col. 2:11).

   Sanctified in the Spirit (1 Cor. 6:11), and in Christ (1 Cor. 1:2).

   Sealed in the Spirit (Eph. 4:30), and in Christ with the Holy Spirit (Eph. 1:13).

   Joy in the Holy Ghost (Rom. 14:17), and in the Lord (Phil. 4:4).

   Joy in the Holy Ghost (Rom. 14:17), and through our Lord (Rom. 5:1).

2. The Holy Ghost dwells in us (Rom. 8:9, 11; 1 Cor. 3:16;

---

[53] Ibid., p. 140 (see above, page 48).

[54] See Prat, *Theology of St. Paul,* ii, p. 394; Bartmann, *Paulus,* p. 76; Wissmann, Πίστις *und Christusfrömmigkeit,* pp. 99 et seq., 109 et seq.

2 Tim. 1:14): Christ in us (Rom. 8:10; 2 Cor. 13:5; Eph. 3:17 [dwell]; Col. 1:27).

The Holy Ghost works in us (1 Cor. 12:11): Christ (Col. 1:29).

The Holy Ghost speaks (prays) in us (Rom. 8:26): Christ speaks in the Apostle (2 Cor. 12:19).

3. We live through the Spirit (Gal. 5:25): Christ is our life (Col. 3:4; Phil. 1:21; Rom. 6:11; Gal. 2:20).

We communicate in the Holy Ghost (2 Cor. 13:13): in Christ (1 Cor. 1:19).

Whosoever are led by the Spirit of God they are the sons of God . . . you have received the spirit of adoption of sons (Rom. 8:14–23: according to Eph. 1:5 we are to be adopted as sons through Jesus Christ.

God shall quicken our mortal bodies because of his Spirit that dwells in us (Rom. 8:11): all shall be raised up in Christ (1 Cor. 15:22).

There is certainly a parallelism between Christ and the Spirit. But there is no question of identity between the two. Paul makes statements about Christ which could not be made about the Spirit. He calls Christ his life in Phil. 1:21, Gal. 2:20, and Col. 3:4; but he never says this of the Spirit. In Gal. 4:19 he says that Christ must be formed in him; this is something which he did not and could not say concerning the Holy Spirit. We could not substitute the Holy Spirit for Christ in Rom. 8:29 where he says that Christians must be conformed to the image of the Son of God. Neither can we speak of the Holy Spirit as he does of Christ in Eph. 4:13, where he says that Christians should attain "the measure of the age of the fulness of Christ".

It may be urged that Paul says in 2 Cor. 3:17: "The Lord is a Spirit"; but whatever this means, it is not a statement that the Lord and the Spirit are identical, for the next sentence reads: "And where the Spirit of the Lord is, there is liberty." There is here a formal distinction between the Lord and the Spirit which would be impossible if the two were identical. The majority of exegetes realize this fact. Windisch,[55] for example, says expressly that this is not an identification of the Lord and the Spirit; it presupposes that they are already known to the readers, and means that both cause the same effects. Most commentators regard it as an exegetical parenthesis which explains that the Lord of Exod. 34:34 is the Spirit (of the Lord).[56] However, Paul could not have said this if he had not felt that Christ and the Spirit are closely connected, and from this point of view the parenthesis cannot be dismissed as a merely casual remark. It is a fundamental phrase, "a cardinal statement",[57] though it does not mean that Christ and the Spirit are metaphysically identical.

Paul declares in 1 Cor. 15:45: "The last Adam (was made) into a quickening spirit": the last Adam here is Christ, but the

[55] *Kommentar zum 2. Korintherbrief,* p. 124.

[56] See W. G. Kümmel, *Kirchenbegriff und Geschichtsbewusstsein in der Urgemeinde und bei Christus* (Upsala, 1943), p. 46, note 19a; K. Prümm, "Israels Kehr zum Geist" in *Zeitschr. f. kath. Theologie,* lxxii (1950), pp. 385–442; against this e.g., P. Benoit in *Rev. biblique,* lix (1952), pp. 129–31. R. Schnackenburg in a letter suggests that Christ is meant by "the Lord" in v. 16, and that verse 17a speaks of Christ the Lord and tells us that he is a Spirit; this statement that Christ is a Spirit is not an identification: like 1 Cor. 15:45 it means that he is the Spirit which gives grace and glory.

[57] Windisch, op. cit., p. 125.

statement does not mean that Christ and the Spirit are identical. Since the resurrection Christ's glorified Body has been free from every trace of earthly weakness and impermanence; it is the organ of Christ who is filled with the Spirit of God and who gives life to all. This glorified Body has been determined and formed by the Holy Spirit, and it is he who possesses it. That is why Paul can say that Christ was made into a lifegiving Spirit.[58]

There is a second difference between Christ and the Spirit, and it proves absolutely that Paul does not regard them as identical. In Paul's eyes Christ is a concrete figure, he bears the marks of Christ crucified. Paul's conception of Christ is particularly clear in Rom. 8:34: "Who is he that shall condemn? Christ Jesus that died: yea that is risen also again, who is at the right hand of God, who also maketh intercession for us." Paul prays to him, and all Christians should do so: "Thrice I besought the Lord that it (the angel of Satan) might depart from me. And he said to me: My grace is sufficient for thee" (2 Cor. 12:8 et seq.). "The same is Lord over all, rich unto all that call upon him" (Rom. 10:12). "In the name of Jesus every knee should bow . . . and every tongue should confess that the Lord Jesus Christ is in the glory of God the Father" (Phil. 2:11). In 1 Cor. 1:2 he describes Christians as "all that invoke the name of Our Lord Jesus Christ". Anyone to whom we pray must be a Person. Paul's deepest longing is to be with Christ, as one friend longs after another; he tells us that he has "a desire to be dissolved and to be with Christ" (Phil. 1:22). In Heaven Christ reigns as King: "To this end Christ died and

---

[58] See Bertrams, op. cit., p. 125.

85

rose again: that he might be Lord both of the dead and of the living" (Rom. 14:9). From Heaven he watches over and guides Christians: "God himself and our Father and our Lord Jesus Christ, direct our way unto you" (1 Thess. 3:11). At the end of time Christ will descend in majesty, surrounded by the angels of Heaven, to judge the living and the dead: "Judge not before the time: until the Lord come" (1 Cor. 4:5); "We must all be manifested before the judgement seat of Christ" (2 Cor. 5:10). Then shall the children of God be revealed (Rom. 8:19): as he says in Col. 3:4: "When Christ shall appear, who is your life, then you also shall appear with him in glory." At the Second Coming he shall bring to naught all kingship and power and authority, and then he shall hand over the kingdom to the Father, "for he must reign until he hath put all his enemies under his feet" (1 Cor. 15:25).

One glance at these texts is enough to demonstrate that when Paul thought of Christ Triumphant he had in mind a concrete definite Person. In his eyes Christ Triumphant was not "the formless Spirit which permeates everything"; he is a Person whose life is inseparable from the Jesus who in this world died on the Cross. Paul does not in any way identify Christ and the Spirit.

It is, of course, perfectly true that Christ and the Spirit are very closely connected, and we must now attempt to elucidate this relationship.

We can begin by recalling two points which have already been established: it has been shown that Paul considers the Spirit as a power rather than as an element; secondly there are texts where Paul speaks of the Spirit of Christ or of the Lord, as in 2 Cor. 3:17: "Where the Spirit of the Lord is, there is liberty." Christ possesses the Spirit; we may say that he controls the Spirit, and that the Spirit is his. Moreover, it is significant that Paul never equates the Spirit with the pre-existing Christ, nor with Christ incarnate. It is Christ, and not the Spirit, who redeemed us; God the Father wrought our Redemption through His Son, Jesus Christ, not through the Spirit. This is clear from various texts: Gal. 2:20: "The Son of God, who loved me and delivered himself for me"; Rom. 5:1: "Let us have peace with God through our Lord Jesus Christ", and 5:9: "Justified by his blood shall we be saved from wrath through him", and 5:11: "our Lord Jesus Christ, by whom we have now received reconciliation."

All the texts which equate Christ and the Spirit refer to Christ's operation on the souls of individuals or on the community, that is, the Church. In other words the reference is always to sharing, possessing, or increasing the new life.

It is, therefore, true to say that when Christ and the Spirit are equated the reference is always to their effect on souls. They are not identified; it is Christ who bears and communicates the Spirit. The presence or operation of Christ is always accompanied by the Spirit. It is through the Spirit that Christ works in us. As Juncker says: "Christ possesses all the power and fulness of the Godhead which is in the Divine Spirit."[59] Paul regarded both Christ and the Holy Spirit as the supernatural vital principle of Christians.

Paul teaches that Christ Triumphant is essentially a Spirit.[60] He tells us that Christ has a spiritual Body, so he may properly be called a spiritual Being. That is why Paul can say: "The last

[59] Juncker, *Ethik des Apostels Paulus,* i, p. 154.
[60] See Bertrams, op. cit., p. 95; Juncker, op. cit.

Adam (was made) into a quickening spirit" (1 Cor. 15:45). It is true that the Apostle has here in mind Christ's role in pouring out the Spirit who operates both in the Christian community and in individuals. But this does not exhaust the content of the verse. It also means that Christ Triumphant is a spiritual Being. But it does not mean that Christ and the Spirit are identical.

Similarly, when Paul uses the phrases "Christ in us" or "the Spirit in us", he is not thinking of Christ in his spiritual Body, but is referring to Christ as the Spirit who gives life to the soul.

It is clear, therefore, that Paul draws a sharp distinction between the Spirit and Christ; in his eyes Christ Triumphant is a Person. Christ has full possession of the Spirit, he is himself a spiritual Being, and he gives the Spirit to men.

There are also places in the epistles where the Spirit appears as a Person rather than as a power, for example, Rom. 8:16; 8:26; 1 Cor. 2:10; 3:16; 6:19; 12:4–11; 2 Cor. 13:13; Gal. 4:6; and 1 Tim. 4:1. It is not at all certain that all these texts refer to the Person of the Holy Ghost, but some of them certainly do so. Paul speaks of the impersonal divine power of the Spirit, and also of a personal Being, distinct from Christ, whom he calls the (Holy) Spirit. A thorough investigation of this point would take us too far afield.[61]

The relationship between the spiritual Christ and the divine Spirit is now clear. But the other question remains: How does Paul come to speak of the indwelling of the (personal) Christ Triumphant, instead of simply saying that the (impersonal) divine Spirit lives and operates in us? It is not difficult to under-

---

[61] See Bertrams, op. cit., p. 144 et seq.; Büchsel, *Geist Gottes,* p. 410 et seq.

stand how he could speak of the impersonal Spirit abiding in us.

Paul's doctrine of the indwelling of the Person of Christ Triumphant may be explained in the following way: When he was converted on the road to Damascus, he saw Christ as a glorified spiritual Being, and ever afterwards he was aware that Christ – whom he had once persecuted in his followers – held his whole being, transformed his soul, transferred him to a new life, and filled him with heavenly power. In view of this it is quite natural that, instead of speaking of an impersonal divine power, he should speak of the Lord Triumphant who held him and changed his being. At Damascus Christ had personally intervened in Paul's life, and had changed him from a persecutor to a vessel of election. Paul could use the expressions which he does, because he regarded Christ Triumphant as a spiritual Being free from the limitations of time and place which bound Christ during his life on earth.

To our minds it is difficult to reconcile the two statements "Christ sits at the right hand of the Father", and "Christ is present in Christians". But they are not incompatible. The idea of the Spirit provides the link between the two. Because of his spiritual existence Christ can sit at the right hand of the Father in Heaven, while simultaneously abiding and working in Christians on earth. The difficulty in understanding this is lessened if we recall that we are not speaking of Christ's physical location when we say that he sits at the right hand of the Father: this expression denotes his divinity; it means that he is raised above the limitations of humanity, and that his Being and operation are divine.[62]

[62] Büchsel, op. cit., p. 410.

On the other hand, as has been shown, when we speak of Christ's indwelling, we refer to the significance of the spiritual Christ for the interior life of Christians on earth. In addition to the evidence already adduced, the meaning of the doctrine of indwelling may also be elucidated by the following consideration. As the epistles show, Paul was acquainted with Old Testament wisdom thought, in which divine Sophia (wisdom) appears as a Person.[63] The language of the Wisdom literature concerning divine wisdom is clearly reflected in Paul's description of Christ as "the power of God and the wisdom of God" in 1 Cor. 1:24.[64] It is said (for example in Wisdom 7:27 et seq.; 8:2 et seq.; 9:1 et seq.; 10:16) that wisdom has entered upon a close relationship with the wise. We read in 7:27: "And being but one, she can do all things: and remaining in herself the same, she reneweth all things and through nations conveyeth herself into holy souls. She maketh the friends of God and prophets." In 10:16 we are told about Moses: "She entered into the soul of the servant of God and stood against dreadful kings in wonders and signs." Wisdom is regarded as a person, and we are told that in addition to its influence on the cosmos, it also abides in the souls of just men. This provides a good parallel to Paul's doctrine.

Another apt parallel is the description in Eph. 2:1 et seq., of the influence of the devil on men: "When you were dead in your offences and sins, wherein in time past you walked

[63] Göttsberger, "Die göttliche Weisheit als Persönlichkeit im AT" in *Bibl. Zeitfragen,* ix, 1–2 (Münster, 1919).

[64] Windisch, *Neutest. Studien f. G. Heinrici* (1914), pp. 220–38; idem, *Kommentar zum 2. Korintherbrief,* p. 125; E. Krebs, *Der Logos als Heiland* (1910), p. 81 et seq.

according to the course of this world, according to the prince of the power of this air, of the spirit that now worketh on the children of unbelief . . . God . . . hath quickened us together in Christ." The prince of the power of this air is Satan, a spiritual being who influences the unbelievers. His spirit is the counterpart to the Holy Spirit who dwells in the faithful; it is a power which penetrates within man and works in him; it is probably identical with sin personified, which is mentioned in Rom. 7:11: "Sin . . . seduced me . . . and killed me."[65] Sin is also personified in 7:17 and 7:20; the former text reads: "It is no more I that do it (that is, whatever he does): but sin that dwelleth in me." Satan – whom Paul conceives as a person – works in the wicked in just the same way as Christ works in the faithful.

To conclude this study of the indwelling of Christ in the faithful:[66] When Paul speaks of the indwelling and operation of Christ in Christians he uses terms which denote a local presence of the Lord Triumphant in Christians. This evidently is connected with the idea of a spiritual being dwelling in men. But his sole aim is to express the truth that Christ Triumphant performs operations of grace on the interior of men. Christ dwells and works in Christians through his activity or through his Spirit. Paul is not thinking of physical presence; he is thinking of influence. The idea is closely paralleled in Rom. 8:11, where he says that God "shall quicken also your mortal bodies because of his spirit that dwelleth in you".

[65] Bertrams, op. cit., p. 158.
[66] See Büchsel in *ZntW* (1949), p. 152; Cerfaux, *Christ in the Theology of Saint Paul*, p. 290 et seq.

4. CONCLUSIONS

We are now in a position to sum up the results of this investigation, and to compare them with other conceptions.

Paul uses various phrases and metaphorical expressions to describe the special relationship which exists between Christians and Christ Triumphant. Fundamentally they all have the same meaning. Sometimes he speaks of Christ abiding in Christians, and elsewhere he says that Christians are in Christ. Both statements convey Paul's conviction that there is an intimate union of life and being between Christians and Christ Triumphant. Christ's act of Redemption lies in the past, but it has enduring effects, and all men who acknowledge Christ are influenced by it. But we mean much more than this when we speak of the union between Christ and Christians. This union entails the continuous outpouring of heavenly powers by Christ Triumphant upon all who believe in him: indeed the faithful live entirely in this sphere of supernatural powers – which is identical with the spiritual Christ – and they are therefore thoroughly penetrated and surrounded by Christ Triumphant (cf. 1 Cor. 12:13). Christ died for men and was raised by God to heavenly life; he now sits at the right hand of God in possession of divine power and majesty. He has completely absorbed Christians into his personal spiritual life; he lives and works in them and has become life for them (see Gal. 2:20; Phil. 1:21; Col. 3:3), while Christians live in him and receive from him continuous supernatural powers. Christ is their vital principle in the new life which as Christians they possess. Christ and his followers are bound in a mysterious union of intimate fellowship in life and being; in

92

this fellowship Christ is the Giver and Christians are the recipients.

Paul regards this union as something real, an objective state, which is brought about by becoming a Christian and thereby being joined to the Person of Christ Triumphant. In moments of spiritual exaltation a Christian may feel that he is fully subject to Christ, and may be aware of Christ's love for him. This is not what Paul means, for Christians are united with Christ quite independently of their momentary disposition of soul.

Moreover, this union is not something which only Paul has attained. It is true of all Christians without exception. Paul considers it a self-evident fact that as soon as a man becomes a Christian he enters upon this vital union with Christ. Naturally he speaks mainly of his own relationship to Christ, but he makes it clear that all Christians enjoy this union, as we see from Gal. 3:27 et seq.; 2 Cor. 5:17; Col. 3:4.

In Scholastic terminology this relationship with Christ can be described as a physical–accidental union between Christ and his followers.[67] Such a union must be carefully distinguished from substantial union, which would mean that the two persons become one entity, in other words that the human being is either annihilated or absorbed into the Divine Person. As Bartmann[68] points out, the new creation of 2 Cor. 5:17 makes a physical change in our spirit and its capacities, and the new life which we receive is something real. But this physical change is not substantial. It is merely accidental, and so it does

[67] Thus also K. Benz in *Theol. Revue* (1919), p. 207; W. Schauf, *Sarx,* p. 144; Meinertz in *Zeitschr. f. Miss.-Wiss.,* xiii (1923), p. 5.

[68] *Paulus,* p. 118.

not produce an indelible natural effect. Its effect is in the order of grace, and it may be undone.

It would be a misconception to regard this union with Christ as a mere alignment of the Christian's will with the will of Christ. For Paul union with Christ is not something merely personal which is attained by subjecting oneself to Christ Triumphant and which essentially consists in this subjection. In the next chapter we shall deal with the effect of Baptism in uniting us with Christ. For Paul Baptism means being "planted together in the likeness of his death" (Rom. 6:5), and we shall see that it is Baptism which unites us with Christ. In view of this it would be erroneous to regard the union as merely a union of wills.

Since this union with Christ has an objective character, it is hardly necessary to point out that it cannot be reduced simply to the Christian's awareness that his entire life is penetrated by the power of Christ in Heaven. Paul makes it quite clear that we are dealing with an objective state in the case of every Christian. This is the fundamental point about the union of Christians with Christ. The Christian is in a new reality; he lives in a new world, and is a new creature: "If then any be in Christ a new creature the old things are passed away. Behold all things are made new" (2 Cor. 5:17). It is true that the new world has not yet come to pass fully, but it does exist in embryo. We have been withdrawn from the old world and have been planted in the new. Paul is speaking of what has actually taken place when he says in Col. 1:13 that God "hath delivered us from the power of darkness and hath translated us into the kingdom of the Son of his love: in whom we have redemption through his blood, the remission of sins." With this qualification we may agree with Bultmann when he says: "The phrase 'in Christ' is used by Paul in an eschatological sense, not in a mystical sense."[69]

These conclusions can be illustrated and completed by a brief survey of modern studies concerning Paul's doctrine of union with Christ. It is particularly interesting at this point to examine the views of those scholars who deny that Paul has a mystical doctrine.

P. Feine is very emphatic that there are absolutely no mystical elements in Paul:[70] he says that the Apostle's preaching and piety have an eschatological rather than a mystical outlook. Moreover, he can find nothing mystical in Paul's conversion. All that Paul says is that Christ has become his absolute sovereign, and that Christ has chosen him as his instrument and has penetrated him with his vital power; he also feels that the powers of the world to come have already taken possession of him, while he ignores earthly interests and is a new creature. But none of this is mystical, for it is derived from the death and resurrection of Christ, regarded as interventions of God in human history through Christ, and it calls for a thorough redirection of life which can be attained only by the greatest effort and activity on the part of men. This redirection of life entails a withdrawal from worldly interests, but we cannot describe such a withdrawal as mystical, for men desire it as a

[69] Bultmann in *Theol. Lit.-Ztg.* (1926), p. 274. Idem, *Glauben und Verstehen* (Tübingen, 1933), p. 257 et seq.: "The phrase 'in Christ' denotes an eschatological and not a mystical fact: in Christ men have justice (2 Cor. 5:21; Gal. 2:17) and freedom (Gal. 2:4), and men belong to the new world, the new humanity, which began with the fact of Redemption."

[70] *Apostel Paulus,* p. 559 et seq.

necessary means of attaining salvation at the General Judgement. Jesus did not preach that we should rest in intimate fellowship with Christ; he preached the suppression of human interests, and so his preaching was fundamentally eschatological. There is not a single case where the phrase "to be in Christ" has a mystical meaning. It means, of course, that Paul feels himself in an intimate vital union with Christ. But that is an outlook which he regards as common to all Christians: he does not consider it personal and individual.

Feine's position is very instructive, and we can accept most of his factual statements without at all subscribing to his denial of mystical elements in Paul's piety. He reaches his conclusions by looking for mystical elements in the Hellenistic sense of the word. In Hellenistic piety mysticism meant a personal individual experience of becoming one with God; it presupposed a pantheistic theology. Feine himself says: "I cannot regard as mystical a relationship between two persons where each retains his separate personality."[71] And if mysticism means the pantheistic absorption in God of Hellenistic piety, it is perfectly true that Paul was not a mystic; the Apostle's clear idea of God as a Person precluded him from adopting any such doctrine.

But if we take mysticism in the wider sense, it is quite correct to speak of Paul's mysticism. There are undoubtedly mystical elements in Paul's spirituality, though it would be a gross exaggeration to describe him as a "mystic" and not a "theologian". There is both mysticism and theology in Paul, and the theological element is predominant.

[71] P. 568.

96

H. E. Weber has written much about this question.[72] He belongs to the school of thought which describes Paul's doctrine of fellowship with Christ as a mysticism of faith. Here is his definition of it: "God has drawn near man by the revelation which he made 'in Christ'. Paul's mysticism is the faith which lives in God's presence in Christ. This faith, which experiences the presence of God, looks forward towards the triumph of eternity when God's presence shall become permanent."[73] In other words, leading one's life in the presence of the living Christ is what is meant by being in Christ. Paul's consciousness is filled with Christ; Christ is the focus of his interest, and the thought of Christ influences him everywhere. Even if he does not positively attend to it, the thought of Christ can lie in the background. "Even when he is not directly aware of it, his subconsciousness, from which thought arises, is filled with it."[74] Christ is the sphere in which Paul's spiritual life is lived. When he thinks or wills or feels, he is conscious of Christ's presence. His whole soul – thought, feeling and willing – is filled with the thought of Christ; and joined to this consciousness is the awareness – or the conviction – of the reality of the vital presence of Christ.

Weber is more profound and more accurate than most others of this school. But his idea of fellowship with Christ, when analysed closely, dissolves into something merely subjective. It is true that he stresses that conduct is influenced by the consciousness of the presence of Christ Triumphant. But he does not

---

[72] *Neue kirchliche Zeitschrift* (1920), p. 213 et seq. See also his books: *Glaube und Mystik* (Gütersloh, 1927), and *"Eschatologie" und "Mystik" im N. T.* (Gütersloh, 1930).

[73] P. 235.   [74] P. 239.

explain how this effect is produced. It is not clear whether it is due really to the living Christ Triumphant, or if it is Paul's own work, achieved by constant intensive concentration of the powers of his soul upon Christ. As I understand Weber, Paul's statements convey to him merely that Christ is present in man's consciousness, but they do not mean that he is objectively present independently of the subject's awareness. This is not a real fellowship of being and life. Weber himself poses the question whether such presence is not merely awareness, and his answer is necessarily that "it is undeniable: in these very texts Paul displays the lively feeling and conviction of reality which is inherent in living religion."[75] Nevertheless he considers that an historical and psychological explanation is not ruled out. Yet Mundle had already pointed out that Paul never distinguishes between the objective presence of Christ and consciousness of his presence, so that we cannot regard consciousness of his presence as the source of "being in Christ".[76] Moreover, it must be remembered that in Paul's eyes the spiritual Christ is really present in the faithful and they in him. Whether such a relationship can be made intelligible, is an independent question. But when we are discussing how Christ can be present we must bear in mind that he exists in a spiritual manner and so is not subject to the same limitations as ordinary men.

Deissner also maintains that a mysticism of faith is the most that can be found in Paul.[77] He says that it is only by faith that Christ dwells in men, and that this applies even to Gal. 2:20. Christ and Paul are two persons; they do not become confused,

[75] P. 245.
[76] *Das religiöse Leben des Paulus*, p. 73.
[77] *Paulus und die Mystik*, pp. 96 et seq., 134 et seq.

but remain two distinct beings who are closely joined by the bond of faith. Furthermore, this faith must not be construed as a mystical elevation to Christ; indeed it is explicitly contrasted with immediate religious fellowship.

E. von Dobschütz is quite uncompromising in his denial of any mysticism in Paul.[78] He claims that when Paul speaks of fellowship with Christ he means a community of outlook. Paul's aim is not absorption in Christ or in God; the Apostle envisages a union with the Lord which safeguards the integrity of the sanctified human person. Von Dobschütz' second statement is quite correct; he is also right when he issues a warning against blunting the definiteness of Paul's ideas and overlooking the fact that all his ideas are intended to influence conduct.

But his description of fellowship with Christ is quite inadequate. He thinks that the mystical phrases – "in Christ" and "Christ in us" – can be reduced to ethical statements or counsels, and that they are simply an unsatisfactory way of expressing something quite different from mysticism. He says that Paul uses the genitive of "Christ" merely to express dependence, and that the passages where it is used express nothing more than moral obligations or mere states of feeling. His view may be summed up by saying that the Christian feels an obligation to imitate Christ and that this moral obligation provides him with supernatural powers; as he himself says: "We have here 'I must' joined to 'I can'; this is a fellowship of outlook which, as well as being the Christian's aim, is also a power which this union provides for men."[79]

[78] *ThStKr*, pp. 95, 314 et seq.; *Der Apostel Paulus,* i, p. 42 et seq.
[79] *ThStKr*, xcv, p. 327.

The most recent author to deal with this problem is F. Büchsel, and he also can find nothing mystical in Paul.[80] He says that the phrase "in Christ" can be understood in various ways, and that there are only twelve places where it denotes being in Christ; furthermore some of these passages refer to Christians in general (Rom. 8:1; 1 Cor. 1:30; 2 Cor. 5:17), others speak of particular individual Christians (Rom. 16:7,11; 2 Cor. 12:2; Phil. 3:9; 1 Thess. 4:16), while the Christian communities are mentioned in Gal. 1:22; 1 Thess. 1:1; 2:14; 2 Thess. 2:1. Being in Christ, he says, means being a Christian in the sense of standing in a personal relationship with Christ, but it is not equivalent to the bare fact of being a Christian. He claims that it is incorrect to understand 2 Cor. 5:17 as meaning "If any man be a Christian, he is a new creature", for those who externally are Christians are not all new creatures. The phrase "in Christ" denotes the ideal Christian, not necessarily any Christian. Only those who enjoy the personal relationship of being "in Christ" are really new creatures. Paul's phrase "in Christ" contains his faith in Christ, while our word Christian abstracts from this faith. The "men in Christ" of Rom. 16:7,11; 2 Cor. 12:2 are those who are guided by Christ as their Lord; they could also be called "servants of Christ" (δοῦλοι). The phrase "in Christ" is paralleled by other phrases: "to be in the flesh, in the Spirit, in the Law, in circumcision, in sin": it means being in a certain definite state because of Christ. The phrase "in Christ" has not a locative meaning; it is used adverbially.

This interpretation of Büchsel's cannot be upheld. Like most Protestant theologians, he denies the role of Baptism in establish-

---

[80] *ZntW* (1949), p. 150 et seq.

ing and promoting union with Christ. He is correct when he says that this union is a relation between two persons. But this is not enough, for union with Christ also signifies a real *union of being* between Christ and the Christian, though it does not mean that the Christian is located in Christ.

Some important facts emerge from this survey of the views of those who deny the existence of Pauline mysticism.[81] Their denial is due to the narrowness of their concept of mysticism; they give the word only the most restricted meaning, and confine it to the effort to be completely absorbed in God. They follow Söderblom in drawing a sharp distinction between prophetic and mystical piety; they regard these as two utterly distinct genera of piety. According to them, a mystic is one who indulges in religious feelings while remaining passive in matters of conduct, and who strives for an ecstatic vision of God in order to become divine.[82] Feine[83] quotes Mehlis[84] with approval: "Mysticism is a form of religious consciousness which desires and strives to bridge over the gap between the transcendent Divinity and the individual soul, so as to reach a perfect union of being even in this life." Von Dobschütz gives a particularly clear explanation of his view: "Was Paul really a mystic? He was, if we are willing to apply the name mysticism to interior piety which works with the understanding and also lets this feeling exercise a practical influence. But can such piety of the heart be called mysticism? The special characteristic of mysticism is that

---

[81] Wilh. Weber, A. Deissmann etc., also speak of Paul's "mysticism of faith" (see infra III, 1).

[82] See Feine, *Der Apostel Paulus,* p. 559 et seq.; H. E. Weber in *Neue kirchl. Zeitschrift* (1920), p. 233 et seq.; Deissner, op. cit., p. 115 et seq.

[83] Op. cit., p. 563.   [84] *Mystik* (1926), p. 22.

it strives for union with God, for becoming free from oneself, and for the ascent to the Infinite. Mysticism is always exclusively a religion of feeling; it luxuriates in the love of God and relegates to unimportance matters of conduct. No one could say that Paul attached importance to momentary feelings of being saved rather than to activeness and good conduct."[85]

Paul's mysticism certainly had nothing in common with the mysticism which these authors describe, and they are perfectly right when they deny that such ideas appear in Paul. There are passages where we may find an emotional colouring in Paul's words about his union with Christ; but it is quite certain that he never reduced fellowship with Christ to indulgence in mystical feelings. Moreover, it is no part of Paul's reaching that the Christian's personality is annihilated by absorption in Christ. The only union which he knows preserves the individuality of the person, and also the relationship of master and servant with Christ. There is no Quietism in his piety; it is most certainly active. And so far from subordinating ethics to mysticism, he stresses the moral obligations of Christians. In Paul's eyes the pious Christian is not one who rests inactive, content with what he has; he is one who strives to live and work in a manner worthy of the Lord. On this point we agree thoroughly with the authors cited above.

Paul had no share in the pantheistic tendencies of Hellenistic mysticism, as we shall show in the fourth section of this work. But scholars like von Dobschütz, maintain that the only possible union with Christ is a union in the consciousness of the Christian: they deny the fact – and even the possibility – of an

[85] *Der Apostel Paulus,* i (1926), p. 42.

objective union. They consider that Paul's fellowship with Christ is merely a relationship between two persons, no different from the relation which exists between any human being and someone whom he respects highly, except that it is a religious bond. This is quite unacceptable, and their idea about a mysticism of faith is no better, for it means that the only spiritual bond between Christ and men in this world is faith. This does not harmonize with Paul's words which teach that there is a real vital union between Christ and Christians.

E. Peterson has traced this school of thought back to the ideas of Albrecht Ritschl and his pupil M. Reischle.[86] They denied the substantial nature of the soul, and said that the soul is merely a complexus of feelings, thoughts and desires. It would follow from this that God's operations on men affect only the conscious activities of the spirit, and that God does not influence the substance of the spiritual life. So it would be impossible to have any real communication of being and life between God and men: the most that we could have is a union of man's will with the divine will, and it must be remembered that God is far from us. It is obvious that the holder of such a philosophical position could not admit any real mysticism in Paul. But, as Peterson rightly observes, a very different attitude to mysticism will be adopted by anyone who admits that God can perform supernatural operations on men in the realm of man's being.

At this point an important question arises. We have described Paul's doctrine of fellowship with Christ, and have defended it. Can such a doctrine really be called mysticism?

---

[86] "Zur Theorie der Mystik" in *ZsystTh*, ii (1924), p. 146 et seq., especially p. 153 et seq.

There is an objective relationship between Christ and Christians; it is a fellowship in life and being which has the sacrament of Baptism as its foundation. If this can be called mystical, then logically all Christians are mystics.[87]

There are two points which can be made in this connection.

To begin with, the name mysticism can and should be applied to this objective relationship which Baptism brings about, for it creates a union of being and life between Christ and man. The essence of mysticism is the establishment of such an immediate fellowship between God and man, and since it is the sacrament which establishes the relationship, it is best described as sacramental mysticism. The word mysticism has a conventional meaning which appears when we speak of the Mystical Body of Christ, or describe Baptism as a mystical death and resurrection. When we use the word mysticism here in that sense, we must note carefully that it refers to the objective and divine side of the union with Christ which Paul teaches.

Paul used the phrases "in Christ" and "Christ in us" to sum up his teaching about this union. And it cannot be repeated too often that this union is not merely a subjective feeling of Christ's nearness. It is an objective relationship in the realm of being between Christ and the faithful. Every man who "believes and is baptized" (Mark 16:16) enters upon a mystical union with Christ Risen and Triumphant.

There is a second point to consider. In addition to the objective and divine aspect there is also a subjective and human side of union with Christ. A Christian can be called a mystic only if,

[87] A number of authors, including some Catholics, prefer to speak of fellowship with Christ rather than mysticism, but this is merely a matter of terminology; they agree with the facts.

in addition to being objectively united with Christ, he is aware of this union and lets it influence him. In other words the objective union with Christ, which Baptism establishes, must become an active union in the sphere of piety and conduct. This takes place when the Christian surrenders his whole soul to Christ and allows the powers of Christ to influence him. In practice the name mystic is applied only when this active union with Christ reaches a particularly high degree, and when all thought, feeling and willing is subordinated to Christ, and the person is guided and moved entirely by the Lord Triumphant.

Paul himself was a mystic in this full sense of the word. His epistles give abundant evidence of this. He is convinced that he dwells "in Christ" and that Christ dwells in him, and he also feels in his weak body the operation of Christ's powers (2 Cor. 12:19; Phil. 4:13), and with the deepest love subjects his soul to Christ. At Damascus he was "apprehended" by Christ; God there "revealed his Son" to Paul, and now Paul's great aim is to be "found (that is, preserved) in him" constantly (Phil. 3:9, 12; Gal. 1:16). His union with Christ provides him with the strength to persevere through all pains, dangers, persecutions, trials and hardships; he can do all things in Christ who strengthens him (Phil. 4:13). Indeed, it is at the times when troubles and cares and pains have almost worn out his human powers that he is most conscious of the powerful influence which Christ exercises upon him: "When I am weak, then am I powerful" (2 Cor. 12:10). That is why he rejoices in his infirmities, for he knows that the power of Christ then dwells in him (2 Cor. 12:9). He is conscious that there is always an intimate union between Christ and himself (see Rom. 9:3; 2 Cor. 12:2), and he is convinced that Christ speaks in him

(2 Cor. 13:3), and that the truth of Christ is in him (2 Cor. 11:10). Indeed, he feels even more closely united with Christ who was crucified and who now sits in glory on the right hand of God. With Christ he is "nailed to the Cross" (Gal. 2:19), he is "dead" and "buried" with him (Rom. 6:3 et seq.); he bears about in his body the death of Christ (2 Cor. 4:10), and his sufferings are the sufferings of Christ (2 Cor. 1:5). He is also certain that he will rise with Christ and be glorified with him (Rom. 6:8; Col. 3:4). Indeed, he goes so far as to say: "I live, now not I: but Christ liveth in me" (Gal. 2:20), and he says this as something self-evident. His self is no longer alive, the old man is dead (Rom. 6:6 et seq.), and a new life has taken its place (Rom. 6:4); he has become a new creature (2 Cor. 5:17). Paul considers that we can speak of life only where Christ is, and so death is gain for him (Phil. 1:21) because it brings Christ near (Phil. 1:23).

Paul does not suggest that only he has these mystical experiences. On the contrary, he is absolutely certain that they are available for every genuine Christian. There are several passages where he makes this clear. In 2 Cor. 13:5 he warns the Corinthian community,[88] where there were serious abuses: "Try your own selves if you be in the faith: prove ye yourselves. Know you not your own selves that Christ Jesus is in you?" He hopes that the community will realize the seriousness of the abuses which have developed, and will appreciate that they are incompatible with Christianity. If the community has experienced and realizes the fact that it is mystically united with Christ, then it cannot avoid this examination. If this is the case,

[88] See above, p. 41.

then the examination will produce the result which Paul expects, and his condemnation of the abuses, and of those who are responsible for them, will be justified. In other words, the latter part of his warning presupposes that they know from experience that they are mystically united with Christ.

The same thought occurs in Gal. 4:6: "Because you are sons (of God), God hath sent the Spirit of his Son into your hearts, crying: Abba, Father." The Apostle believes, and he takes for granted that the Galatians believe, that this prayer is possible only because the Spirit of God's Son dwells in Christians. He tells the Romans to "reckon that you are dead to sin, but alive unto God, in Christ Jesus our Lord" (6:11) and to behave accordingly. Three further texts are 1 Cor. 3:1 where he describes the Corinthians as "little ones in Christ" – this is the counterpart of being "perfect" (1 Cor. 2:6); in Gal. 4:19 he says "I am in labour again until Christ be formed in you"; and in Eph. 3:17 he prays that "Christ may dwell in your hearts". All three of these texts assume that "to be in Christ" is a feature of ordinary Christian life. The objective mystical union with Christ, which Baptism establishes, can and must be expressed in the life of every Christian. Each man can experience it in the heavenly powers which surround him, and he can perfect the union by an ever more intimate and thorough dedication of himself to Christ.

If we leave aside the numerous texts where Paul speaks of the influence of the Spirit on the faithful[89], it is true that he generally confines his remarks to the objective mystical rela-

---

[89] We can abstract here from these texts, for they have only an indirect bearing on our theme; they concern primarily the idea of the Spirit.

tionship which exists between Christ and every Christian.[90] This is the explanation of the fact which J. Weiss finds so strange, that there is a "mystical fervour" in comparatively few of the texts where the phrase "in Christ" occurs.[91] For Paul, fellowship with Christ is not merely a momentary experience which occurs at times of high spiritual exaltation; it is a reality, an objective fact which does not depend on perception of the operations of Christ. It is true, of course, that these operations can be perceived, but they are real whether we notice them nor not. When a man becomes a Christian he is "in Christ" and is continually under Christ's influence, even if he is not aware of it. That is why the phrase "in Christ" describes the fact of being a Christian, which is an objective relationship with Christ.[92]

[90] See Rom. 8:1; 16:7, 11; 2 Cor. 5:17.

[91] *Urchristentum*, p. 360.

[92] See also Schmitz, *Christusgemeinschaft*, p. 244 et seq. Paul's extraordinary mystical experiences are discussed by, for example, J. Baruzi, "La mystique paulinienne et les données autobiographiques des épîtres", in his book: *Création religieuse et pensée contemplative* (Paris, 1951), pp. 8–96, and by E. Benz, *Paulus als Visionär* (Wiesbaden, 1952). I have been unable to consult Chester C. McCown, "The Sources of Pauline Mysticism", in *Munera studiosa* for W. H. P. Hatch, ed. by Shepherd and Johnson (Cambridge, 1946), pp. 46–67, and A. A. Fulton, "The Mysticism of Paul the Apostle" in *Evangelical Quarterly*, xx (1948), p. 172 et seq.

III

The Means of Union with Christ

Now that the nature of union with Christ has been examined, the problem arises of how this mystical relationship is brought about. Before attempting an answer, it is worth while defining the problem which we are facing. We are not concerned here with the Comparative Religion problem of the origin of Paul's ideas, nor with how he came to believe that the relation between Christ and Christians is a mystical relationship. Our problem is to elucidate Paul's teaching on how this mystical relationship comes about: When and how does a man enter upon this mystical fellowship of life and being with Christ?

Paul's mysticism has an objective and divine aspect, as well as the subjective and human side. We must therefore consider its origin both on the part of God and on the part of man.

1. GOD'S ACTION IN BAPTISM

Most Protestant scholars consider that union with Christ is brought about by faith.[1] We may add to them all those who

---

[1] There is a lengthy account of this in Wissmann, Πίστις und Christus-frömmigkeit, p. 129.

deny that there is any mysticism in Paul, and those who will admit nothing more than a mysticism of faith.

Here is how P. Wernle sums up their ideas: "Through faith in Christ, Paul finds the justice which observance of the law did not bring. And from this faith there surges forth a mystical fellowship with Christ which is not simply a higher degree of faith, nor in any way opposed to faith. This fellowship is the deeper meaning and value of faith, for it is an interior contact with the object of faith, and it transforms the individual into Christ – or the Spirit of Christ – who is grasped in faith."[2] It is clear from this passage that Wernle is very sceptical about Paul's mysticism and that he would prefer to avoid the word altogether. The idea that the Christian is in Christ as in a vital element, always seemed to him a gross exaggeration. He considers that this "so-called mysticism" is something completely artificial and formal, and that a profound term like mysticism is utterly unsuited to describe it.[3] Wernle and others of his school regard what we call mystical union with Christ as being fundamentally only faith in Christ, even though it is a faith of a particularly interior and affective kind: to use a metaphor, faith is the bud, and mysticism is the flower which develops from the bud. In other words, mystical union with Christ is simply fully developed faith in Christ. Such writers take no account of a real objective fellowship of life and being between Christ and Christians.

This view is quite unacceptable, for it has already been shown that there is an objective side to Paul's mysticism; it is a real union of life and being, and not merely a grasping of Christ

[2] *Zeitschrift f. Theologie und Kirche,* xxv (1915), p. 65.
[3] Ibid., p. 69.

by faith. There is no doubt that this was what Paul taught. Moreover, he taught that this objective relationship is established by a sacramental act, namely by Baptism. He says clearly that mystical union with Christ is brought about by this act. We will now consider Paul's statements about this matter, and then investigate what role, if any, is played by faith in the process.

Let us begin with Paul's language. He speaks of Baptism into (εἰς) Christ, or into the name of Christ: 1. Rom. 6:3: "Know you not that all we who are baptized in Christ Jesus are baptized in his death?"; Gal. 3:27: "As many of you as have been baptized in Christ have put on Christ." 2. 1 Cor. 1:13 et seq.: "Were you baptized in the name of Paul? I give God thanks, that I baptized none of you but Crispus and Gaius: lest any should say that you were baptized in my name." The Greek verb βαπτίζειν "to baptize" always had the connotation of being plunged into an element. Hence Paul's phrase "to be baptized into Christ" probably means to be plunged or sunk into the Person of Christ, understanding Christ in a local sense; it therefore signified being brought into a most intimate union and vital relationship with him. However, this interpretation is meaningless if applied to 1 Cor. 10:2, and it has therefore been challenged when applied to Rom. 6:3; those who challenge it say that "in" means "in the name of"; they suggest that it refers to dedication to the Person of Christ.[4] It is not at all clear that they are correct.[5]

The idea is expressed more clearly in Gal. 3:27, where Paul

---

[4] See Schnackenburg, *Heilsgeschehen,* p. 18 et seq.

[5] K. L. Schmidt in *Eranos-Jahrbuch,* xiii (1945), p. 213: Baptized into Christ, literally: plunged into Christ; βαπτίζειν means "to plunge", and this cannot be separated from the sublime "to baptize".

speaks of putting on Christ as one puts on a garment and is completely enveloped in it. If we examine the metaphor, we discover that, like the phrase "in Christ", it denotes the sphere into which the person is transferred by Baptism. This sphere is the spiritual Christ.[6] Paul's language shows that Baptism creates such an interior relation and union with Christ that the person who is baptized can be said to be in Christ. Indeed in Rom. 16:7 he uses precisely this expression to describe Andronicus and Junias, who, he says, were in fellowship with Christ (γεγόνασιν ἐν Χριστῷ) before him. Though he does not mention Baptism here, there is no doubt that he is thinking of it. An even clearer case is Gal. 3:28 where, having spoken of putting on Christ, he says: "You are all one in Christ Jesus." They have put on Christ in Baptism, and thereby they are in Christ. The Christians as such are not simply a number of individuals, they are one great unit, for they are in the one Person, Christ.

[6] The metaphor is not elucidated by referring to the practice in the Mystery Religions of putting on the cloak or the mask of the god (thus Dibelius, *Paulus und die Mystik,* p. 63 et seq.). Unlike the Hellenistic thinkers, Paul thought eschatologically, and in terms of universality not of individuals. The metaphor of "putting on Christ" probably reflects the idea of wearing a heavenly garment which is ready for all souls. The mythology of the oriental Gnostics identified the heavenly prototype of original man with a garment; as the soul returned home from darkness to the world of light it was clothed in the heavenly robe which came to meet it, and salvation was thereby attained (see the "Pearl Hymn" in *Acts of Thomas,* 112 et seq.). In the light of this idea it is understandable that Christ as Redeemer should envelope the redeemed like a garment. "In Paul there are faint isolated echoes of this. But the great difference is that he suppresses or ignores the pantheistic equation of God and man, Saviour and saved. When applied to Christ the metaphor has a different meaning." Thus A. Oepke, *Galaterbrief,* p. 69; Käsemann, *Leib und Leib Christi* (1933), p. 87 et seq.

So Paul's language shows that to his mind Baptism creates the mystical union of men with Christ.

This conclusion is confirmed and supported by the texts where he speaks expressly of the effects of Baptism: Rom. 6:1 et seq.; Col. 2:10 et seq.

The Epistle to the Romans contains Paul's most important statements about the effects of Baptism, and these deserve further comment.[7] In Rom. 5:20 he said that the law increased sin, but that the effect of this was that grace was given still more abundantly. He now faces the objection which may be raised, that it is therefore better to remain in sin so that grace may be given more abundantly. His answer to this error appears in 6:2 et seq., where he says that it is out of the question for us to remain in sin: "We that are dead to sin, how shall we live any longer therein?" (verse 2). In the following verse he shows by reference to Baptism that Christians are really dead to sin: "Know you not that all we who are baptized in Christ are baptized in his death?" In other words, as you well know, death to sin has become a reality in Baptism. The following verse paraphrases this statement, and adds the purpose of this death: "For we are buried together with him by baptism into death: that, as Christ is risen from the dead by the glory (that

---

[7] The most recent examination of this is R. Schnackenburg, *Heilsgeschehen* (1950), and H. Schwarzmann, *Die Theologie des hl. Paulus nach Röm. 6* (Heidelberg, 1950). Ὁμοίωμα of verse 5 is discussed at length by J. Schneider in *ThWb*, v, 191–5. O. Casel's view (presence of the Mysteries) is defended at length by V. Warnach, "Taufe und Christusgeschehen nach Röm. 6" in *Archiv f. Liturgiewissenschaft*, iii (1954), pp. 284–366; he is impugned by R. Schnackenburg in *Münchener Theol. Zeitschr.*, vi (1955), pp. 32–53, and by E. Stommel in *Römische Quartalschrift*, 1 (1955), pp. 1–21.

is, the power) of the Father, so we also may walk in newness of life (that is, in a new life)" (verse 4). He means that it is absurd to continue in sin after Baptism, for the whole purpose of dying with Christ in Baptism is the release of the body from sin, so that we are under no further subjection to sin. Moreover, this death should be for us the passage to a new kind of life, just as Christ's death was followed by his new life. Paul attaches great importance to this thought, so much so that he again paraphrases it in verse 5.

The language of verse 5 is somewhat obscure, and there is disagreement about its meaning and about how it should be translated. Some exegetes render it: "If we have been planted together with the likeness of his death, we shall be also (planted together with) the likeness of his resurrection." The meaning would then be that the death and resurrection of Christ are sacramentally present in Baptism, and they are the likeness of his actual death and resurrection. Those who receive Baptism are most intimately joined with the salutary effects of Christ's death and resurrection, these effects being present in Baptism. In this sense we can say that they die (in Baptism) at the same time as Christ. This exegesis is adopted by O. Casel, H. Schlier, and Joh. Schneider.

A second way of interpreting this verse is to supply "with Christ" and to translate: "If we have been planted together (with Christ) in the likeness of his death, we shall be also (planted with him) in the likeness of his resurrection." Grammatically the first version is preferable, but the supplying of the words "with Christ" to produce the second version is suggested by verse 4: "We are buried together with him by Baptism". If this second version is correct, then the meaning is that Baptism imitates the death (and resurrection) of Christ, and by Baptism the subject undergoes the same death as Jesus, and also, like Christ, experiences a real resurrection. By this (sacramental) death and resurrection he grows with Christ. But this growth here and now with Christ cannot be separated from the historical redemptive act of Christ's death and resurrection.

Whichever interpretation is followed, the whole context makes it clear that Paul means that Baptism incorporates man not only into Christ's death, but also into his resurrection. Baptism communicates to the subject not only the event of Christ's death, but also the event of his resurrection. The two are joined together. Just as Christ was raised to a new life and now lives entirely for God (verse 10), so the Christian is also raised to a new life which he is enabled and obliged to lead. The entire argument aims at demonstrating this obligation, and Paul again stresses it in verse 11: "So do you also reckon that you are dead to sin, but alive unto God, in Christ Jesus our Lord."

Paul's teaching here is of importance for the solution of our problem. The entire argument assumes that Baptism creates such an intimate union between man and Christ that the Christian undergoes exactly what Christ underwent in his death and resurrection, namely death to sin (verse 10) and the attainment of a new life (verses 4, 9, and 10). Indeed, we can only do full justice to Paul's thought by saying that the Christian has gained a share in Christ's own death and resurrection, he has died with Christ and has risen again with him. This can be true only if a real union of life has been established between Christ and the Christian, if they have in some sense "been planted together" and have become a unity.

The correctness of this interpretation is confirmed by verse 11, where he calls upon the Christians to "reckon that you are dead to sin, but alive unto God, *in Christ*". By Baptism, which plants us together with Christ, man is put into the state of being "in Christ". But Christ has undergone death, which for him is dying to sin, and he has risen again, which carried with it for him the gaining of a new life – a life "unto God" (verse 10): similarly it must be true that one who is baptized is dead to sin and alive unto God. This is automatically the state of one who is "in Christ".

In Col. 2:11 et seq. there is a close parallel to Rom. 6:1 et seq. There also, dying with Christ is connected with Baptism. There are numerous other passages where Paul speaks of Christians dying with Christ and rising again with him, without mentioning Baptism (Gal. 2:19; 5:24; 6:14; Rom. 7:7; 2 Cor. 5:14; Phil. 3:10; Col. 2:20; 3:3; Eph. 2:5 et seq.). But these passages show close kinship in thought and language with Rom. 6:1–11, and it is quite clear that they regard Baptism as the place where this happens. These texts, therefore, also may be adduced as proofs that it is Baptism which establishes fellowship with Christ.

It is clear from a careful reading of Rom. 6:1 et seq., that Paul considers Baptism the means of establishing mystical union with Christ; he regards one who is baptized as being "in Christ". This teaching emerges even more clearly from what he says about the "Body of Christ".

Those who believe in Christ constitute the Body of Christ. He tells the Corinthians: "You are the Body of Christ and members of member" (1 Cor. 12:27), and the same idea occurs in Rom. 12:4 et seq.: "As in one body we have many members, but all the members have not the same office: so we, being many, are one body in Christ: and everyone members of one another", while in Eph. 5:30 he simply says: "Because we are members of his body." Side by side with this concept we find another idea, which in the last analysis is really another form of the doctrine of the Body of Christ – the idea that the faithful taken together constitute one personality: in Gal. 3:28 he says: "You are all one in Christ", and in the following verse he says that Christians are the seed of Abraham, having said a few verses earlier (3:16) that the seed of Abraham is one. It is obvious that Paul here is thinking of Christ as a personality which embraces all Christians and joins them into a unit.

All Christians are incorporated into the Body of Christ, into Christ who embraces all the faithful. The means by which this incorporation is brought about is Baptism. This is made quite explicit in a number of texts, especially in 1 Cor. 12:13. In that passage Paul points out that the human body has many limbs, but the limbs, in spite of their number, make up only one body. The same, he says, is true of Christ: "For in *one* Spirit were we all baptized into (that is, so as to make) *one* body, whether Jews or Gentiles, whether bond or free." In other words Baptism has incorporated the faithful into the Body of Christ, it has made them into the Body of Christ.

An equally significant text is Gal. 3:26. The whole passage from 3:7 onwards is devoted to showing that the true children of Abraham are those who believe in Christ, and not the Jews who observe the Law. Scripture tells us that Abraham received a promise that all nations should be blessed in him. He received this promise because of his faith; it was given to him and to his seed. The Scripture uses the singular number "seed", for it refers to Christ. The Law cannot qualify this promise, for it was merely our guide to Christ "that we might be justified by faith" (verse 24). The Law has now fulfilled its role: "After the faith is come, we are no longer under a pedagogue", we are no longer subject to the Law (verse 25). Now "you are all the children of God, by faith in Christ Jesus" (verse 26).

To demonstrate this point he refers to Baptism in the following verses. These are the important verses for the present purpose: "For as many of you as have been baptized in Christ have put on Christ. There is neither Jew nor Greek: there is neither bond nor free: there is neither male nor female. For you are all one in Christ Jesus. And if you be Christ's, then are you the seed of Abraham, heirs according to the promise" (verses 27-9). We may paraphrase the thought in the following manner: Because by Baptism Christians have put on Christ and now are in Christ, they constitute one Person with Christ ("one in Christ") and participate in his Being. Since he is the Son of God (see Gal. 1:16; 4:5), they also are "sons of God" (see Rom. 8:14 et seq.). Since Christ is the seed of Abraham to whom the promise was given, they also are the seed of Abraham and sharers in the promise.

So once again we reach the conclusion that Baptism unites men mystically with Christ; it causes them to "be in Christ".

Consideration of the other effects which Paul attributes to Baptism provides further proof. He says, as we have seen, that Baptism establishes a mystical union of life between man and Christ. He also ascribes other effects to the sacrament: it gives men the Spirit (of Christ), it kills the old man of sin, it produces new life in man, and thereby it guarantees our resurrection from the dead. There is an inseparable bond between mystical

118

union with Christ on the one hand, and on the other, possession of the Spirit and the new life ("Christ-life").

Büchsel thinks it strange that Paul never says that we receive the Spirit in Baptism. But there are various texts (for example, 1 Cor. 6:11; 12:13) which imply that Baptism communicates the Spirit to men. Paul's silence about the matter – if he really is silent about it – is probably due to the occasional nature of his writings.[8] But it seems to me that Paul does mention the giving of the Spirit in Baptism. In 1 Cor. 12:13b he says: "In one Spirit we have all been made to drink." This follows so closely on the reference to Baptism in the first part of the verse, that we may quite legitimately regard it as a new metaphor for the reception of the Spirit at Baptism.[9] There is another reference to Baptism in 1 Cor. 6:11, where Paul says to the Corinthians: "You are washed: but you are sanctified: but you are justified: in the name of our Lord Jesus Christ and the Spirit of our God." He is here drawing a sharp contrast between their former life ("such some of you were") and their present state, so it is clear that he has Baptism in mind. In the Epistle to Titus he teaches that Christians receive the new life in Baptism through the renovation which the Holy Spirit works; he says that God saved us "by the laver of regeneration and renovation of the Holy Ghost" (3:5).

It is true that Paul does not mention Baptism when he deals expressly with the giving of the Spirit. This is true of Rom. 5:5: "The charity of God is poured forth in our hearts by the Holy Ghost who is given to us"; Gal. 4:6: "God hath sent the Spirit

---

[8] *Geist Gottes*, p. 426 et seq.
[9] Thus, among others, Lietzmann and Allo, ad loc.

of his Son into your hearts"; Rom. 8:15: "You have received the Spirit of adoption of Sons."

In spite of this silence there are passages where it is clear that he has Baptism in mind, for example, 2 Thess. 2:12: "God hath chosen you firstfruits unto salvation, in sanctification of the spirit"; Gal. 3:2: "Did you receive the Spirit by the works of the law or by the hearing of faith?"; Eph. 1:13: "In whom (that is, Christ) you also, after you had heard the word of truth (the Gospel of your salvation), in whom also believing, you were signed with the holy Spirit of promise." Finally it is noteworthy that in Gal. 3:26 et seq., the rights of Christians as sons and heirs are said to derive from their Baptism.

The connection between Baptism and the new life is mentioned more often and more clearly. It will be sufficient for the present purpose to select some examples.[10] Paul teaches that Baptism annihilates the old man, frees us from the body of sin, and breaks the bonds of sin. Thus Rom. 6:6: "Our old man is crucified with him, that the body of sin may be destroyed, to the end that we may serve sin no longer" (cf. Gal. 5:24: "They that are Christ's have crucified their flesh, with the vices and concupiscences";[11] Rom. 6:11: "Reckon that you are dead to sin"; Col. 2:11: "In whom (that is, Christ) also you are circumcised with circumcision not made by hand in despoiling of the body of the flesh: but in the circumcision of Christ (that is, Baptism)."

---

[10] The texts in question appear in E. Sommerlath, *Entstehung des neuen Lebens*, p. 100 et seq.; Juncker, *Ethik Pauli*, i, p. 109 et seq.; J. Müller, *Der Lebensbegriff des hl. Paulus* (Dissertation, Münster, 1940), pp. 27–51.

[11] Crucified by the act of Baptism, as the aorist shows. The active voice refers to the decision which Christians have taken by receiving Baptism.

In addition to these effects Baptism also creates in man a new life: for man it is a resurrection, a rebirth, and it is also a pledge of the future resurrection from the dead. Rom. 6:4 tells us that because of Baptism Christians are expected to "walk in newness of life". They must consider themselves and act as "alive unto God" (6:11) and as "alive from the dead" (6:13). According to Col. 2:12 et seq., in virtue of their Baptism (2:11) Christians have "risen again" and have been "quickened" with Christ. And even their bodies shall rise again, because by Baptism they have been planted with Christ who died and rose again (Rom. 6:8; Phil. 3:11; cf. Rom. 8:17).

Elsewhere Paul speaks of the new life which is sent to Christians without expressly attributing it to Baptism. But in these cases he always uses the aorist,[12] thereby pointing back to a particular past fact which produced the effect he speaks of. This fact can only be Baptism.

This new life is real "Christ-life"; it is the life of Christ Triumphant himself which fills and penetrates Christians. Paul says this explicitly in Col. 3:3 where he calls Christ "your life", in Gal. 2:20 where he says: "I live, now not I: but Christ liveth in me", and in Phil. 1:21 where he declares that for him to live is Christ. In Paul's teaching death to sin and the gaining of the new life is the same thing as entering upon mystical union with Christ.

At this point the problem arises, what part does faith play in the establishment of this mystical union? There is no need to examine again the theory that Paul teaches a "mysticism of

---

[12] See Col. 3:1: "If you be risen with Christ"; Eph. 2:5 et seq.: "hath quickened us together in Christ . . . and hath raised us up together."

121

faith", which would mean that we are united with Christ when we grasp him by faith. That has already been rejected. It is obvious that such a view deprives Baptism of its whole effect, and reduces it to a mere ceremonial rite.

What role is ascribed to faith by the scholars who admit that it is Baptism which unites us to Christ? Most of them say that Baptism and faith create union with Christ. This is the view of the Catholic B. Bartmann, who appeals to the Council of Trent for support:[13] "It is well known how often Paul demands faith as the condition and beginning of the new life. But, as we shall see, he understands it in a comprehensive sense to mean the acceptance of the entire Christian economy of salvation, and there is no doubt that Baptism is a part – and a very prominent part – of the Christian economy." Unfortunately Bartmann does not develop his thought, and, moreover, he is inaccurate, for he speaks of union with God.

On the other hand, Meinertz speaks to the point: "Man enters upon mystical fellowship with Christ through Baptism and faith. In the Pauline sense faith is the acceptance of God's entire economy of salvation, and it includes the sacrament of Baptism."[14]

The Protestant scholars E. Sommerlath,[15] E. Wissmann,[16] and especially W. Mundle[17] have examined the problem thoroughly. Sommerlath says that fellowship with Christ is a Baptism-fellowship and a faith-fellowship, and that Baptism is the principal ele-

---

[13] *Paulus*, p. 95.
[14] *Zeitschr. f. Miss.-Wiss.* (1923), p. 2.
[15] *Ursprung des neuen Lebens*, p. 99 et seq.
[16] Πίστις *und Christusfrömmigkeit*, p. 110 et seq.
[17] *Glaubensbegriff*, p. 123 et seq.

ment, for it is the objective means of communicating the new life. Paul, he says, considers union with Christ due primarily to Baptism, and it is by Baptism that we win a share in Christ's vital powers. When Paul wished to expound the practical effect of being a Christian, and especially when he was showing how it should influence conduct, he often stressed that it is Baptism which makes men Christians; in spite of the fact that his whole message was devoted to faith, he never says that faith is the direct means by which one becomes a Christian. Fellowship with Christ is something objective which is established by Baptism. It is by faith that the Christian personally grasps this fellowship and develops it fully by leading a Christian life. Our fellowship with Christ has to assert itself constantly against the attacks of the life of the flesh. Moreover, the new life remains hidden until it reaches its consummation in the resurrection of the body (Col. 3:2). These two points show clearly the place of faith in the new life.

These scholars rightly stress that Baptism is the objective communication of the new life, and therefore of fellowship with Christ. We may say without qualification that Baptism, and not faith, establishes the mystical relationship with Christ.[18] Baptism really immerses us in the spiritual Christ, it incorporates us into his Body, and transfers us to a new sphere of life. And this is never due to an act of man's; it is always the effect of God's action on men, "by whom (God) you are called into the fellowship of his Son" (1 Cor. 1:9); "of him are you in Christ Jesus" (1 Cor. 1:30). God has sent the Spirit of his Son into our hearts

[18] O. Schmitz (*Christusgemeinschaft*, p. 132) is therefore wrong when he says: "Whoever believes in Christ is thereby in Christ; there is no factual causal link between one state and the other."

(Gal. 4:6; Rom. 8:15), and has given us the pledge of the Spirit (2 Cor. 1:22; 5:5). He has raised us up to life (the new life in Christ) (Col. 2:13; Eph. 2:5).

It is also significant that when Paul is speaking of the origin of fellowship with Christ he generally uses the passive voice (see Rom. 6:4 et seq.; 1 Cor. 12:13; Gal. 2:19; Col. 2:11 et seq.; 3:1; Eph. 2:10).

This conclusion might be impugned by citing texts like Gal. 3:2, 14, 26, where Paul seems to say that we receive the Spirit – or become sons of God – by faith. But that is not the real meaning of these texts.[19]

In Gal. 3:2 he says explicitly that they received the Spirit by hearing the *preaching* of faith: "This only would I learn of you: Did you receive the Spirit by the works of the law or by the hearing of faith?" In this passage Paul is contrasting the Old Testament with the New. "Faith" here is something objective (= the faith), which Paul's preaching had brought to the Galatians, namely the message of the salvation which Christ achieved. As we shall soon see, faith, that is the acceptance of this message, is necessary before one can become a Christian by Baptism and by receiving the Spirit in Baptism. Exactly the same idea appears again in Gal. 3:14.

Gal. 3:26 should be translated: "You are all the children of God by faith in Christ Jesus." The Galatians have become sons of God by being established "in Christ". The phrase "by faith" simply denotes the necessary condition for incorporation in Christ. In the verse immediately following Paul says explicitly

[19] On the whole matter see Wissmann, op. cit., especially p. 112 et seq.; Mundle, op. cit., p. 131 et seq.

that this incorporation is brought about by Baptism, not by faith: "For as many of you as have been baptized in Christ have put on Christ."

Col. 2:12 does not provide an argument either. Paul here declares that those who are buried with Christ "are risen again by the faith of the operation of God who hath raised him up from the dead". This does not mean that faith is the cause which produces fellowship with Christ, for in the early part of this verse he expressly connects death and resurrection with Baptism. Faith is mentioned here because it is the necessary condition for the reception of Baptism.

In Phil. 3:9 Paul attributes justification to faith, but this text does not affect our conclusion. He says: "not having my justice, which is of the law, but that which is of the faith of Christ Jesus, which is of God: justice in faith". This text is really a parenthesis in the passage Phil. 3:8–12. In this passage fellowship with Christ is connected closely with justifying faith, though elsewhere the two are separated. In Paul's eyes they are not independent. He connects them very closely. By Baptism man is liberated from sin and thereby justified (Rom. 6:7) and simultaneously he reaches the state of "being in Christ". Justification and sacramental re-creation form one single act.[20] In Phil. 3:9 faith has the wide sense of accepting the Christian message, and this includes receiving Baptism (see page 129 et seq.). There is not the slightest reason for thinking that Paul considered faith as the source of fellowship with Christ.

Sommerlath is incorrect when he maintains that Paul teaches that the whole new life of fellowship with Christ is granted to us

[20] Mundle, op. cit., p. 135.

not by Baptism alone, but by Baptism and faith.[21] He bases this view on Gal. 2:20; Rom. 1:17; and Eph. 3:17.

In the Epistle to the Galatians the Apostle makes two statements. He declares that because he has been crucified with Christ (2:19b) in Baptism he no longer has a life of his own, but Christ lives in him. He also says that the life which he still lives in the flesh is led in the faith in the Son of God who delivered himself for Paul (2:20). There is a certain polarity between these two statements, but the meaning is perfectly clear. The mystical death in Baptism has killed the old man and given him a new life, his present life in Christ. His everyday human life, "the life in the flesh" still continues, but it is led on a new plane, namely "in the faith". Faith does not establish the new life, but it fosters it, and protects and develops it. In other words faith perfects the new life. The faith to which Paul refers is the faith of one who is already baptized and justified, who has become a new creature.

Sommerlath also says that what makes faith of such importance is the fact that it is the indispensible organ by which man personally accepts the fellowship with Christ which Baptism establishes, and by which this fellowship affects his conduct.[22] This statement is at least inaccurate, and it cannot be accepted. There is no doubt whatever that one who is baptized must express the new life in his conduct. Paul himself teaches this,[23] as we see from his repeated use of the imperative when he is speaking of the matter (see Rom. 6:1–7:6; 8:12–17; Gal. 5:13–25; 6:16; 1 Cor. 6:9–11; Col. 3:1 et seq.). But there is

---

[21] Op. cit., p. 117 et seq. [22] See Mundle, op. cit., p. 131 et seq.
[23] See below, III, 3.

not a single place where Paul connects the faith with this injunction. In his eyes the old man is dead, and a new creation is actually present: "The old things are passed away. Behold all things are made new" (2 Cor. 5:17). Moreover, he never speaks of man personally accepting this life, or grasping it by faith. What he does say is that the life of the Christian should draw the consequences of being a Christian: "If we live in the Spirit, let us also walk in the Spirit" (Gal. 5:15); "Whereunto we are come . . . let us also continue under the same rule" (Phil. 3:16). We can do so, and it is obligatory for us. Our body of sin is already destroyed (Rom. 6:6), our flesh is crucified (and therefore dead) with its vices and concupiscences (Gal. 5:14). Paul's injunctions follow from these facts: You must walk in newness of life (Rom. 6:4), serve sin no longer (6:6), let sin not reign in your mortal body (6:12), no longer fulfil the desires of the flesh (Gal. 5:16); you must by the Spirit mortify the deeds of the flesh (Rom. 8:13) and yield your members to serve justice unto sanctification (Rom. 6:19). There is never a word about faith in this connection, though he occasionally mentions the Spirit (Rom. 8:13 et seq. and Gal. 5:18: "led by the Spirit"; Gal. 5:22: "the fruit of the Spirit").

The only apparent exception is Eph. 3:17, where Paul prays to God that he may grant the readers of the Epistle "that Christ may dwell by faith in your hearts". Even if faith is here considered as the means by which Christ's mystical indwelling takes place,[24] this solitary text is hardly sufficient to support Sommerlath's view. The recipients of the Epistle are already in fellowship with Christ, so we cannot interpret this text to mean

[24] Dibelius, *Eph.*, ad loc.; see further Mundle, op. cit., p. 158, note 2.

that faith establishes union with Christ. Obviously faith is here equivalent to the new life which they possess as Christians. Paul's prayer here is for the same object as in the preceding verse, namely that the indwelling of Christ ("Christ-life") should appear in them with ever greater power. Moreover, this text does not refer to an action on man's part. It speaks of an action of God's.

However, Sommerlath is perfectly correct when he points out that both faith and Baptism play a part, and we are not obliged to exclude one or the other. Faith accompanies union with Christ.[25] It is Baptism that produces the new life, and the source of this life is the mystical union with Christ Triumphant. But the full majesty of this life is hidden from us; it will not be revealed until the future, when Christ will come from Heaven and "will reform the body of our lowliness, made like to the body of his glory" (Phil. 3:21). Our "life is hidden with Christ in God" (Col. 3:3). "The revelation of the sons of God" (Rom. 8:19), "the (full) adoption of the sons of God" (Rom. 8:23) will take place in the future. What we have received is a pledge of complete salvation (2 Cor. 1:22; 5:5; Eph. 1:14; cf. also Rom. 8:23).

Therefore, although we are in union with Christ, there is still room for faith. By faith we mean confident trust, something akin to hope, that God will complete the work which he has begun in us. That is what Paul means when he says: "Knowing that while we are in the body we are far from the Lord. For we walk by faith and not by sight" (2 Cor. 5:6 et seq.). But this is not a per-

---

[25] Op. cit., p. 120. See also Wissmann, op. cit., pp. 48, 55, and especially Mundle, op. cit., p. 168 et seq.

manent state: "If we be dead with Christ (through Baptism) we believe that we shall live also together with Christ" (Rom. 6:8), or, as he says in 1 Thess. 4:13: "If we believe that Jesus died and rose again: even so them who have slept through Jesus, will God bring with him." (Cf. also 2 Cor. 4:13 et seq.) Elsewhere, instead of using the term faith, Paul speaks of waiting (1 Cor. 1:7; Phil. 3:20 et seq.; 1 Thess. 1:10; Rom. 8:23: "waiting for the adoption of sons of God, the redemption of our body"), or of the enduring of the hope (1 Thess. 1:3; 2 Thess. 3:5). But this firm enduring hope is based on the faith that God who raised up Christ will also raise up Christians to a life in glory.

This brings us to the most important part which faith holds in regard to fellowship with Christ. Faith does not establish union with Christ, but it is the indispensible condition for the establishment of this union. We can say without qualification that without faith there is no union with Christ. Union with Christ means an extremely close relationship with Christ Triumphant, a real participation with him in his being and life. But this relationship presupposes faith in the resurrection of Christ, in his spiritual existence, and in the possibility of him influencing human life. Only one who has attained this faith can enter upon a mystical relationship with Christ. In other words, faith is the necessary condition for receiving Baptism, which establishes union with Christ.

When Paul speaks of faith he means the agreement of the intellect with the content of the Gospel message, in other words the voluntary acceptance of the message of salvation as divine truth; faith entails obedient subjection of oneself to the Gospel as to a binding rule of conduct (see Rom. 1:5; 6:16; 16:19, 26;

2 Thess. 1:8).[26] It is not possible to mark out with absolute certainty what exactly Paul understood by the Gospel, but there is no doubt that it is particularly concerned with Jesus Christ and the salvation which he brought.[27]

In a number of places Paul gives a summary of the main points of his message (1 Thess. 1:9 et seq.; Rom. 1:3 et seq.; 1 Cor. 15:1 et seq.; 2 Tim. 2:8). They may be summarized thus:

1. The coming into the world of the pre-existing Son of God as the Messias who had been awaited from the family of David (Rom. 1:3; Gal. 4:4; 2 Tim. 2:8);

2. His death upon the Cross for sinful mankind (1 Cor. 1:23; 2:2; 15:3; Gal. 3:1);

3. His resurrection from the dead and his exaltation into heavenly kingship (this is the central point of Paul's message; Rom. 1:4; 4:24; 10:9; 2 Cor. 4:14; 5:14 et seq.; 1 Thess. 4:14; 2 Tim. 2:8);

4. The expectation of the Second Coming of Christ to save his people from the threatening wrath of God (1 Thess. 1:10; Rom. 5:9; Tit. 2:13);

5. When preaching to Gentiles he stressed faith in the one true living God (1 Thess. 1:9, and the Areopagus Discourse Acts 17:22–31), who has reconciled mankind to himself through his Son Jesus Christ (Gal. 4:4; 2 Cor. 5:19 et seq.).

[26] On this matter see Mundle, *Der Glaubensbegriff des Paulus* (1932).

[27] See Mundle, ibid., p. 39 et seq. (Paul's Gospel means more than his missionary preaching); E. Molland, *Das paulinische Evangelium* (Oslo, 1934), pp. 57–78; R. Asting, *Die Verkündigung des Wortes im Urchristentum* (Stuttgart, 1939), pp. 417–25; G. Friedrich in *ThWb,* ii, 427 et seq.

Naturally there were other points in the Gospel which Paul preached both to Jews and Gentiles. But Paul demanded that anyone who wished to enter the Christian religion should accept his message and should obediently comply with the demands of the Gospel. Faith in this sense is the indispensible preliminary before anyone can be admitted to Baptism.

Furthermore, this faith necessarily leads to Baptism. And therefore, just as we can say "No Baptism without faith", so we can also say "No (genuine) faith without Baptism." If it does not lead to Baptism it is not genuine faith. Neither Paul, nor anyone else in primitive Christianity, knows of such a thing as a "believer" who has not been baptized (Rom. 6:1 et seq.; 1 Cor. 1:13–17; Gal. 3:27; Eph. 4:4; 5:26; Tit. 3:5). Indeed, it is instructive to observe Paul's use of the verb πιστεύειν "to believe": the aorist πιστεῦσαι "to become a believer" can mean "to become a Christian" (Rom. 13:11; 1 Cor. 3:5; 15:2; Gal. 2:16; Eph. 1:13); and the present πιστεύειν can mean "to be a Christian" (the present participle appears frequently: "the faithful", Rom. 1:16; 4:11; 10:4; 1 Cor. 14:22 etc.). Also the substantive πίστις "faith" is often used for "Christianity" (Gal. 1:23; 3:23, 25; Rom. 1:8; 1 Thess. 1:8; 1 Cor. 15:14, 17; Eph. 4:5 etc.).

"To be in Christ" has for Paul the same meaning as "to be a Christian, to belong to the Church as the Body of Christ". That is why he can interchange the two ideas "to be in Christ" and "to be (live, stand) in the faith". In Gal. 2:20, for example, "I live in the faith" means, I live as a Christian; and "Stand fast in the faith" in 1 Cor. 16:13 (similarly Col. 1:23; 2:7) means, stand fast in the Lord (1 Thess. 3:8; Phil. 4:1; likewise 1 Cor. 1:30; Rom. 16:11; Col. 2:6).

131

To sum up, when Paul uses the word "faith" he does not refer to grasping the living Christ, nor to surrendering oneself to him. Faith for Paul was rather the acceptance of the message of the salvation which God had wrought through Christ, and therefore profession of the Christian religion. But the man who accepts this message with faith, is not thereby united mystically to Christ. This union is produced only by Baptism.

2. GOD'S ACTION IN THE CALLING OF PAUL

Paul's conversion to Christianity took place in a unique manner. Near Damascus Christ Triumphant appeared to him and made him a disciple.[28] Paul's own statements about this event oblige us to ask how mystical union with Christ was established in his case. The question may be framed thus: Did he enter into fellowship with Christ at the moment when Christ appeared to him near Damascus? After that act of grace (Gal. 2:9; 1 Cor. 15:10) did he feel and know that he was mystically united to Christ Triumphant?

One's first reaction is to return an affirmative answer, and many scholars do so.[29] Indeed, a number of them maintain that

[28] See K. Pieper, *Paulus. Seine missionarische Persönlichkeit und Wirksamkeit* (Münster i. W., 1926), p. 20 et seq.; W. G. Kümmel, *Röm. 7 und die Bekehrung des Paulus* (Leipzig, 1929) (pp. 139–60: Die Bekehrung des Paulus); R. Bultmann, "Neue Paulusforschung" in *Theol. Rundschau N. F.,* vi (1934), pp. 229–46 (Conversion pp. 231–6); J. Munck, "La vocation de l'apôtre Paul" in *Studia theol.,* i (Lund, 1948), pp. 131–45. The question whether the "Damascus experience" was the source of Paul's doctrine of union with Christ, is thoroughly examined (and answered negatively) by Mundle, *Glaubensbegriff,* pp. 114–23.

[29] E.g., Deissmann, *Paulus,* p. 105; Heitmüller in *Zeitschr. f. Theol. und Kirche,* xxvii (1917), p. 147. Others are mentioned in Mundle, op. cit., p. 115, note 3.

Paul's entire doctrine of mystical union with Christ is derived from his experience of conversion at Damascus. Wilhelm Weber has written a book attempting to prove this.[30]

Any examination of this question must be based on Paul's own evidence. The relevant passages are Gal. 1:11 et seq.; 1 Cor. 9:1; 15:8; 2 Cor. 4:6; Phil. 3:7 et seq. There are obscurities in these texts, but we can establish two facts from them: 1. Christ appeared in divine glory to Paul; 2. he personally had a profound influence on Paul's life.

According to 1 Cor. 15:8 Paul had a vision of Christ: "Last of all, he was seen also by me, as by one born out of due time." There is no doubt that this vision marked the beginning of his life as a Christian, and led to his conversion. When speaking of it Paul mentions that he was then active as a persecutor of Christians – an activity which he regretted bitterly – and we are justified in regarding the vision as the beginning of the change from persecutor to Apostle. And when Paul says in 1 Cor. 9:1: "Am not I an apostle? Have not I seen the Lord Jesus Christ?" he must be referring to this vision on the road to Damascus. The vision was obviously the beginning of his conversion into an apostle, for he not only juxtaposes the two, but evidently he connects them as cause and effect (see also Gal. 1:16; Acts 22:21).

Although 2 Cor. 4:6 does not explicitly mention the appearance of Christ on the road to Damascus, yet its form of expression shows the influence of that experience.[31] He says that God has illuminated the hearts of the faithful – as distinct from the

[30] *Christusmystik* (1924).

[31] Kümmel, op. cit., p. 147: "It is highly probable that Paul is here referring to the vision at Damascus in which God let his glory in Christ

unbelievers (verse 4) – so that they recognize the divine majesty of Christ: "For God, who commanded the light to shine out of darkness, hath shined in our hearts, to give the light of the knowledge of the glory of God, in the face of Christ Jesus." This passage can have only one meaning. Hitherto Paul had hated Jesus bitterly, and had savagely persecuted him in his followers. But he suddenly saw Jesus in heavenly glory, and simultaneously realized that this Jesus was truly the divinely sent Messias and that he had risen from the dead and reigns in divine glory in Heaven.

But these texts tell us nothing about how Paul became united with Christ. They explain how the persecutor changed into an apostle, but not how he entered upon mystical union with Christ. We must now examine Gal. 1:11 et seq. and Phil. 3:7 et seq., to see whether they settle the problem.

In this passage of the Epistle to the Galatians Paul is proving that the Gospel which he preached to the Gentiles was communicated to him directly by a revelation from God, and was not learned from men. He demonstrates that he could not have received or learned it from men either before or after his conversion. Before his conversion he was a bitter enemy of the Christian mother community, and afterwards he had no contact with it except for very short periods. In other words, he adduces a kind of alibi to prove the divine origin of his Gospel. In verse 15 he continues: "But when it pleased him who separated me from my mother's womb and called me by his grace, to reveal his Son in me, that I might preach him among the

shine forth; the vision amounted to a new creation for Paul." Bultmann in *Theol. Lit.-Ztg.* (1950), p. 209: Paul is here referring to his conversion.

134

Gentiles: immediately I condescended not to flesh and blood, neither went I to Jerusalem to the Apostles who were before me: but I went into Arabia and again I returned to Damascus." Unlike 1 Cor. 9:1 and 15:8, there is here no mention of a vision of Christ which converted him. Paul says here that God revealed his Son in him, and he tells us that the reason for this revelation was the commission to preach to the Gentiles. If we connect this with verse 12 where he stresses that he received his Gospel "by the revelation of Jesus Christ", it seems to follow that Paul himself considered that he had been called to preach to the Gentiles and had learned the Gospel through a special interior revelation from Christ; the vision at Damascus and this revelation would be two separate events. Yet the common view is that the vision of Christ and the revelation of the Gospel, together with the commission to preach, took place all at the same instant.

The text does not make it clear whether the revelation took place at the moment of the vision, or only during the following hours or days. There is no cogent argument for thinking that the two were simultaneous. On the other hand, verses 16b and 17 forbid us to separate them widely. When Paul writes "to reveal his Son in me (ἐν ἐμοί)", the last phrase does not mean "through me", as in 1 Cor. 7:14, nor does it mean "to me", as in Gal. 1:24; in either case he would have used a simple dative. The phrase must be rendered "in me", for elsewhere the verb ἀποκαλύπτειν is not followed by the preposition. This expression reflects the fundamental interior revolution which the vision produced in Paul. It cannot be used to uphold a mystical interpretation of the vision at Damascus, as A. Oepke[32] has

[32] *Galaterbrief,* ad loc.

pointed out. At Damascus Christ appeared in his glory and showed Paul that he is alive, living in a spiritual manner. In addition to this, Christ also revealed himself as a personal power with a profound influence on Paul's life. It was at this moment that Paul first realized that Christ Triumphant is a power which penetrates and directs his life and being. But this revelation was something extraordinary; in the strict sense of the word it was a miracle. But it cannot be simply equated to the fellowship with Christ which, according to Paul, every Christian enjoys permanently.

The vision of Christ of 1 Cor. 9:1, the appearance of the risen Christ of 1 Cor. 15:8, and the revelation of the Son by God of Gal. 1:16, were one single event in Paul's life, which happened at a definite time and place; this event converted him to Christianity, and was connected with his commission to preach to the Gentiles.[33] In 1 Cor. 15:5–8 he lists it with the other appearances of the risen Christ, and places it last on the list. This vision was of an entirely different nature from the visions and revelations which Paul often received afterwards as a Christian. In 2 Cor. 12:1 he speaks of "visions and revelations", and in verse 7 he mentions "the greatness of the revelations"; Gal. 2:2 tells us that he went to Jerusalem "according to revelation". It is particularly significant that in 2 Cor. 12:1 he describes the Lord as the author of the visions and revelations, and, according to verse 9, the Lord Himself answers Paul's threefold prayer. Acts also reports a number of

[33] This is demonstrated by Kümmel, op. cit., pp. 143–8, against G. P. Wetter ("Die Damascusvision" in *Festgabe f. A. Jülicher* [Tübingen, 1927], pp. 80–92).

136

cases where Christ intervened in Paul's life by visions and revelations (18:9; 22:17; 23:11; 27:23).

Phil. 3:7–14 is a difficult passage to interpret, but it is of
importance for deciding whether Paul attributed his (personal)
fellowship with Christ to the vision at Damascus and not to
Baptism.

The Apostle is here engaged in a polemic against the judaistic
agitators. He begins by declaring that the true circumcision are
the Christians "who in spirit serve God and glory in Christ
Jesus, not having confidence in the flesh" (that is, in natural and
historical privileges) (3:3). He then speaks of himself, and points
out that he would have as much right as anyone to have confidence in the flesh, for he has the privileges which derive from
Jewish ancestry and observance of the Law (3:4–6). But he
has reckoned as "loss" for Christ's sake all that was "gain" for
him (3:7); in other words, he has realized the worthlessness of
what he used to value. This reassessment caused a complete
break in his life. It did not precede and cause his conversion.
On the contrary, it was brought about by the appearance of
Christ Triumphant at Damascus. In verse 8 he adds that he
still holds his new evaluation; he still counts everything "loss"
(that is, worthless) for the sake of Christ; to know Christ
surpasses all other things, and for the love of Christ he has
suffered the loss of all things. Indeed he declares with even
stronger emphasis that he considers all things foolishness (dung)
in order to win Christ and to be found in him.

The exegesis of the last verse presents difficulties. The main
verb (ἡγοῦμαι) is in the present tense, so it cannot refer to the
past events which led up to his conversion; the allusion must be
to the purpose or the final effect of his conversion, which had

not yet been fully attained when Paul was writing. At Damascus Christ had "apprehended" him (verse 12c), and now Paul must keep "apprehending" or taking possession of Christ, and qualify for the description of "being in Christ". The phrase "wherein I am also apprehended" refers to being in Christ, that is, to incorporation into his Body; it means being a true Christian. One who is "in Christ" in this manner possesses a justice which does not come from the Law, but from God; Paul has this justice because of his faith in Christ (verse 9). The purpose clause in verse 10 is dependent on the last clause of verse 8, and it develops the thought: "that I may know him and the power of his resurrection and the fellowship of his sufferings". The knowledge of which he speaks here is not a theoretical intellectual knowledge; it is a practical knowledge, an experience and an interior search. The two following expressions explain what this knowledge is: "the power of his resurrection" is the power which the risen Christ possesses, by which he creates in men a new life of an entirely different kind; it is the "newness of life" (Rom. 6:4) in which Christians ought to walk. In short, it is the supernatural power of the Spirit which the risen Christ gives us. "The fellowship of his sufferings" means suffering like Christ and with Christ, sharing in the sufferings which were laid upon Christ (Col. 1:24). Paul is probably thinking of the daily death which he mentions in 1 Cor. 15:31 ("I die daily"), of the perpetual crushing of the outward man (2 Cor. 4:16), of the continual bearing in his body of the death of Christ (2 Cor. 4:10). The new life enables him to suffer with Christ, to be made "conformable to his death", which is Paul's own paraphrase for "the fellowship of his sufferings". By doing this he receives the guarantee that he shall rise bodily from the dead, thereby attaining the consummation for which he is striving (3:11). He goes on to reject the suggestion that he believes that he has already finally attained his aim of knowing Christ (3:10). This is certainly not the case. But he can justifiably claim that all his powers are devoted to the attainment of this aim. He admits that he can do this only because at his conversion he was apprehended by Christ Jesus and drawn into the fellowship of his resurrection and sufferings (3:12).

Paul here draws a sharp distinction between Christ's action and his own. Christ intervened irresistibly in his life, and attached Paul to himself. Ever since that moment Paul has no longer belonged to himself, and his whole being has been subject to Christ; he is aware of being entirely bound to Christ. It was not Paul who created this relationship, but Christ Triumphant; it was Christ who took the initiative. In regard to himself Paul can only say "I am apprehended". When he says that he has not already attained, he means that he is not yet a perfect disciple of his crucified and risen Lord, but that on his part the fellowship with Christ must be deepened, and his interior man must be continually renewed and perfected (2 Cor. 4:16). Therefore, like a good runner, he keeps his eyes fixed on the goal, namely the "knowledge of Christ", and he avoids no exertion or sacrifice in his apostolic life, provided that he can finally attain the prize, namely the call to heavenly glory on the Last Day (3:13 et seq.).

The phrase "knowledge (gnosis) of Christ" (γνῶσις Χριστοῦ Ἰησοῦ verse 8; γνῶναι αὐτόν verse 10) calls for comment. R. Bultmann[34] says that Paul is using Gnostic terminology here,

---

[34] Art. γνῶσις in *ThWb*, i, 680–719, especially 710 et seq.

though he admits that the meaning is Christian. Paul explains the "knowledge of Christ" as being "found in him" (verse 9 et seq.), by which he means being drawn into the scheme of salvation by faith. When he speaks of "knowing" in verse 10, he is referring to experiencing the power of the resurrection and of the fellowship of Christ's sufferings. He is not thinking of passing beyond normal human existence through ecstasy, as was the idea in Gnosticism and in the Hellenistic Mysteries. The Gnostics had described individual experiences. This is not what Paul does. He is expounding what it means to be a Christian.

Dibelius in a number of writings[35] has maintained that the "knowledge of Christ" is the salvation which one who believes in Christ obtains, namely constant union with Christ Triumphant, from which the Christian derives the powers which are listed in verse 10. He claims that the word gnosis bears the technical meaning which it has in Hellenistic mysticism; it does not refer to intellectual knowledge, but to perception of the Godhead in vision and to the transformation of the seer. He cites as parallels to this 2 Cor. 3:18; 4:6, and the prayer from the Mimaut papyrus (K. Preisendanz, *Papyri Graeci magici* i 58, v. 599 et seq.). The prayer reads: "We rejoice that thou hast shown thyself to us: we rejoice that while we are still in the body thou has deified us by the knowledge of thyself (ὅτι ἐν πλάσμασιν ἡμᾶς ὄντας ἀπεθέωσας τῇ σεαυτοῦ γνώσει)." He says that in Phil. 3:9 the phrase to "be found in him" has its full mystical meaning, and denotes becoming one with Christ. He considers that in verse 12 the object of the verb "apprehend" is

[35] Most recently in *Glaube und Mystik bei Paulus*, p. 688, note 1; *Philipperbrief* [3], p. 89 et seq.; *Paulus und die Mystik*, p. 68.

140

Jesus Christ, and that Paul is speaking here of full union with Christ. Moreover, he gives the word τελειοῦσθαι the full force which it had in Hellenistic mysticism.

Bultmann and Dibelius are correct when they identify Paul's terminology as Gnostic or Hellenistic.[36] But he never mentions an ecstatic vision of Christ nor a transformation wrought by such a vision. And there is no justification for speaking of a union between the Christian and Christ similar to the union with the Divinity of Hellenistic mysticism, for this union was absorption. Dibelius himself points out that the difference between Paul's gnosis and the "knowledge" of the mysteries is shown in verse 14: man becomes like Christ, not by a dedication ceremony, but by work, struggling and suffering. As Michaelis well says, to "know him" in verse 10 refers to the union with Christ which we can experience in the present life, and to the possibility and reality of ever closer fellowship with him.[37]

The conclusions which we have reached at this point may be summed up thus: By the vision at Damascus, Christ Triumphant made a deep impression on Paul's life, and divided it into two fundamentally opposed parts, for he changed the fanatical persecutor into an eager disciple and apostle. From this point onwards Paul had only one aim in life: to make his union with Christ ever more interior and more complete, and to let his whole life be ever more thoroughly penetrated by the vital powers which Christ gave him. There is no doubt that he considered the vision at Damascus as the turning point of his life.

The texts which have been examined do not make the

[36] This is denied by J. Dupont, *Gnosis*, pp. 34–6. See Bultmann in *Journal of Theol. Studies* (1952), pp. 10–26.

[37] *Philipperbrief*, p. 59.

slightest mention of Baptism. Are we justified in inferring that Paul's fellowship with Christ began with the vision at Damascus and not with his Baptism? Such a conclusion would be premature.

In Phil. 3:7–14 the theme is not precisely the cause and the beginning of his fellowship with Christ. That passage deals with his perpetual endeavour to perfect and to develop on his part the fellowship with Christ Triumphant who has taken possession of him. The phrase "to be found in him" presupposes that such a fellowship with Christ is already in existence. Perhaps we have here an implicit reference to Baptism, even though it is not mentioned explicitly. So the conclusions which we have already reached must be supplemented by an investigation of the role which Baptism played in Paul's life.

There is no doubt that Paul was baptized. Acts tells us that he was baptized three days after the vision (Acts 9:9; 9:18). The silence of the Epistles cannot weaken the evidence of Acts on this point, for Paul takes it for granted that Baptism is universally practised throughout the Christian communities (see 1 Cor. 10:2; 1:14 et seq.), and he regards it as the means by which the Spirit is communicated and by which we are incorporated into the Body of Christ (1 Cor. 12:13). In various passages he includes himself when he speaks of Baptism, for example, Rom. 6:3: "Know you not that *all we* who are baptized in Christ Jesus are baptized in his death?"; 1 Cor. 12:13: "In one Spirit were *we all* baptized into one body." It is true that he uses the second person in Gal. 3:27 and Col. 2:10 et seq., which would seem to confine Baptism to his readers. But in these passages he is arguing vigorously in order to make them appreciate the rights and obligations which *they* have as a result of *their* Baptism.

142

Paul was baptized, and he was convinced that his Baptism had been a major influence on his life as a Christian. As we see from 1 Cor. 12:13 and Rom. 6:3 et seq., he considered that Baptism was the origin of his incorporation into the Body of Christ, of his participation in the death and resurrection of the Lord, and of his faith in the future resurrection from the dead (Rom. 6:8). In Gal. 2:19 he also attributes to Baptism the indwelling of Christ in him: "With Christ I am nailed to the cross. And I live, now not I, but Christ liveth in me."

Dibelius maintains that in Gal. 2:19; 5:24; 6:14; Rom. 6:6 Paul holds that his own union with Christ is totally independent of Baptism. Such a view would be out of harmony with the ideas of the Greek Christian communities,[38] and it is quite unacceptable. It is true that "being crucified with Christ" is a new Christian picture. But in the eyes of Paul and of the Roman community Baptism is a symbol not so much of being buried with Christ (this idea occurs only in Rom. 6:4; Col. 2:12), as of Christ's death. Thus he speaks of being "baptized into his death" and of being "buried together with him by Baptism into death" (Rom. 6:3 et seq.), of becoming "dead to the law" (Rom. 7:4), and of "being made conformable to his death" (Phil. 3:10). To Paul's mind it was not Christ's burial, but his death on the Cross, which was the redemptive act (Col. 2:14) – indeed it was the central thought of his preach-

---

[38] *Die Isisweihe des Apuleius,* p. 46. W. Bousset shows greater insight in *Kyrios Christos,* p. 108, where he says: "It is as if a mysticism of a more personal type appears here (i.e., in 'union with the cross'). But it also originated with the liturgy and the sacrament." Bousset lays great stress on the part which liturgical mysticism played in Paul's life (Ibid., p. 84 et seq.; p. 106 et seq.).

ing (see 1 Cor. 1:17 et seq.); and it was natural for him to substitute for "buried with Christ" the phrase "crucified with Christ" – though he does so only four times. Moreover, there is surely significance in the connection of crucifixion with Baptism in 1 Cor. 1:13 where he says: "Was Paul then crucified for you? Or were you baptized in the name of Paul?"

The significance which Paul attached to his own Baptism appears also from the important place which union with Christ's suffering occupies in his thought, as we see from Rom. 8:17; 2 Cor. 4:10; Gal. 6:17; Phil. 3:10 et seq.[39] The thought in these texts is that the sufferings of Christians are sufferings of Christ, and that they make man like Christ who has passed through suffering and death. This idea is inseparably linked with the concept of Baptism as a participation in Christ's death, which he expounds in Rom. 6:2 et seq.

Paul, therefore, considered that Baptism played an important part in bringing about his union with Christ. And so, when the question arises of the point at which his union with Christ began, there seems to be a double answer: on the one hand at the vision, when he was seized irresistibly by the power of Christ Triumphant, on the other hand at his Baptism. It might be said that this answer is self-contradictory, and that his union with Christ certainly began when he was personally seized at Damascus, and not at his Baptism, even though he was baptized shortly after the vision.[40] This is not the case. Paul makes it quite clear that Baptism is the means by which the permanent spiritual-real union with Christ takes place, the Spirit of Christ is communi-

[39] See below III, 3.
[40] Thus Deissmann, *Paulus,* p. 115: "At any rate, it was the vision at Damascus, and not Baptism, which was the decisive factor for Paul."

cated to us, and we are incorporated into his Mystical Body. Naturally Christ can make an extraordinary intervention into a man's life, and can attach the man irresistibly to himself. But even in such a case we cannot dispense with Baptism, for it is Baptism which establishes the objective side of union with Christ, namely incorporation into the mystical organism which is the Body of Christ. Only Baptism kills the old man, produces the new creature, and lays the title for the resurrection from the dead. If we once see that there is an objective side to union with Christ as expounded by Paul (see above II, 4), we cannot gainsay these consequences which derive from Paul's own teaching.

Bousset's view[41] cannot be accepted when he draws a distinction between "sacramental mysticism", which he equates with magic, and "spiritual mysticism". He claims that before Paul the Greek Christian communities practised a sacramental mysticism which involved the Christians as a group: Paul, he says, transformed this into a personal mysticism, and developed it by giving it a spiritual and ethical reinterpretation. But in Rom. 6:2 et seq. Paul speaks of a real death and resurrection with Christ, and he takes it for granted that this doctrine is known to the Roman community. There is not the slightest evidence that he had given a spiritual reinterpretation to this teaching. He does insist vigorously on the moral conclusions which Christians must draw from this doctrine. But once again there is no reason to think that these conclusions were new to the readers, and that hitherto they had considered Baptism as nothing more than a natural action with magic effects. Undoubtedly some members

[41] Op. cit., p. 107 et seq.

of the communities did not always apply these lessons in their conduct, and some of them had a rather magical idea about Baptism; there is abundant evidence that this was the case at Corinth, as we see from texts like 1 Cor. 10:2–13; 11:27 et seq.; 15:29. Even at the present day clergy sometimes encounter the same phenomenon. But there is no evidence that Paul gave a spiritual and moral reinterpretation to what was originally a liturgical action. Yet it must not be overlooked – it is an important fact – that he never tires of reminding the Christians of the great obligations which lie upon them because they have died and risen again with Christ in Baptism. This is one of the more important effects of the union with Christ which Paul describes.

3. MAN'S ACTION

As we have seen (III, 1) Baptism is the means by which the objective mystical relationship with Christ is established. By this sacrament man is withdrawn from the sphere of death (and of the flesh, sin, and the Law) and is transferred to the "sphere of Christ", which is another name for the "new life". In virtue of Baptism man is "in Christ" and Christ is in him; he is a member of the Mystical Body of Christ, a "new creature".

But fellowship with Christ is not complete as soon as Baptism has been received; there is still room for perfecting the process of being mystically united to him. The sacramental relationship must become an ethical relationship also. Christ, with whom we are united by Baptism, is not only the giver of heavenly powers; he is also a model for our conduct. His death, into which the Christian has been baptized, is a supreme ethical act; it was performed through obedience to his heavenly Father (Phil. 2:8) for the thoroughly ethical-religious purpose of liberating mankind from sin. That is why the mystical fellowship with Christ is not complete until it becomes an ethical-religious relationship. In other words, the union of being which Baptism creates must develop into a union of behaviour.

Paul stresses this point vigorously. He uses many expressions to urge Christians to let their conduct reflect what they are. It is not enough to possess the new life, they must also "walk in newness of life" (Rom. 6:4); instead of being content with having the Spirit, they must also "walk in the Spirit" (Gal. 5:25) and be "led by the Spirit" (Rom. 8:14; Gal. 5:18). Since the Christian has been freed from the servitude of sin and has become a servant of God, he must devote his whole being to God's service (Rom. 6:17 et seq.).

Paul teaches that the Christian life should be a constantly increasing growth into fellowship with Christ. He is well aware that there are many degrees of personal union with Christ. He explicitly distinguishes between "children" and the mature or "perfect". He regrets to say that the Corinthians have not yet grown out of childhood: "I could not speak to you as unto spiritual, but as unto carnal. As unto little ones in Christ. I gave you milk to drink, not meat: for you were not able as yet" (1 Cor. 3:1 et seq.). He complains that "you are yet carnal. For, whereas there is among you envying and contention, are you not carnal and walk you not according to man?" (3:2, 3 et seq.). He is worried that the Galatians may fall away from Christ, and he says to them: "My little children, of whom I am in labour again, until Christ be formed in you" (Gal. 4:19). By Baptism each man becomes a new creature, and he is obliged to express in his conduct the figure of Christ with whom he is mystically united. This is where the Galatians fail; the image of Christ has grown fainter in them, and has almost disappeared. That is why the Apostle is so concerned that the figure of Christ should again be visibly expressed in his beloved children.[42] Indeed, he has this same concern for all whom he has won for Christ. The aim of all his activity is to preach Christ in all wisdom to all men so "that we may present every man perfect in Christ Jesus" (Col. 1:28). The same idea can be found in Eph. 4:13 et seq.: "until we all meet . . . unto a perfect man, unto the measure of the age of the fulness of Christ: that henceforth we be no more children . . . but . . . in charity we may in all things grow up in him who is the head, even Christ". This passage refers to the Church, the community of the faithful, but it includes the thought that each individual Christian must grow to maturity in charity, for that is the only way in which the community of Christians, the Body of Christ, can reach perfect form and maturity. We may add that Paul did not consider himself free

[42] That is how the majority of exegetes understand the metaphor, for example J. Behm in *ThWb,* iv (1942), 761: "The mystical idea is that Christ lives in Christians. . . . In order that the faithful may have this 'Christ-life', Christ must be formed in them, in a sense he must become man again in each of them (an idea which became widespread in later mysticism). The metaphor of the child developing in its mother's body is intended to convey the idea of Christ attaining full formation and mature existence in the Christian." H. Schlier (*Galaterbrief,* p. 151 et seq.) gives a different explanation: he refers it to the formation of the Body of Christ (the Church) by the birth which takes place through the apostolic preaching: "Paul is thinking of the members of the community as a whole; he is not referring to individual members in whom Christ dwells, though naturally the community is born by Christ becoming strong in individuals." See also above I, 3, page 44.

from this duty of growing. His deep desire was "that I may gain Christ: and may be found in him" (Phil. 3:8).

We must realize the seriousness with which Paul regards this duty of each and every Christian to perfect the "Christ-life" which he has received in Baptism. It becomes clear when we consider various other injunctions. It has long since been noticed that the Epistles contain a number of ethical commands which seem inconsistent with his high estimation of the effects of Baptism. The injunctions quite often are phrased in such a manner as to suggest that the readers are not yet in mystical union with Christ, but have still to reach this relationship.[43] Here are the texts in question:

1. Imperative	*2. Indicative*
Put off the old man with his deeds (Col. 3:9; Eph. 4:22; cf. Rom. 6:13).	Our old man is crucified with him, the body of sin destroyed (Rom. 6:6; 2 Cor. 5:14,17b).
Mortify your members which are upon the earth (Col. 3:5,8).	They that are Christ's have crucified their flesh, with the vices and concupiscences (Gal. 5:24).

[43] The most recent writing on this is: W. Gutbrod, *Die paulinische Anthropologie* (Stuttgart, 1934), pp. 205–16; P. Althaus, *Römerbrief* (*N. T. Deutsch* 6), Excursus on Rom. 6; A. Oepke, *Galaterbrief*, Excursus, p. 109 et seq.; E. Percy, *Die Probleme der Kolosser- und Epheserbriefe* (Lund, 1946), pp. 116–22; H. Schlier, *Galaterbrief*, pp. 128–30, 192–6; A. Kirchgässner, *Erlösung und Sünde im N. T.* (Freiburg i. Br., 1950), pp. 147–57; Wendland, *Theol. Lit.-Ztg.* (1952), p. 462 et seq.; E. Moscy, "Problema imperativi ethici in justificatione paulina" in *Verbum Domini*, xxv (1947), pp. 204–17; 264–9; G. Bornkamm, *Das Ende des Gesetzes,* (Munich, 1952), pp. 34–50; L. Nieder, see below IV, 3, note 124.

Let not sin therefore reign in your mortal body, so as to obey the lusts thereof (Rom. 6:12; cf. 13:14b).

In whom (Christ) also you are circumcised with circumcision not made by hand in despoiling of the body of the flesh: but in the circumcision of Christ, buried with him in Baptism (Col. 2:11 et seq.). You are not in the flesh (Rom. 8:9).

Put ye on the Lord Jesus Christ (Rom. 13:14).

As many of you as have been baptized in Christ have put on Christ (Gal. 3:27).

Put on the new man who according to God is created (Eph. 4:24; Col. 3:10).

If there be any in Christ a new creature (2 Cor. 5:17).

That Christ may dwell by faith in your hearts (Eph. 3,17).

Christ liveth in me (Gal. 2:20; Rom. 8:10; Phil. 1:21; Col. 1:27).

Walk then as children of the light (Eph. 5:8; 1 Thess. 5:6,8) Let us therefore cast off the works of darkness and put on the armour of light (Rom. 13:12; cf. Eph. 6:11–17).

You were heretofore darkness, but now light (Eph. 5:8; 1 Thess. 5:4 et seq.).

Purge out the old leaven that you may be a new paste (1 Cor. 5:7).

You are unleavened (1 Cor. 5:7).

Let us walk in the Spirit (Gal. 5:25).

If we live in the Spirit (Gal. 5:25).

If you are led by the Spirit

The law of the spirit of life, in

you are not under the law (Gal. 5:18; cf. Rom. 8:4).	Christ Jesus, hath delivered me from the law of sin and of death (Rom. 8:2).
If by the Spirit you mortify the deeds of the flesh, you shall live (Rom. 8:13; Gal. 5:16).	You are not under the law, but under grace (Rom. 6:14).
Be reformed in the newness of your mind (Rom. 12:2).	We . . . beholding the glory of the Lord . . . are transformed into the same image (2 Cor. 3:18).

It is evident at a glance that there is a formal contradiction between the statements in the two columns. Naturally Paul did not mean them to contradict each other in substance. How are they to be reconciled?

Joh. Weiss suggests that the indicative sentences are extremely clever paradoxes, such as are characteristic of all mysticism.[44] But this does not harmonize with the facts. Paul is perfectly serious in these statements about the effects of Baptism. There is nothing to suggest that they are mere outbursts of enthusiasm. Paul is declaring facts when he says that the Christian is a new creature, that the old things are passed away, and that all things are made new (2 Cor. 5:17). And he is equally earnest in his injunctions, as we see from their large number, and from the emphatic form in which he casts them.

The only explanation which fits the facts is that we have here a merely formal contrast; the paradox is purely verbal. The

44 *Urchristentum*, p. 405.

source of the confusion lies in the fact that Paul uses the same terms for two different things, namely for the result of the sacrament of Baptism and for his ethical injunctions. In spite of his use of one set of terms, it is quite clear from the Epistles that he considered these two things utterly different.

It is obvious that in the actual life of the Christian there is a strong contrast between the ideal and the reality. The ideal Christian life is entirely free from sin and is completely directed by the union with Christ; but in reality the flesh, and sin which derives from it, have not yet lost all their power. In principle the flesh is dead, but so long as the Christian lives in the flesh it continues attempting to assert its domination. That is the meaning of Gal. 5:16 et seq.: "I say then: Walk in the Spirit: and you shall not fulfil the lusts of the flesh. For the flesh lusteth against the spirit: and the spirit against the flesh. For these are contrary one to another: so that you do not the things that you would." So although the body of sin (Rom. 6:6) is destroyed, the possibility and the danger of sinning remain. There are two hostile powers in the Christian which struggle incessantly to win the Christian. By Baptism man becomes a divine sinless being. But this is not all; the reception of Baptism obliges him also to keep up a constant resistance to sin. When a man becomes a Christian, sin does not lose all its power. Paul candidly recognizes that there is still much imperfection and sinfulness in the Christian communities.

Nevertheless there is an essential difference between Christian life and life before the coming of Christ. In the past man was subject to the dreadful necessity of being sinful, he was enslaved to the sinister power of sin (Rom. 6:17 et seq.), whereas he now knows that this power is broken and that he is in a position to put up a successful resistance to his former master. His mysterious union with Christ Triumphant gives him the power to overcome impulses and passions which spring from the flesh, for, though deprived of its rights over man, the flesh is not yet dead. Union with Christ also enables man to produce the fruits of the Spirit, which Paul enumerates as: Charity, joy, peace, patience, benignity, goodness, longanimity, mildness, faith, modesty, continency, and chastity (Gal. 5:22). This explains his insistence on the fact that "if you live according to the flesh, you shall die: but if by the Spirit you mortify the deeds of the flesh you shall live" (Rom. 8:13); again in Gal. 5:21 he says: "I foretell you, as I have foretold to you, that they who do such things (that is, the works of the flesh) shall not obtain the kingdom of God."

Paul's teaching is quite clear. But his injunctions are cast in language which appears to contradict his teaching about the effects of Baptism. However, they must be interpreted in the light of his attitude to sin.

Paul considered that Baptism establishes the new life and withdraws man from the sphere of the flesh. He did not teach that the Christian's conduct thereby becomes perfect. The objective foundation which is established by Baptism must be expressed in the Christian's conduct. Man's activity must follow God's action.[45] The paradoxical form of his injunctions helps us to appreciate the great importance which the Apostle attached to morality.

[45] Schlier agrees with this, op. cit., p. 196: "The imperative orders the Christian to fulfil what has been said of him, that is, to show openly and practically by his conduct the hidden – but real – effect of Baptism, to demonstrate and confirm by his conduct his sacramental being."

An examination of Paul's "mysticism of suffering"[46] enables us to get a still deeper appreciation of his thought. Paul suffered enormously (2 Cor. 1:5), and when speaking of his sufferings he often calls them "sufferings of Christ" (2 Cor. 1:5; Phil. 3:10; Col. 1:24). He tells the Galatians that "I bear the marks of the Lord Jesus Christ in my body" (Gal. 6:17) – a reference to the wounds and scars which he received in the exercise of his apostolate. It was a custom in antiquity for believers to be branded with the mark of their god, which sealed them as dedicated to him. In the same way the brand of Christ was stamped upon Paul by the numerous assaults and persecutions which he suffered as an apostle (2 Cor. 6:4 et seq.; 11:23 et seq.). To the Corinthians he describes himself as "always bearing about in our body the mortification of Jesus" (2 Cor. 4:10). This is not a reference to the doctrine of Gal. 2:19 and Rom. 6:6 of being crucified with Christ in Baptism; here he is thinking of the

---

[46] On "mysticism of suffering" see A. Steubing, *Der paulinische Begriff "Christusleiden"*, Dissertation, Heidelberg (Darmstadt, 1905); Bartmann, *Paulus*, p. 137 et seq.; Deissmann, *Paulus*, p. 157 et seq.; W. Weber, *Christusmystik*, p. 74 et seq.; Mundle, *Das religiöse Leben des Apostels Paulus*, p. 78 et seq.; O. Schmitz, *Christusgemeinschaft*, p. 190 et seq.; *Lebensgefühl des Paulus*, p. 109 et seq.; Windisch, 2 *Kor.-Br.*, p. 40 et seq.; J. Schneider, *Passionsmystik des Paulus* (1929); G. Wiencke, *Paulus über Jesu Tod* (1939), p. 126 et seq.; Dibelius, *Paulus und die Mystik*, p. 64 et seq. – On Col. 1:24 see also J. Schmid: *Bibl. Zeitschrift*, xxi (1933), pp. 330–44; Windisch, *Paulus und Christus*, pp. 244–8; G. Kittel in *ZsystTh*, xviii (1941), pp. 186–91; H. Schlier in *ThWb*, iii, 143 et seq.; F. Hauck, ibid., 806 et seq.; A. Oepke, ibid., 109 et seq.; E. Percy, *Die Probleme der Kolosser- und Epheserbriefe* (1946), pp. 128–34; Th. Preiss in *Rev. d'histoire et de philosophie relig.* (1938), p. 205 et seq.; M. Carez, ibid. (1951), pp. 343–53; B. N. Wambucq in *Verbum Domini*, xxvii (1949), pp. 17–22.

sufferings of his life as a Christian and an apostle. In the course of this life he constantly experiences in his body the death of his Lord, Jesus Christ (1 Cor. 15:31; 2 Cor. 4:11). This statement means that his pains and sufferings are the same as those which Christ once had to endure (2 Cor. 4:7 et seq.), or that they are falling upon him for Christ's sake (2 Cor. 4:11).

He describes his sufferings in these terms because he endures them as one who is mystically united with Christ (see 1 Cor. 12:26). But there is a further and more profound explanation of Paul's language. As Rom. 6:2 et seq. teaches, union with Christ is above all fellowship with his death and life, a fellowship with Christ who died and rose again. In Baptism we die and rise with him sacramentally. But this must be fully manifested and made effective in the Christian's life: the Christian must become absolutely like Christ who died and rose again. The only way to be like Christ who died is to bear patiently the sufferings and tribulations which God ordains. In this way the Christian becomes "conformable to his (Christ's) death" (Phil. 3:10), and this conformity is a pledge that at the resurrection of the dead "the body of our lowliness" will be "made like to the body of his glory" (Phil. 3:21). For in Christ's own case, God raised him from the dead and exalted him because of the obedience with which he endured the death on the Cross (Phil. 2:8 et seq.).

Paul's utterances about his sufferings and troubles show that this was how he regarded and evaluated them. In 2 Cor. 4:7 et seq., he writes that he can courageously stand up to all sufferings and persecutions in spite of the weakness of his body; he attributes this unexpected fact to the power of God. He says that God has deliberately chosen as his instruments men who are weak; God's purpose in so doing was to ensure that nothing would obscure his power. Paul continues: "Always bearing about in our body the mortification of Jesus" – the reference is to the continual perils, persecutions and tribulations which afflict his body and leave their traces on him (cf. Gal. 6:17) – "that the life also of Jesus, may be made manifest in our bodies" (verse 10). He immediately paraphrases this verse so as to make it even clearer: "For we who live are always delivered unto death for Jesus' sake; that the life also of Jesus may be made manifest in our mortal flesh" (verse 11). The life of Jesus, of course, means the new life which Christ has gained from the Father through his resurrection. This life grows from our fellowship with Christ's death. Does this manifestation of the life of Jesus take place at the resurrection of the body, or is Paul thinking of the victorious surmounting of all perils and the strengthening of the inward man, as in verse 16? The first possibility cannot be ruled out, for in verse 14 he says explicitly that he is thinking of the Second Coming of Christ: "Knowing that he who raised up Jesus will raise us up also with Jesus and place us with you." He then again states his motive for enduring suffering: "For which cause we faint not: but though our outward man is corrupted, yet the inward man is renewed day by day. For that which is at present momentary and light of our tribulation worketh for us above measure exceedingly an eternal weight of glory" (verse 16 et seq.).

The theme of the whole passage is the manifestation of the life of Jesus to Paul both in this life and in eternity. During his life in this world he has often been aware of his "infirmity", and he has frequently found that it is on such occasions that the power of Christ descends most abundantly upon him (2 Cor. 12:9). "For which cause", he adds, "I please myself in my infirmities, in reproaches, in necessities, in persecutions, in distresses, for Christ. For when I (the outward, physical man) am weak, then am I (the inward, spiritual man) strong" (2 Cor. 12:10).

Elsewhere he declares that sufferings make our resurrection from the dead secure, for example in Rom. 8:17: "And if (we are) sons (of God), (we are) heirs also; heirs indeed of God and joint heirs with Christ: yet so, if we suffer with him, that we may be also glorified with him." A share in Christ's suffering gives us a share in his glorification.

The same conviction is revealed by Phil. 3:10 et seq. Paul wants to know Christ and to know the power of his resurrection and the fellowship of his sufferings, while he conforms himself to the death of Christ, in order finally to attain the resurrection from the dead. This text can only mean that Paul considers fellowship in Christ's death an indispensible condition for attaining fellowship in his life – including the resurrection of the body. That is why it is so important for him to share in Christ's sufferings until he becomes conformable to Christ's death; in this way he will attain the "prize of the supernal vocation", as he calls the resurrection in verse 14.

2 Cor. 13:3 et seq., is somewhat obscure, but it also deals with the same theme: "If I come again, I will not spare. Do you seek a proof of Christ that speaketh in me, who towards you is not weak, but is mighty in you? For although he was crucified through weakness, yet he liveth by the power of God. For we also are weak in him: but we shall live with him by the power of God towards you." Paul means that he lives "in Christ" and must therefore express in his life both the strength and the infirmity of his Lord. That, he says, is how you should understand my present weakness, to which you are taking exception.

But I am certain that I shall be glorified with Christ at his Second Coming, and I will apply to you the power of the risen Christ which I already have as a help in my present work. If you do not reform, "Christ in me", who is living and powerful, will make himself known to you as judge and avenger.[47]

Paul is far from thinking that suffering is of importance only in his own case. Like the whole primitive Church, he was convinced that all kinds of sufferings and troubles are a part of Christian life. When Christ was leaving the world he told his apostles: "In the world you shall have distress" (John 16:33). Paul himself told the newly converted Christians of South Galatia that they should continue in the faith in spite of troubles, for "through many tribulations we must enter into the kingdom of God" (Acts 14:21). Again he sent Timothy from Athens to Thessalonica to strengthen the faith of the Christians there, and to warn them against wavering in the present crisis; he adds: "Yourselves know that we are appointed thereunto. For even when we were with you, we foretold you that we should suffer tribulations: as, also, it is come to pass, and you know" (1 Thess. 3:1–4). And St. Peter writes: "Dearly beloved, think not strange the burning heat which is to try you: as if some new thing happened to you. But if you partake of the sufferings of Christ, rejoice that, when his glory shall be revealed, you may also be glad with exceeding joy" (1 Peter 4:12 et seq.). The Epistle of Barnabas has the same teaching: "So, says he, those who wish to see me and reach my kingdom must go through distress and suffering to grasp me" (7:11).[48] It has been pointed out that this

[47] Windisch, op. cit., p. 419.
[48] See also Rom. 8:17, 35 et seq.; 12:12, 14; 2 Cor. 1:4, 7; 1 Thess.

doctrine of Paul's derives from Jewish tradition, for the Jews held that Israel's place in the world was inseparable from suffering. But there is a major difference between Paul's doctrine and the Jewish view, for the Jews believed that the Messianic community, far from being a suffering community, would be the triumphant Empire of Israel.

Paul himself appreciates this law of suffering. He had much more than a normal share of troubles and sufferings (2 Cor. 1:4 et seq.; 4:8; 7:4; 11:23 to 12:10). Yet he bears them patiently, indeed cheerfully, for he is convinced that the great weight of suffering which has befallen him is a source of plentiful blessing, not only for himself but also for the entire Church. He says repeatedly that he suffers on behalf of his communities, as in Eph. 3:13 where he asks the readers not to waver because of the tribulations which he is undergoing on their behalf, for these tribulations will help them to reach glory in the future. And the meaning of 2 Cor. 1:6 is probably that the tribulations which his apostolate involves are to their advantage, for he can preach the Gospel to them only if he takes upon himself the sufferings which his office entails.

The most important statement of this doctrine appears in Col. 1:24: "(I) now rejoice in my sufferings for you and fill up those things that are wanting of the sufferings of Christ, in my flesh (that is, by my bodily sufferings), for his body, which is the Church." Even at the present day exegetes disagree about the exact meaning of this text.

Paul certainly does not mean that the sufferings of Christ have some defect which he must supply by his life of sacrifice, so as to

2:14; 2 Tim. 2:12; Ignatius, *Magn.* 9, 2; *1 Clem.* 35:4; *2 Clem.* 17:7; 19:3; 20:2, 4.

159

complete the work of Redemption. To begin with, he never uses the word "sufferings" (θλίψεις) when speaking of Christ's redemptive work; in such cases he uses the words Death, Blood and Cross, as in Col. 1:20: "making peace through the blood of his Cross". Moreover, it would never have occurred to Paul, nor to any other Christian to speak of a defect in the Redemption which was wrought by Christ's death. Christ fully and entirely discharged the burden of suffering laid upon him by the Father, and thereby completed the Redemption. At the present day exegetes agree on these points.

Some commentators, such as Percy, put forward the following interpretation of the verse in question: Paul regards his own sufferings as a continuation of Christ's sufferings; his sufferings produce favourable results for the Church – both for its interior growth and for its expansion – and in this respect his sufferings may be said to complete the sufferings of Christ. But such a process could not be called "filling up what is wanting of the sufferings of Christ" in any proper sense.

The "sufferings of Christ" cannot mean the sufferings which Christ himself underwent. In view of this fact many exegetes, including Schlier, Hauck and Oepke, suggest that Paul is not speaking of the historical Christ. They maintain that he is speaking of the mystical Christ who is united in one body with the totality of the faithful. In this verse, they say, Paul means that the Church has still to undergo a certain burden of suffering, and that he is vicariously discharging this burden by bearing the sufferings of imprisonment.

Oepke says that this passage is based on the idea of Christ as the Universal Man. As the Person who appeared on earth he has made satisfaction for men's sins. As head of the new humanity he enjoys a heavenly existence. But, in so far as he with his (mystical) "Body" still belongs to this world, he must yet fulfil a certain amount of suffering which is determined by God. And, in so far as Paul is a member of the Body of Christ, his sufferings are the sufferings of Christ, and they contribute to the hastening of complete Redemption.

This interpretation is very popular, and was held even by St. Augustine. But it is open to the objection that the idea of Christ suffering in his followers cannot be clearly found in the New Testament. Moreover, this interpretation would render the passage tautologous: "I fill up those things that are wanting of the sufferings of (the Mystical Body of) Christ for his (mystical) body, which is the Church." Finally, it is hard to believe that Paul could have claimed to be discharging by his own sufferings the burden of suffering which God had laid upon the entire Church.

The "sufferings of Christ" can only be Paul's own sufferings. We have here a "characterizing genitive" which tells us that Paul must bear these sufferings because he is "in Christ" or in the new "Christ era" (see I, 2). God has laid down a certain amount of suffering for Paul to bear, and he has not yet entirely discharged it. Elsewhere in the Epistles he also uses the phrase "sufferings of Christ" to describe the sufferings which the performance of his apostolic mission entails. He says in 2 Cor. 1:5 that "the sufferings of Christ abound in us", and, according to Gal. 6:17, "I bear the marks of the Lord Jesus in my body.' In the course of his touching declarations in 2 Cor. chapter 4, he describes himself (verse 10) as "always bearing about in our body the mortification of Jesus, that the life also of Jesus may be made manifest in our bodies".

161

By means of these "sufferings of Christ" man is made like Christ crucified, and they assure us that we shall share in Christ's heavenly glory (Phil. 3:10 et seq.). "If we suffer with him . . . we may be also glorified with him" (Rom. 8:17; cf. 2 Tim. 2:11 et seq.). "We who live are always delivered unto death for Jesus' sake: that the life also of Jesus (that is, the new life of Christ Triumphant) may be made manifest in our mortal flesh" (2 Cor. 4:11). It follows that these "sufferings of Christ" are a great blessing for Christians, for they express in the life of the Christian the death and resurrection with Christ which was sacramentally effected by Baptism.

In Col. 1:24 Paul makes a further point about his "sufferings of Christ": they are profitable to the Body of Christ, that is, to the whole Church. He is firmly convinced of this, and this conviction is the reason for his great and profound joy when surrounded by tribulations.

The examination of Paul's "mysticism of suffering" gives us a clearer and deeper insight into his teaching. He sets great store by God's action in Baptism, which gives us a mystical and sacramental fellowship with Christ's death and resurrection. But he is equally insistent that by their conduct Christians must display a moral fellowship with Christ. It is only when this moral fellowship has been established that our heavenly calling attains its goal. God's action in Baptism must be reproduced in man's conduct. The sacramental relationship with Christ must be made an ethical relationship also.

IV

The Specifically Christian Character of Pauline Mysticism

1. A PROBLEM OF COMPARATIVE RELIGION

THE conclusions in II, 4, have demonstrated that Paul's mysticism is not a "mysticism of faith"; the Apostle's teaching is that a real mystical fellowship of life and being exists between the Christian and Christ Triumphant.

But mysticism is not a clearly defined, unambiguous concept. As Leo Baeck has said: "There is no such thing as mysticism pure and simple. Each religion develops its own mysticism according to its special nature. We do not encounter a universal mysticism; instead we find the mysticism of Buddhism, of Taoism, of Neo-platonism, of Judaism, of Christianity, of Islam."[1]

It is therefore not enough to say that Paul teaches that there is a real mystical relationship between Christians and Christ. This description is too vague. The specific character of Pauline

[1] *Ursprung und Anfänge der jüdischen Mystik,* Vorträge des Institutum Judaicum an der Univ. Berlin i (Giessen, 1927), p. 94.

163

mysticism must be defined more closely, and the best way to do this is to contrast it with contemporary Hellenistic mysticism, which owed much to Oriental influence.

The relation between Paul and pagan mysticism is a matter of dispute among scholars, and the last word has not yet been said about it. Eminent scholars hold views on this subject which are quite irreconcilable with one another.

On the one hand, there is the Comparative Religion school represented principally by the classical scholars A. Dietrich[2] and R. Reitzenstein, and by the theologians W. Heitmüller[3] and W. Bousset[4]. Of these, Reitzenstein has done most to connect Paul with the stream of Oriental-Hellenistic mysticism. In his book on the Hellenistic mystery religions, which first appeared in 1910 and reached its third edition in 1927, he presents Paul as the great mystic who owes to Hellenism his most precious possession, namely the belief in his apostolate and in his liberty. Even before his conversion he was a mystic; he was a loyal follower of the Jewish Law. But Hellenistic moral writings and revelation literature affected his outlook and helped to prepare the ground for his conversion. He adopted certain phrases and figures of speech from these sources, but this was not their main effect on Paul. His principles were all derived from Hellenistic mysticism.[5]

Reitzenstein's views were impugned by the Protestant theologian K. Deissner. His book *Paulus und die Mystik seiner*

[2] *Eine Mithrasliturgie* (Leipzig, [1]1903, [3]1923).

[3] *Taufe und Abendmahl bei Paulus* (Tübingen, 1903).

[4] *Kyrios Christos* (Göttingen, [1]1913, [2]1921).

[5] Reitzenstein also expounded his ideas in: *Das iranische Erlösungsmysterium* (Bonn, 1921), and in *Studien zum antiken Synkretismus* (1926; in collaboration with H. H. Schaeder).

Zeit ("Paul and the mysticism of his time") appeared in 1918 and reached a second edition in 1921.[6] Deissner denies that Hellenistic mysticism had any influence worth mentioning on Paul; the only concession he makes to Reitzenstein's view is that Paul borrowed some terms from the mystery religions.[7] But he stresses that these were mere borrowings of terminology; Paul did not take over any Hellenistic ideas. On the contrary, so far from being an exponent of these notions, Paul attacks the fundamental assumptions of the mystery religions.

There is not space here to enter upon a full-scale examination of this difficult problem. In any case we are not concerned with establishing Paul's independence of Hellenistic mysticism. Our task is to contrast the fundamental ideas underlying the two systems, so as to clarify the specific nature of Paul's mysticism.

There is no doubt that Deissner's criticism of Reitzenstein is sound, and in large measure we must agree with what he says about Paul. However, he takes mysticism in the narrow sense of pantheistic divinization, and denies that there is in Paul any mysticism properly so called. In this respect his work is defective. He followed Nathan Söderblom in drawing a sharp distinction between prophetic and mystical piety. But if mysticism be understood in the sense which we have given it, there is no foundation for such a distinction.

---

[6] G. Heinrici's work *Die Hermesmystik und das N.T.*, which was published posthumously by E. v. Dobschütz (Leipzig, 1918), had less influence. It was challenged by Reitzenstein in *Gött. Gel. Anzeigen* (1918), pp. 241–74, and by H. Windisch in *Theol. Tijdschrift*, lii, pp. 186–240.

[7] These are: "put on Christ" Gal. 3:27; "perfect" Phil. 3:15; "mystery" Col. 1:25 et seq.; "transformed" 2 Cor. 3:18. Probably the phrase "in Christ" should be added to this list.

No doubt it may be made in theory, but it can be applied only in the rarest practical cases. Both forms of piety appear intimately interwoven in the case of many saints, indeed in most cases: they are vividly aware of the infinite gulf which separates them from God and of their strict moral obligations, and they are happy in the thought that they enjoy a most intimate fellowship of life with God; one or the other of these elements may be predominant. There is no abstract formula which can sum up Augustine, Bernard of Clairvaux, Francis of Assisi, Bonaventure, or St. Teresa of Ávila. And it is equally out of the question to say simply that a religious spirit like Paul showed one or the other type of piety. Such formulae are utterly inadequate for doing justice to the flow of life.

It is possible to call Paul a mystic, or rather, to recognize the mystical element in his theology and piety, without considering him an exponent of Oriental-Hellenistic mysticism. We will demonstrate in detail that his mysticism is essentially different from this pagan mysticism.

There are three facts which make this difference essential:

1. Paul derived from Judaism a strictly monotheistic concept of God; according to this concept God is a personal spiritual Being, superior to the world. Hellenistic mysticism, on the other hand, was pantheistic, or at least it had pantheistic tendencies.

2. There is a clearly defined eschatology in Paul's theology, as there was in the Old Testament, Judaism, and the rest of primitive Christianity. There is no such thing in Hellenistic mysticism.

3. Paul's mysticism is Christ-mysticism. He is aware that he is mystically united with a Person who once lived on this earth, underwent suffering and death, was raised up by God's

power, and now sits at the right hand of God. Pagan mysticism of his time was a mysticism of infinity.

These three points are of importance; indeed, they are fundamental to the relationship with God. On these matters there is absolute incompatibility between Paul and Hellenism. This fact inevitably gives Paul's mysticism a specific character of its own.

2. THE FUNDAMENTAL IDEAS
OF ORIENTAL-HELLENISTIC MYSTICISM

Before entering upon the comparison of Paul's mysticism with the mysticism of the Hellenistic world, we will outline the main principles[8] which underlay the latter.

[8] Literature on this question: Reitzenstein, *Hellenist. Mysterien-religionen* ([3]1927). Reitzenstein-Schaeder, *Studien zum antiken Synkretismus* (1926). Bousset, *Kyrios Christos*, p. 112 et seq., p. 163 et seq. J. Kroll, *Die Lehren des Hermes Trismegistos* (1914; reviewed by Bousset in *Gött. Gel. Anz.*, clxxvi [1914], pp. 697–755). Deissner, *Paulus und die Mystik seiner Zeit* ([2]1921; reviewed by Posselt in *PhilolWschr* [1918], p. 865 et seq.; [1921], p. 433 et seq.; Dibelius in *Deutsche Lit.-Ztg.* [1921], p. 724 et seq.). Dibelius, *Die Isisweihe* (1917). H. E. Weber in *Neue kirchl. Zeitschr.* (1920), pp. 258–60. Geffcken, *Religiöse Strömungen*, p. 61 et seq. Bräuninger, *Untersuchungen zu den Schriften des Hermes Trismegistos* (1926; reviewed by M. Dibelius in *Gnomon* [1929], p. 161 et seq.). Van Randenborgh, *Vergottung und Erlösung* (1927). K. Deissner, "Erlöser und Erlösung im Urchristentum und Hellenismus" in *Deutsche Theologie*, ii (1929), pp. 119–26. Heigl, *Antike Mysterienreligionen* (1932). Festugière, *L'idéal religieux des Grecs*, pp. 87–169. Hopfner, *Die orientalisch-hellenistischen Mysterien* (1935). Jonas, *Gnosis und spätantiker Geist*, i (1934). Dodd, *The Bible and the Greeks*, pp. 97–248: Hellenistic Judaism and the Hermetica. Bornkamm, Art. μυστήριον in *ThWb*, iv, 809–20. Nilsson, *Geschichte der griechischen Religion*, ii (1950), pp. 555–672. On the Hermetic writings see alo K. Prümm, *Religions-*

First a word about sources. By far the most important sources
for this Oriental-Hellenistic mysticism are the so-called Hermetic writings, which get their name from Hermes Trismegistos, the Egyptian god of revelation. The Hermetic Corpus
consists of eighteen tracts – which are partly mutilated – as
well as a work called "Asclepius" which survives in Latin; to
these we can add a considerable number of fragments which
are preserved by the fifth century A.D. writer Johannes Stobaeus.[9]
The Hermetic Corpus is of importance for us.

The eighteen tracts claim to be revelations from Hermes and
other Egyptian gods. They are best described as pagan-Gnostic

geschichtliches Handbuch für den Raum der altchristlichen Umwelt (reprinted
Rome, 1954), pp. 535–600; for Poimandres H. Gundel in Pauly-
Wissowa, Realenc. d. klass. Altertumswiss., xxi, 1 (1951), 1193–1207.
See also H. Schlier, "Der Mensch im Gnostizismus" in Anthropologie
religieuse (edited by C. J. Bleeker, Leyden, 1955), pp. 60–76.

[9] Published by Parthey (1854, incomplete); Reitzenstein re-edited
some of the tracts in his Poimandres (1904); Tract I appears also in Reitzenstein–Schaeder, op. cit., p. 154 et seq. The most recent edition of the
whole is W. Scott, Hermetica I (Oxford, 1924), Text; II–III (1925–6),
Commentary (Scott's text has been vigorously criticized by the textual
scholars: see Pfister in PhilolWschr [1925], p. 615 et seq.; [1927], No. 19;
Reitzenstein in Gnomon I [1925], p. 249 et seq.; III [1927], p. 266 et
seq.), IV (1936), Testimonia with introduction, appendices and indices
by A. S. Ferguson. The text appears with a French translation, brief
introductions and notes: Corpus hermeticum, Texte établi par A. D. Nock
et traduit par A. J. Festugière, 4 vols. (Paris, 1945–54). The Corpus is
examined thoroughly in Festugière's four volume work: La révélation
d'Hermès Trismégiste (Paris, 1944–54); there is an outline of this by
Festugière himself in L'Hermétisme (Lund, 1948) (Offprint from Bulletin
de la Société des lettres de Lund, 1947–8). The Anthology of Stobaeus
contains thirty one otherwise unrecorded excerpts from Hermetic writings. There is also a number of fragments in Lactantius, Cyril of Alexandria, and other writers (see Scott I and IV).

revelation literature. There is no uniformity in their ideas about cosmology, anthropology, and theology. Bräuninger[10] following Bousset[11] demonstrated that the tracts fall into two groups which originated in two utterly different schools of thought. The so-called Oriental group uses the terminology of Greek philosophy, but its thought is entirely eastern (I, IV, VI, VII, XII, 1 Scott, XIII). These tracts are an extremely valuable source for Oriental-Hellenistic mysticism. Their nature appears most clearly in their presentation of the two central ideas of Gnosis and Heimarmene. Gnosis here means the transcendental mystical vision of God, while Heimarmene is regarded as an obscure disastrous force. The other main group of these tracts is the so-called Hellenistic group (V, VIII, XII, 2 Scott, XIV), which does not go beyond Greek philosophy. The ideas in these tracts are principally Stoic, with a certain influence of Platonism. This second group of tracts does not concern us here. Finally IX, X, and XVI are "mixed tracts".

It is not possible to establish the date of their composition. Reitzenstein thinks that they were produced in Egypt at some time during the first three centuries of our era; he considers that they were intended for readers who had received a Greek education.[12] Others think that they are later than this. Deubner[13] dates them to the third century of our era, while Geffcken[14]

---

[10] *Untersuchungen zu den Schriften des Hermes Trismegistos,* Phil. Dissertation (Berlin, 1926).

[11] *Gött. Gel. Anz.* (1914), p. 697 et seq.

[12] *Hellenist. Mysterienreligionen,* p. 47.

[13] Chantepie de la Saussaye, *Lehrbuch der Religionsgesch.,* ii (1925), p. 489.

[14] *Religiöse Strömungen,* p. 14; *Der Ausgang des griechisch-römischen Heidentums* (1920), p. 78 et seq.

thinks that a considerable portion goes back to the first century
A.D. Scott is inclined to place their composition in the third
century, though he does not rule out the possibility that some
parts date from the second century. Like Lagrange,[15] he considers that they contain a mixture of Platonic thought – derived
particularly from the "Timaeus" – and Stoicism. On the other
hand, Reitzenstein, Bousset, Geffcken, Norden, Deubner,
Bräuninger, Büchsel, and Windisch claim to find in them strong
traces of Oriental religious speculation. I prefer this second
view.[16] It is disputed whether some of the tracts show Christian
influence. Lagrange insists that there is such influence in I and
XIII.[17]

There are other sources also, namely some parts of the
magical papyri, particularly the so-called Liturgy of Mithras.
The ideas behind the Greek-Oriental mysteries also are relevant.

As these sources show, the aim of Oriental-Hellenistic mysticism was to achieve the divinization of man. This divinization
takes place by man ascending completely into the godhead and
becoming entirely one with it. This unity is attained by Gnosis,
particularly in its highest form – the vision of God. The whole
process is based on the doctrine that the better part of man, the
"essential man", is a portion of the godhead itself, which can
escape the domination of Heimarmene and attain complete rest

[15] "L'hermétisme" in *Rev. biblique* (1924), p. 481 et seq.; (1925),
p. 82 et seq.; p. 368 et seq.; p. 547 et seq.; (1926), p. 240 et seq.

[16] See Büchsel, *Geist Gottes*, p. 118 et seq.

[17] As Heinrici had already done in *Die Hermesmystik* (1918). Windisch
is more conservative in his review of Heinrici's thesis (*Theol. Tijdschrift*,
lii [1918], pp. 186–240). He admits the possibility of Christian influence
on I, XIII, IV, but narrows his views still further in *ZntW* (1924), p. 280.
See also E. Meyer, *Ursprung und Anfänge des Christentums*, ii, pp. 371–7.

and happiness by returning to its source; this return is effected by release from the prison of the body and ascent to God.

Heimarmene,[18] (*fatum,* fate) according to these tracts, is the source of all evil in the world. It works in close conjunction with the stars. The usual teaching of the Hermetic tracts is either that it works through the seven planets (Stobaeus, *Ecl. I,* 82, 5 Wachsmuth; Scott I, 434: "the stars are subservient to destiny"), or that the planets work through fate (I, 9: "The Demiourgos as god of fire and of air has created seven rulers [the planets], which surround the visible world by their courses [or spheres]; their influence is called fate"). Heimarmene is also connected with the twelve signs of the Zodiac, which are called masters of destiny (XIII, 7; Apuleius, *Metamorph.* 11, 23 et seq.).[19]

As he begins his (voluntary) descent from the upper world, the "spiritual" primitive man has, so to speak, no attributes. He comes first to the province of the Demiourgos where he receives garments, as it were, in the sphere of each of the planets; each of these garments is a "psychic" quality corresponding to the particular planet in whose sphere he is.[20] "In

[18] On Heimarmene see Kroll, *Lehren des Hermes,* p. 214 et seq.; Reitzenstein, op. cit., pp. 67, 255, 300 et seq.; Bräuninger, op. cit., p. 10 et seq.; p. 29 et seq.; Bousset in *Gött. Gel. Anz.* (1914), p. 171 et seq.; Jonas, *Gnosis,* i, pp. 156–210.

[19] The Egyptian astrologers had a solar calendar, and the Zodiac was the basis of their astral system. So in Egyptian astrology the number twelve took the place which was occupied in the Babylonian system – with its lunar chronology – by the number seven, derived from the planetary system (Jonas, *Gnosis,* i, p. 201, note 1).

[20] Cf. Servius on *Aeneid,* vi, 714: "As the souls descend they take with them the indolence of Saturn, the irascibility of Mars, the lust of Venus, the avarice of Mercury and the craving for power of

this way he is clothed with garments of the soul, and they make man earthly even before he has a body." "In this way, the powers of the world keep adding qualities, and this process is a gradual corruption of the original being. In other words, these gifts from the planets are really burdens which combine to create man's earthly nature. After receiving this unwholesome endowment man finally breaks through the system of the spheres and reaches this lower world where he takes on a body, and in spite of his alien origin he has become a member of the lower world."[21] Heimarmene, as the power of stellar compulsion, is the source of man's wicked impulses, and so it is the principle of all the evil on earth.

Because of the dualism in man's nature, he is subject to Heimarmene: "Alone of all living things on earth he is of a double nature, mortal in his body and immortal in the essential man. Though immortal and ruler of everything, yet he has a mortal lot, and is subject to fate. Though superior to the world of the spheres, he has become a slave to the government of the spheres; bisexual, from an ambivalent father, always sleepless, from a sleepless father, he is dominated (by a yearning for love and sleep)" (I, 15). But fate dominates only man's bodily nature, and so man can always withdraw from the influence of fate, for his soul is incorporeal and immortal since it comes from the heavenly region which is above the planets. Man withdraws from the influence of fate when he climbs back to God through the sphere of the planets and becomes united with God. In the course of this ascent the soul discards one after another the

Jupiter: these confuse the soul and prevent it from using its own energy and powers." Jonas, *Gnosis,* i, p. 182, note 1.

[21] Jonas, *Gnosis,* i, p. 181 et seq.

burdens which the planets imposed on him as he descended (cf. I, 16; XIII, 7). The goal of this ascent is divinization, which automatically involves complete liberation from the domination of fate. The ascent is accomplished by means of Gnosis.

Gnosis is communicated by Nous, "the divine spirit which is a person or is personified".[22] Thus we read in XII, 1, 9: "Nous, which is the self of God, dominates everything – fate, the law, and all else; and it is not impossible for Nous to raise the self of man above fate, or, if man is unmindful, to subject him to fate."[23] According to X, 9, Nous is the instrument of Gnosis, and according to IV, 6, it is Nous which reveals divine matters to us and puts the knowledge of God within our reach. So Nous is the divine Spirit which makes man capable of the Gnosis of God. In Tract IV Hermes teaches Tat (this is the mystic's name) that God has sent upon the earth a mixing bowl filled with Nous, and has told the souls of men through his herald: "Plunge into this mixing bowl, thou who canst, thou who believest that thou shalt ascend to him who sent the bowl, thou who knowest for what end thou wast born. All who have grasped the message and plunged into the Spirit, have participated in knowledge (Gnosis) and become perfect men, since they have received Nous. But all those who ignore the message receive the Logos but not Nous, and so they are in ignorance about the purpose and source of their birth. . . . But those who have participated in the gift which God has sent are immortal instead of mortal, unlike the rest of mankind."[24] In other words,

[22] Bräuninger, op. cit., p. 23; also p. 15 et seq.

[23] See Reitzenstein, op. cit., p. 408.

[24] See Norden, *Agnostos Theos* (1913), p. 102. See also Dodd, *The Bible and the Greeks,* p. 236.

Gnosis bestows the divine nature, which primarily means immortality.

Various passages of the tracts describe how the soul ascends to God so as to become divine and escape from the power of Heimarmene. The first tract, which is called *Poimandres,* describes the ascent after death of the soul which possesses Gnosis (§§ 24–6). Reitzenstein considers that this is the oldest surviving Gnostic document, and thinks that its author was a contemporary, or even a predecessor, of Philo, whose approximate dates are 20 B.C. to A.D. 40.[25] Dodd dates this tract to the early second century or the end of the first century.[26]

Poimandres tells us that when the material body has been laid aside "man struggles upwards through the spheres, and he gives to the first circle his power to wax and wane,[27] to the second craftiness, to the third the illusion of cupidity, to the fourth magnificence, to the fifth pride which resists God together with rashness, to the sixth avarice, and to the seventh treachery and deception. Being then divested of the power of the spheres he reaches the eighth circle with his own power, and joins those who are there in praising the Father. Those who are there join in rejoicing at his arrival. He becomes like them and hears powers which dwell beyond the eighth sphere and which

---

[25] *Studien zum antiken Synkretismus,* p. 32.

[26] *The Bible and the Greeks,* pp. 200–9. *Poimandres* is not influenced by early Christian writings. There is a certain relationship in ideas, especially with the Fourth Gospel (Dodd, op. cit., pp. 204, 247 et seq.). Nilsson, *Griech. Religion,* ii, p. 384: "In *Poimandres* we find an early stage of developed Gnosticism, so it cannot be earlier than the second century."

[27] The seven planets in the order: Moon, Mercury, Venus, Sun, Mars, Jupiter, and Saturn. On the whole passage see Reitzenstein, *Studien,* p. 26 et seq.

praise the Father with loving voice. Then one after another they ascend to the Father, they go into the powers, and becoming powers themselves they ascend into God. That is the good end of those who have possessed Gnosis – to become divine".[28] The goal of Gnosis has been attained.

But only a comparatively small number of men share in Gnosis and attain divinization, for two requirements must first be fulfilled: knowledge of self and piety. Knowledge of self means knowing the divine origin of one's nature (I, 18; IV, 4; X, 15), and piety means humble worship of God (I, 22; VI, 5; IX, 4). The great mass of men who are not Gnostics do not achieve salvation after death. They go to the Underworld, where they are tortured and coerced by avenging spirits and enter the bodies of animals.

So *Poimandres* teaches that men who have attained Gnosis achieve union with God in their "incorporeal nature"; but this union takes place only after the separation of body and soul. The only possible inference from this is that the final union with God is not attained until after death, and that the possession of Gnosis does not by itself produce this union in the present life. This is the explanation of the phrase "the good end" (τέλος) in § 26. Reitzenstein has pointed out parallels in Plato (*Symp.* 210e and 211b), where in a similar context "the end" (τέλος) is contrasted with "the beginning of vision".[29]

---

[28] Translated with reference to K. Latte's German version, *Religionsgeschichtl. Lesebuch*[2], v, 74. On the idea of the soul's ascent through the spheres to God in order to attain divinization (immortality) see M. P. Nilsson, "Die astrale Unsterblichkeit und die kosmische Mystik" in *Numen, International Review for the History of Religions* (ed. R. Pettazzoni, Leyden, i, 1954), fasc. 2.   [29] *Hellenist. Mysterienreligionen,* p. 290.

But beside this doctrine we also find the idea that man can become divine even during his corporeal life. This is particularly important for our present purpose. The principal source for this doctrine is Tract XIV. It is in the form of a confidential instruction of Hermes the Father (the mystagogue) to the mystic; the subject of the instruction is rebirth. The tract shows the rebirth taking place during the discourses of Hermes, and we learn of its various stages from the utterances of the mystic.[30]

Here is a summary of this tract: (§ 1)We are told that in an earlier instruction Hermes had declared that no one could attain salvation before rebirth. The mystic had asked to learn the doctrine about rebirth, and he had been told that he must first withdraw from the present illusory world. He has now done so. (§ 2) Now Hermes begins to instruct him: The seed from which the new man is born is true goodness; the begetter is the will of God; the divine son, who is begotten, is All in All, he consists of all the powers of God. (§ 3) Concerning his own rebirth Hermes can only say this: I once saw in myself a transcendental vision, which was granted me by the mercy of God, and I rose above myself into an immortal body. Since then I am no longer the earlier person, but I have been (re)born in the spirit. The earlier composite form has disintegrated. I have no longer any colour, I cannot now be touched nor measured . . . You see me with your eyes, but you cannot appreciate what I really am, for you are looking with the body and with human vision. I can no longer be seen with human eyes.

(§§ 4–6) While the Father is giving this description of his

[30] It is analysed by Reitzenstein, *Poimandres,* p. 214 et seq.; *Hellenist. Mysterienreligionen,* p. 47 et seq.; p. 407. See also Jonas, *Gnosis,* i, pp. 200–2; Dey, *Palingenesia,* pp. 117–25.

rebirth, the son begins to experience a transformation. He no longer sees his own body, but he still sees the Father's body, though, as he has learned, it is merely an illusion. The mortal form changes daily. With the passage of time it becomes greater and smaller, for it is like a phantom. What is real is transcendental, and in order to attain birth in God he must learn to see reality. (§ 7) When the mystic protests that this is impossible for him, Hermes warns him: Draw him (that is, God) into you and he comes; will it and it takes place; subdue your corporeal sensations and the birth oft he Godhead will become a reality in you. You must purify yourself from the irrational tormentors who dwell in matter. The son asks whether there are such spirits in him and is told: Not few, but many terrible ones. They are the following twelve: ignorance, grief, intemperance, lust, injustice, avarice, deception, envy, craftiness, anger, imprudence, and malice.[31] These torment the inner man who, so to speak, is imprisoned in the body. They are driven out, one after the other, by the good divine powers which descend into man and together form the new man. (§§ 8-10) While Hermes is instructing the mystic about the various divine powers, they descend into him and drive out the tormentors (that is, the vices). The divine powers are: knowledge of God, joy, continence, steadfastness, justice, unselfishness, truth, goodness, life, and light. "When the ten divine powers which drive away the twelve tormentors are present, the spiritual birth has taken

[31] The twelve vices which are introduced into man's soul from outside under the influence of the stars, correspond to the twelve signs of the Zodiac, which Egyptian astrology considered the masters of fate. See Reitzenstein, *Poimandres,* p. 271; Bräuninger, op. cit., p. 19 et seq.; p. 29.

place and through this birth we are divinized."[32] (§ 11) Now the mystic says that he has become a new being and can see transcendentally. He cries out as in ecstasy: "I am in Heaven, on earth, in water, in the air. I am in the animals, in the plants, in my mother's body, before my mother's body (that is, not yet conceived), after my mother's body (that is, already born), I am everywhere." He expresses here the pantheistic feeling of being raised beyond time and space. Reitzenstein says: "It is the feeling of being the Aëon, the god of the world, which now is the 'man' or the 'soul'."[33]

(§ 14) He then asks whether this "body", which is composed of the ten divine powers (that is, the transcendental body, the new man), can ever disintegrate. The reply is that the physical body which is perceived by the corporeal senses is utterly different from the body which originates in the new birth. The one is corruptible, the other incorruptible, the one mortal, the other immortal. "Do you not know that you have become god and the son of god, just like me?" (§ 15) The mystic now wishes to hear the hymn which the soul of the dead hears when it reaches the eighth sphere, the song of praise which, according to *Poimandres* (§ 26), – to which he explicitly refers – the divine powers sing. This request can only mean that he wishes

[32] See Jonas, *Gnosis,* i, p. 202: The psychic self is replaced by the spiritual self in this way: By divine grace the divine powers descend to the mystic who has prepared himself by asceticism, they expel from him one by one the tormentors (vices) which have occupied the space of the soul, i.e., which constitute it, and they take the place of these vices. So they simultaneously destroy the astral psyche and create from its elements the "Logos" (= the spirit).

[33] *Hellenist. Mysterienreligionen,* p. 49.

to share in the supreme consummation. (§ 16) The Father grants his wish. Poimandres has told him no more than was described there (in Tract I), for he knew that the mystic could know and hear for himself all that he wished. He is now the world god, and the powers which praise the Father are the powers in him. (§§ 17–20) God's Logos praises the Father in him, and in the word offers the All to him as a spiritual sacrifice.

The rebirth, which is described in this tract, amounts to attaining in this life what Poimandres teaches us will be the soul's experience after the death of the body. Poimandres describes it as happening in reality: in Tract XIII it takes place in mystery. The soul loses its wicked impulses one after the other, while the divine powers enter in turn, drive out the vices, and constitute the divine being which is the new self. When the twelve vices are wiped out, there is no longer any connection with the stellar powers, and man is therefore free from Heimarmene, which is stellar compulsion. This may be summed up as salvation through divinization.

In *Poimandres* divinization takes place after death, when the soul really ascends through the spheres of the planets. In the rebirth mystery, it is achieved by theurgic actions. Hermes tells how he himself was divinized by an ecstatic vision which God granted him, and his teaching obviously aims at communicating the same ecstatic vision to the mystic. From his statements we learn that the ecstasy which produces rebirth is a form of dying and going to Heaven: in this ecstasy the old (natural, corporeal) man dissolves, and a new divine being is born. The discarding of the twelve vices corresponds to the journey of the soul through the spheres of the planets. In both cases the final result is divinization. The mystic is everywhere, he is above time and space, and has become the Aeon.

This idea recurs elsewhere. In the Mysteries of Isis (Apuleius, *Metam.* 11, 21) the initiate undergoes a "voluntary death" *(mors voluntaria)* and attains a "new life guaranteed by grace" *(precaria salus;* cf. *quodam modo renatus).* The rebirth at initiation is also equated to death in the "Preaching of the Naasene", a work which Reitzenstein considers[34] was composed about A.D. 100 for a Phrygian-Jewish community by a thoroughly hellenized Oriental. In § 28 we read: "It is prescribed that whoever has been initiated into the minor (Mysteries, that is, the Eleusinian mysteries), should then have himself initiated into the greater. 'Greater death earns greater reward'." The quotation at the end of this statement is from Heraclitus. The so-called *Liturgy of Mithras*[35] also teaches that the mystic cannot be reborn and become a son of God by going to Heaven, unless he first leaves his corporeal body behind: on his return he will resume it again, unimpaired and unchanged. Here, as in Tract XIII, the mystic becomes divine in ecstasy; but according to the *Liturgy of Mithras* he really goes to Heaven in this ecstasy.

The doctrine of rebirth is also attested in the final prayer of Asclepius from pseudo-Apuleius, which is preserved in the Mimaut papyrus.[36] "We rejoice that thou hast revealed thyself to us; we rejoice that by the knowledge of thyself thou hast

[34] *Hellenist. Mysterienreligionen,* p. 12.

[35] Reitzenstein, ibid., p. 46; p. 169 et seq.; A. Dietrich, *Mithrasliturgie* (³1923). Text and translation also in Preisendanz, *Zauberpapyri,* i, pp. 88—101 (v. 475-830).

[36] Reitzenstein, op. cit., p. 66; p. 285 et seq. Translated by Preisendanz, ibid., p. 59 (v. 599-609).

180

made us divine (ἀπεθέωσας τῇ σεαυτοῦ γνώσει)[37] while we are still held in the body. We can return thanks to thee only by knowing thy greatness. We have known, thou life of human life; we have known, thou womb of all knowledge; we have known, thou womb made fruitful by the Father; we have known, thou Father ever fruitful. Having worshipped so great a Good, we can make only one petition: Grant that we may remain secure in thy knowledge, while we take care never to swerve from this kind of life."

The Hermetic rebirth of Tract XIII is equalled in importance by the initiation into the Mysteries of Isis, which Apuleius describes[38] in his *Metamorphoses* (Book XI). In the Hermetic mystery the rebirth takes place while Hermes speaks, and there is no liturgical action properly so called. In the other case however, there is a mystery in the proper sense, where the sacred action is the central feature. The day of the initiation arrives only after a long preparation which includes instruction by the priests, fasting, purifying baths, and baptism. When the candidate has solemnly cut himself off from the community, he is led by the High Priest into the sanctuary. He is forbidden to tell what happens to him there. He gives only the following information (§§ 23 et seq.):

"I travelled to the boundary of death, I trod Proserpina's

[37] In ps.-Apuleius, *Asclepius,* Epilogue 41b it reads: "ac numine tuo salvati gaudemus, quod te nobis ostenderis totum; gaudemus, quod nos in corporibus sitos aeternitati fueris consecrare dignatus".

[38] Explained in Reitzenstein, *Iranisches Erlösungsmysterium,* p. 163 et seq.; *Hellenist. Mysterienreligionen,* p. 220 et seq.; J. Berreth, *Studien zum Isisbuch in Apuleius' "Metamorphosen"* (Dissertation, Tübingen, 1931); Dey, *Palingenesia,* pp. 86–100; W. Wittmann, *Das Isisbuch des Apuleius* (Stuttgart, 1938).

threshold, and after travelling through all elements I returned again. At midnight I saw the sun shining brilliantly, I stood before the eyes of the lowest and highest gods, and I worshipped them from near. Now I have told you what you have heard and cannot understand. Now I will tell only the things that can be revealed to the uninitiated without sin. Morning came, and when the sacred rite was finished I came forth, initiated with twelve robes . . . I was ordered to walk upon a wooden plank before the image of the goddess in the middle of the temple, wearing a brightly embroidered linen robe. A precious cloak hung behind me from my shoulders to my ankles. Wherever you looked I was adorned with brightly embroidered beasts, Indian dragons and Hyperborean griffins, feathered winged creatures, which suggest another world. The initiates call this the heavenly robe. In my right hand I held a lighted torch; my head was decorated with a chaplet from which white palm leaves arose like rays. When I was adorned like the sun and stood like a statue, suddenly the curtain was pulled back and the people came to see me."[39]

This ceremony can only mean that the community of mystics was to worship the new initiate. The twelve robes signify that he has taken on twelve different forms;[40] he probably did this as he travelled through the elements. It is similar to the putting on of the divine powers, which is mentioned in Tract XIII.[41] The salvation which the goddess grants to the mystic consists principally of his release from the unholy force of fate. The priest told the mystic (11,15): "Hostile events have no power over

---

[39] Translated from Latte's version, *Religionsgeschichtl. Lesebuch*,[2] v, 40.
[40] See Reitzenstein, *Hellenist. Mysterienreligionen*, p. 226.
[41] See Bräuninger, op. cit., p. 20.

you, whose life our majestic goddess has chosen for her service." The mystic himself praises the goddess in similar terms in his prayer of thanksgiving: "Thy hand disentangles the inextricably interwoven threads of fate, calms the storm of misfortune, and checks the destructive course of the stars" (11,25).[42]

3. PAULINE AND HELLENISTIC MYSTICISM CONTRASTED

Paul's doctrine is really mystical, and so it need cause no surprise to find many contacts between him and Hellenistic mysticism, particularly in terminology. The problem which faces us now is whether his mysticism is akin to Hellenistic mysticism, or are they fundamentally different. We must now discuss the nature of the two systems.

1. To begin with, Paul's doctrine is essentially concerned with union with Christ. He does not speak of mystical union with God; Christ is the term of the union which he describes. This fact has emerged clearly from what has been said about his use of the phrase "in God", which very seldom occurs in Paul, and hardly ever expresses the same idea as the phrase "in Christ" (II,1).[43] It is by Christ that Paul is apprehended (Phil. 3:12), God

---

[42] See Reitzenstein, op. cit., p. 255.

[43] It need hardly be pointed out that this is not a denial of the possibility of union with God. The point is that Paul does not speak of union with God. It is of course true that fellowship with Christ entails union with God, for the Spirit of Christ, who operates in us through Christ, is the Spirit of God. In the strict sense Paul's doctrine of union refers to union with Christ, which is established through Baptism, and which creates a mystical fellowship between each person who receives Baptism and the Crucified and Risen Christ. This must not be considered as simply interchangeable with union with God.

183

has revealed his Son in Paul (Gal. 1:16), he was baptized in Christ's death (Rom. 6:3), he was crucified together with Christ (Gal. 2:19), Christ is his life (Gal. 2:20; Col. 3:4; Phil. 1:21), and Christ's resurrection is the pledge of Paul's own resurrection (Rom. 6:8). He speaks here of Christ who has a spiritual existence and who has been exalted to the right hand of God; but this Christ is the same Person as Jesus of Nazareth, who lived on this earth in the form of a servant, and who died on the Cross for the salvation of mankind (Phil. 2:5 et seq.).

There is no difficulty in seeing the fundamental reason for the fact that Christ is the term of union in Paul's mysticism. It was through Christ that God redeemed us. By his death and his resurrection into glory, sin and death were destroyed, and the new life was created. And through him salvation is made available to individual men. The death and resurrection to a new life which Christ has undergone are prototypes which must be fulfilled in Christians. Christ was predestined by God to be the first born from the dead and the first born of many brothers (Col. 1:18; 1 Cor. 15:20; Rom. 8:29). When the individual man enters upon fellowship with him he is freed from the servitude of sin and of death by putting off the old man of sin, and he is transferred to a new sphere of life. This fellowship with Christ is also a pledge that at the General Resurrection he shall be clothed with a spiritual body and shall thereby attain the last and supreme end of the work of Redemption. In view of this teaching we must describe Paul's doctrine as union with Christ.

Nevertheless this mystical union is in no sense a fusion of the two persons, it does not represent a unification of the Christian with Christ. It is a union of two persons where each fully preserves his personality. Paul speaks of union with Christ or fellow-

184

ship with him; he does not teach that we become one with him.
Both Christ and Paul retain their separate personalities; they
enter upon a union, a *unio mystica,* but it is not a fusion of
substance. Man does not lose his individual personality, and the
spiritual Christ is not represented as a vague force which permeates the many. It is true that there are passages – particularly
Gal. 2:20 – which seem to hint that Christ is impersonal in some
such way. But this is merely apparent, as has been demonstrated
in II,4. It is true that Paul says that Christ "liveth in me" (Gal.
2:20), or "for me to live is Christ" (Col. 3:4); but he never
makes an equation between himself and Christ, saying "I am
Christ". What he does say is: "my life is Christ", meaning by
"life" the new life which has taken the place of the old. This is
utterly different from saying that he is Christ, for it simply
means that Christ is the new vital principle of the Christian.
Because Christ Triumphant is a distinct Person from the Christian who is united with him, it is possible for the Christian to
pray to Christ and to regard himself as Christ's servant. Paul
here presents a unique blend of immanence and transcendence.
The Christian is in Christ and Christ is in him, and yet he
knows that Christ sits in glory on the right hand of God (Col.
3:1; Rom. 8:34), and he eagerly awaits his Second Coming in
divine majesty (Phil. 3:20).

The special nature of this union with Christ is illustrated
especially by the Pauline idea of the Mystical Body.[44] In Gal.
3:27 et seq., for instance, he says: "You have put on Christ . . .
you are all one in Christ." He does not say "you are Christ".

[44] On the Mystical Body see the present author's book: *Die Kirche als
der mystische Leib Christi* (1940).

185

His meaning is that because you are "in Christ" you form with Christ one unified whole, and therefore you are no longer separate individuals; instead you have become a common person in and with Christ: the seed of Abraham, the heir of the promise. Christ Triumphant embraces all of you, and makes you members of his Body. At the same time each member of this Body, of this common personality, retains his own personality: "You are the body of Christ and members of member" (1 Cor. 12:27). Each has his own individual function, but all are permeated by the Spirit of Christ. When we take into account that Paul describes Christ as the head (Col. 1:18; Eph. 1:22), it is clear that the members remain distinct.

Hellenistic mysticism is utterly different from this. Its idea of God is pantheistic, or, at least, has pantheistic tendencies. The mystic aims at knowing and becoming like God, and becoming one with him; but this god is an impersonal principle, he is not a person. This is certainly true of the mystical theory, and it is clearly expressed in the Hermetic writings. Much the same applies to the mysteries also; their divinities are simply personifications of the powers of nature. This is the only way to understand the following inscription on a statue of Isis: "O goddess Isis, thou who alone art all *(una quae es omnia)*, the mighty Lord Arrius Balbinus dedicates thee to thyself" (C. I. L. x, 3800). The same explanation must apply to the terms in which the initiate praises the goddess in Apuleius, *Metamorphoses*, 11,25: "The gods of Heaven love you, and the gods of the underworld worship you; you cause the earth to revolve and the sun to shine; you rule Heaven and tread upon Hell; the stars obey your command, the cycle of the seasons follows it, the gods rejoice in it and the elements serve it. At your nod the breath of the wind blows, the cloud brings nourishing moisture, the seed springs up, and the bud grows" (cf. also 11, 5).

This creates a radical difference between Hellenistic and Pauline mysticism. The Greek mystics did not aim at entering upon a vital union with the Godhead and receiving into themselves the vital powers of the Godhead; their goal was absorption into the Godhead as a drop of water is absorbed in wine. As Bousset aptly says: "Greek mystical piety had as its goal, not so much life in or with the Godhead, as mystical identity with the Godhead."[45] Their great desire was a thorough and complete ascent and absorption into the Godhead after death. This is expressed very clearly in *Poimandres* § 26: "Having become (divine) powers, they ascend into God." Indeed, they aimed at becoming one with God even in this life through ecstasy; according to Tract XIII the man who has been reborn has become another; he is God, God's son, the All, in the All. He no longer has corporeal substance, but participates in incorporeal being and is composed entirely of divine powers; he is raised above time and space. As Bousset points out,[46] it is a shock to realize that this doctrine effaces any fundamental distinction between divine and human.

This equation of god and man has even more absurd effects in the magical papyri, where many of the mystical ideas appear in crude forms.[47] For example, the mystic of the prayers to Hermes makes this petition: "Come into my spirit and my mind

---

[45] *Kyrios Christos*, p. 113.   [46] Ibid., p. 115.

[47] See Reitzenstein, *Poimandres*, p. 15 et seq.; *Hellenist. Mysterienreligionen*, p. 27; Deissner, *Paulus und die Mystik*, p. 80; Festugière, *L'idéal religieux*, pp. 281–328 (the religious significance of the magical papyri).

for the whole course of my life, and fulfil all the wishes of my soul. For you are I, and I am you. What I say shall always take place." He addresses Hermes in the following terms: "You are I, and I am you. Your name is mine, and mine is yours, for I am your image", and "I know you, Hermes, and you know me. I am you, and you are I."[48]

This idea assumes other forms in the liturgical mysteries. For example, in the Mysteries of Isis the candidate is dressed like the Sun god and is set up on a podium to be worshipped by the followers of Isis. Obviously at that moment he is regarded as the godhead incarnate.[49] But after that glorious hour the prosaic life of everyday returns, though the initiate believes that he has escaped for ever from the power of fate: the dedication must be renewed later (Apuleius, *Metamorphoses,* 11, 26 et seq., 29); indeed, it must be completed in the following year by initiation into the Mysteries of Osiris.[50]

There is no need to stress that this idea of mystical union has absolutely nothing in common with Paul's teaching. Bousset points out that Paul's position has no parallel in these ideas, for he preserves completely the gulf between the faithful and Christ.[51]

[48] These passages are in Preisendanz, *Zauberpapyri* ii: XIII, 792–794; VIII, 49–50 and 36–37.

[49] O. Casel in *Jahrbuch für Liturgiewissenschaft,* xv, p. 356 et seq.: Mystische Ineinssetzung wie im Kultbild. By initiation Apuleius (Lucius) becomes a *simulacrum divinum.* Certainly the Taurobolium ceremony was regarded as having a divinizing effect, as we see from the description which Prudentius gives in *Peristeph.* X, 1046 et seq. (hunc . . . omnes salutant et adorant eminus).

[50] See also Perdelwitz, *Die Mysterienreligion und das Problem des 1. Petrusbriefes* (Giessen, 1911), p. 48 et seq.   [51] Op. cit., p. 115.

Attempts have been made to adduce parallels to Paul's utterances about mystical indwelling. But these alleged parallels are purely accidental, and prove nothing. Reitzenstein[52] refers to the Egyptian Insinger papyrus which says: "Know the greatness of God, so that you may have it abiding in your hearts" (XXXV, 17; similarly XXXVI, 3); "Thot (?) is (?) heart and tongue of the pious; behold (?), his house is the god" (XXXV, 19). He also points out a passage in Tract X (§ 21): "Nous enters the pious soul and leads it to the light of knowledge." But these are merely theoretical abstractions. They contain no personal element such as is always attached to Paul's phrases "in Christ" and "Christ in us".[53]

In some of the magical texts the magician attempts to bring the godhead into his soul by adjurations[54] ("Enter, show thyself to me"). Such texts provide a parallel to possession by a prophetic spirit (see above II, 1), but not to Paul. The magician is trying to draw the godhead into himself simply to enable him to perform some magic act. Any parallelism between these texts and Paul does not extend to their substance. The same comment applies to a passage from the *Metamorphoses* of Apuleius (11, 25), which Clemen[55] has compared with Gal. 2:20. When Lucius was leaving Corinth, where he had been initiated, he prostrated himself before the image of Isis, tearfully kissed its feet, and prayed to her: "I will hide deep in the shrine of my heart thy divine countenance and thy sacred being *(numen sanctissimum)*, and I will always preserve it and keep it before my eyes." This text

---

[52] *Poimandres*, p. 237.
[53] Thus Bousset, op. cit., p. 116, note.
[54] *Poimandres*, p. 25 et seq.
[55] *Neutestamentl. Studien f. G. Heinrici* (1914), p. 32.

refers to very intimate contemplation. It has nothing to do with mystical indwelling.

The Comparative Religion school insists that the theology of Baptism which we find in Rom. 6:2 et seq., has an exact parallel in the cult of gods who die and rise again. In these mysteries the initiate shares in the lot of the god, and thereby he participates in the god's destiny; in other words he is freed from the bonds of death and from the oppression of fate, and he obtains a pledge of eternal life and of divinization (σωτηρία). Bousset maintains[56] that the differences between Paul and these mysteries do not outweigh their agreement on fundamentals: "In mystical fellowship the votary man undergoes the same experiences as the divine hero originally underwent, as a pattern and as the principal subject of these experiences. What the faithful experience is only the victorious issue of what began in the past. When contact is made the electric current passes through." Bousset alleges that Paul's theology of Baptism is not original.[57] Before his time these pagan mystical ideas had influenced the Gentile Christian communities; they considered that as Baptism is the act by which men are initiated into Christianity, it is a death and resurrection of the subject analogous to the death and resurrection of Christ. Bousset adds that these communities still regarded Baptism as something quite human and magical. He claims that this theory existed before Paul came on the scene; Paul adopted it and emended it, so as to transform it into a doctrine which could be used in moral preaching.[58]

It is, of course, correct to say that some kind of parallel may

[56] *Kyrios Christos,* p. 139.   [57] Ibid., p. 134.
[58] This is also Lietzmann's view, *Röm.,* p. 64.

be drawn between the two systems. But the resemblance is not very great, and it does not support the far reaching conclusions which have been drawn.

According to Bousset, the myth of the god who dies and rises again was widespread in the religions which were under oriental influence, and this myth is one of the characteristics of the mystery religions. But this statement cannot be proved from our sources.[59] The only gods who were supposed to die and rise again were Osiris, Adonis, Attis, and probably also Dionysus. Leipoldt[60] suggested that the same was true of Heracles Sandon, who was an object of special worship in Tarsus, Paul's birthplace; but he can adduce no evidence to support his conjecture. Indeed, it is significant that we commonly find legends about many of these gods dying; but only a few of them rise again, and the resurrection stories are often obscure, and occur in very late sources. The feast of Adonis, for instance, was mainly mourning for the dead god; his resurrection played almost no part. "We hear little about a resurrection of Adonis."[61]

[59] On what follows see: J. Leipoldt, *Sterbende und auferstehende Götter* (1923; with a full bibliography); F. Nötscher, *Altorientalischer und alttestamentlicher Auferstehungsglaube* (1926), p. 85 et seq.; M. Brückner, *Der sterbende und auferstehende Gottheiland* (1920); Lietzmann, *Röm.*, p. 63 et seq.; E. B. Allo, "Les dieux sauveurs du paganisme gréco-romain" in *Revue des sciences philos. et théol.*, xv (1926), pp. 5–34; L. de Grandmaison, "Dieux morts et dieux ressuscités" in *Rech. de science relig.*, xvii (1927), pp. 97–126; J. Prüssner, *Sterben und Auferstehen im Hellenismus und im Urchristentum* (Dissertation, Greifswald, 1930); W. Goossens, *Les origines de l'eucharistie* (Louvain, 1931), pp. 252–84; Th. Klauser, *Reallexikon für Antike und Christentum, Art. Auferstehung*, i, 919–38 (G. Bertram and A. Oepke); Wiencke, *Paulus über Jesu Tod*, pp. 115–26; P. Althaus: Excursus on Rom. 6:1–14.

[60] Op. cit., p. 75.   [61] Leipoldt, op. cit., p. 18.

Attis is a better example, for the literary evidence is supplemented by the monuments. But it was only at a late date that the idea of death and resurrection became attached to the cult of Attis; the earliest evidence of this connection comes from the fourth century of our era. In the case of Dionysus there is no direct reference to a resurrection. The legend only tells that his opponent Lycurgus, who is responsible for Dionysus' death, is blinded by Zeus, and must soon die. This is taken as a reference to the resurrection. "There is no doubt that Lycurgus is the lord of winter, while Dionysus is the power of the plant world which sleeps in winter."[62]

Moreover, Bertram (Col. 928; see note 59) makes the good point, that apparently the first to apply the definite ideas of death and resurrection to the Hellenistic mystery gods were the early Fathers of the Church. The word resurrection occurs in the *Dialogue* with Tryphon of Justin Martyr (69, 2) where he says that the Greeks tell how Dionysus, after being dismembered and dying, rose again and went to Heaven. According to Origen (commentary on Ez. 8) the votaries of Adonis rejoice because their god has risen from the dead. Lucian, on the other hand, speaks of the feast of Adonis in his work "Concerning the Syrian goddess". The feast was held in midsummer when the vegetation was parched and withered; all that Lucian says about the feast (chap. 6) is: "When they have wept and lamented enough, they first offer a sacrifice to the dead, to Adonis, as if he were dead; then on the next day they display him as alive and lead him (from the Underworld) to the light of day." The events which are recounted in the various myths can hardly be de-

[62] Ibid., p. 25.

192

scribed as resurrection; return to life would be a more accurate term for them. Indeed, the mystery religions used other terms which usually have nothing to do with resurrection; their terminology conveys the point that what the initiated expected was not resurrection, but immortality and eternal life; this is what the mysteries promised to their initiates. Gnosticism and the mysteries have no interest in a resurrection of the body, for such an idea would be incompatible with the Orphic and Platonic doctrine that the body is the tomb of the soul (σῶμα – σῆμα).

The question which concerns us is whether these cults claim to link the fate of the mystic with that of the god. In the case of the Adonis cult there is no evidence in our sources to indicate such a relationship. Attic pottery with scenes of the festival of Adonis has been found in tombs, and in Roman times scenes from the Adonis story were carved on sarcophagi. But these discoveries do not entitle us to draw any definite conclusion.

It is different in the case of Osiris. But in pre-Hellenistic times every dead person – originally only royalty – was equated to Osiris, whose kingdom they enter at death. There was no need for initiation into the mysteries in order to share his lot; it was enough to observe the funeral rites. An Egyptian text says: "He (the deceased) will live as truly as Osiris lives; as truly as Osiris is not dead, he shall not perish; as truly as Osiris is not destroyed, he shall not be destroyed".[63] We learn from Apuleius (*Metamorphoses*, 11, 30) that by being initiated into the mysteries of Osiris, Lucius becomes the god Osiris.

[63] F. Cumont, *Die orientalischen Religionen im römischen Heidentum* ([2]1914), p. 116.

193

There is an interesting report in the mid-fourth century writer Firmicus Maternus which may refer to the mysteries of Attis.[64] Here is his account of the so-called Hilaria Festival, which was held on March 25: The mystic community laments loudly for the dead god whose effigy has been laid on a bier. A light is brought and the priest anoints the throats of all, saying in an undertone the verses: "Be of good heart, mystics, for the god is saved (σεσωσμένος), and he shall be salvation (σωτηρία) from suffering for us also." This rite means that the mystic, having shared in the ritual representation of the death and revival of the god, shall participate in his "salvation". In this context salvation obviously means immortality, a life of happiness after death. That was how Firmicus understood it, for he says mockingly to the mystic: "You expect that your god will thank you, reward you with similar gifts, and give you a share in his. You wish to die as he dies, and to live as he lives."

Damascius, whose approximate dates are 458 to 533, tells us[65] that he and Isidorus performed the feat of descending into the cave at the temple of Apollo at Hierapolis in Phrygia; this cave was supposed to be the entrance to the Underworld, but they were not killed by the fumes which arose from it. Only the Galli, the priests of Cybele, were supposed to be able to make this descent without danger. During the night after this venture he dreamt that he was Attis, and that the mother of the gods held in his honour the Hilaria festival, which in the cult of Attis

---

[64] *De errore prof. relig.* XXII. See also H. Hepding, *Attis* (1903), p. 168 et seq. Nilsson, *Griech. Religion,* ii, p. 612, thinks that the words of the priest while anointing derive from the Mysteries of Osiris.

[65] In his *Vita Isidori;* cf. Hepding, *Attis,* p. 74; Nötscher, op. cit., p. 102 et seq.

was the feast of resurrection and joy. "This", he tells us, "revealed to me our salvation from Hades." He evidently believed that the rite makes the mystic become Attis himself, and thereby assures him of salvation from Hades, that is, of gaining immortality. It is interesting to notice the lateness of these two pieces of evidence.

The same idea underlies the form of Taurobolium which can be described as "blood baptism".[66] The candidate descends into a pit, wearing a hood which has been perforated. A bull – or, in the case of the Kriobolium, a ram – is slaughtered over the hood, so that the warm blood flows over the mystic and drenches his whole body. He then comes up from the pit, and is worshipped as a god by the community. This ceremony must be repeated after twenty years. So far as is known, the Emperor Helagabalus was the first to hold this blood baptism. There is no epigraphical evidence concerning it before the year A.D. 305.

The sources give us no further information about the theology of these cults. All the other information which we find in works on Comparative Religion is conjecture. The only other material for deciding our question is our knowledge about the idea of rebirth in the mysteries (see above IV, 2), though they do not connect the lot of the mystic with that of the god.

A passage from Tertullian's *De Baptismo,* chapter 5, is often cited as referring to the Eleusinian mysteries, but it makes no such reference.[67] The correct text reads: "Moreover, they (the

[66] See Cumont, op. cit., p. 79 et seq.; Reitzenstein, *Hellenist. Mysterienrelig.,* pp. 22, 45; Nötscher, op. cit., p. 105 et seq.; Dey, *Palingenesia,* pp. 65–81.
[67] F. J. Dölger in *Antike und Christentum,* i (1929), pp. 43–53.

pagans) purify their farm houses, dwellings, temples, and whole towns by sprinkling them with water. Indeed, they 'baptize' themselves wholesale on the feast of the 'Games of Apollo' and the 'Pelusia'. And they imagine that this effects rebirth *(in regenerationem)* and expiates their broken oaths. Likewise the ancients used to cleanse with purifying water anyone who had defiled himself by murder" (cf. Ovid, *Fasti,* 2, 35–46). In this passage Tertullian is speaking of baths to which the pagans attributed the power of regeneration, in the sense of taking away sin and the divine penalties attached to it. So the word *regeneratio* has here the wider sense of rebirth from the life of sin.

It will at once be evident that the pagan mystery religions contained ideas similar to those which Paul developed in Rom. 6:2 et seq.[68] Yet those ideas could not have been more widespread than the cult of the god who dies and rises again, and to the best of our knowledge, such cults were confined to a narrow field. Moreover, the sources of our information are extraordinarily late. This does not rule out the possibility that the cult was older, but it does impose great caution on anyone who wishes to draw conclusions from these sources. Certainly there is no real parallelism between the idea of rebirth by itself and Paul's teaching in Rom. 6:2 et seq., for rebirth does not necessarily entail a connection between the lot of the believer and that of the god.

Furthermore, in regard to the myth of the god who dies and rises again, we must not lose sight of the fundamental differences between this myth and Paul's concept.[69] The main differences may be enumerated as follows:

[68] This is also the view of Deissner, *Paulus und die Mystik,* p. 125.
[69] See ibid., p. 125 et seq.

i. These gods are divinities of vegetation or of the stars. Their death and resurrection simply represents the yearly death and reawakening of nature.[70] In the case of Christian Baptism, on the other hand, we are dealing with an historical Person, who, as a fact, did once die and rise again.

ii. These mystery gods do not die for the sins of men, as Jesus did. When hunting, Adonis was wounded by a wild boar, and died in the arms of his beloved Astarte. Attis died after unmanning himself in a fit of madness, when Cybele, his first love, had become jealous and killed the nymph to whom he gave his love.

iii. The mystic becomes the god, so that rebirth takes place through divinization. By contrast, the Christian is never simply equated to Christ; the distinction is always preserved.

iv. Ethical ideas play no really important part in the relationship between the mystic and the god; only his nature is affected. Paul, on the other hand, regards Baptism as the source of ethical obligations for one who is baptized.[71]

v. When the mysteries hold out the promise of "salvation", they mean principally liberation from the influence of fate and the attainment of immortality. For Paul "salvation" is freedom from sin (cf. "dead to sin"). It follows that there is nothing in common between the significance for the faithful of the death of Jesus and what the initiate hoped to gain from the death of Adonis, Attis, or Dionysus. Hellenism shows no acquaintance with the idea that true salvation is freedom from sin and guilt.

vi. The mysteries had no doctrine corresponding to Paul's

---

[70] See Leipoldt, op. cit., p. 59, and K. Holl, *Urchristentum und Religionsgeschichte* (Gütersloh, 1925), p. 12 et seq.

[71] See above III, 3 and also p. 236 et seq.

conception of the growth of the baptized with Christ into a mystical organism, the Body of Christ.

We must agree with Büchsel's judgement: "A thorough evaluation of the material which Leipoldt has assembled shows that internally, from the point of view of religious content, the relationship between Paul and Christ has virtually nothing in common with the relationship between these gods who die and their votaries."[72]

There is no possibility that Paul took from these mysteries any material for his doctrine of Baptism. However, it is probable that at least the fundamental ideas in the theology of Rom. 6:2 et seq., were not first proposed by Paul himself, and it is not impossible that the missionaries to the Gentiles had explained the significance of Baptism by adopting the idea of a connection between the lot of the god and that of the initiate. By doing this they would be making use of the concepts and thoughts of their hearers, probably as a means of refuting the pagans' ideas, exactly as Paul did in the Areopagus discourse: "What you worship without knowing it, that I preach to you" (Acts 17:23). The theme of the preaching would be that the false doctrine of the pagans concerning their so-called gods (1 Cor. 8:5) is full reality in Christ.

This would not be a borrowing of material. It is merely the infusion of a new content into a form of thought and expression which already existed. Paul actually did this when he called Baptism a "putting on of Christ" (Gal. 3:27; Rom. 13:14), for this phrase was current in ancient religion and was used in the mysteries.[73]

[72] *Geist Gottes,* p. 301, note 1.
[73] See Leipoldt, op. cit., p. 54; Deissner, *Paulus und die Mystik,* p. 129; Dölger, 'Ιχθύς, i, p. 115 et seq.; ii, p. 238, note 1.

As Leipoldt says: "Evidently this is an attempt on the part of the Gentile Christians or their missionaries to preach to the Hellenists in their own language about Jesus and Christian piety."[74] But it would be quite wrong to maintain with Bousset, Lietzmann, Dibelius and others, that these Gentile Christians had a natural and magical conception of Baptism, and that Paul was the first to give the theology of Baptism an ethical bearing (see above III, 3). Christian Baptism was always regarded as a sacrament in the proper sense of the word; it was never looked upon as a piece of natural magic. Any man who wished to receive it had to be "converted" and to believe, and to undertake for the future, ethical obligations.[75] In Rom. 6:1 et seq. there is not the slightest indication that Paul was producing a new, hitherto unheard-of doctrine, when he spoke of the ethical obligations of those who are baptized in 6:6–11 (cf. "Know you not").

2. The mystical relationship between Christ and Christians of which Paul speaks, is not something final; it is only provisional.[76] It is incomplete in two respects, both in its extent and in

[74] Op. cit., p. 73. Deissner, "Erlöser und Erlösung" in *Deutsche Theologie,* ii (1929), p. 123: "Paul utilized the myth of the god who dies and rises again (Rom. 6) to impress upon his hearers the intimacy of the union with Christ: but underlying these teachings is the memory of Christ's death as a death for sin." The possibility is admitted also by Bartmann, *Dogma und Religionsgeschichte* (1922), p. 81 et seq., and O. Casel in *Jahrbuch für Liturgiewissenschaft,* v (1925), p. 232.

[75] See Feine, *Apostel Paulus,* p. 341 et seq.

[76] See Mundle, *Das religiöse Leben des Paulus,* p. 93 et seq.; Deissner, op. cit., p. 131 et seq. (on this see Posselt in *PhilolWschr,* xli [1921], p. 439 et seq.); Schmitz, *Lebensgefühl des Paulus,* p. 49 et seq.; K. L. Schmidt, "Mystik und Eschatologie im Urchristentum" in *ZntW* (1922), p. 277 et seq.; Lohmeyer, Σὺν Χριστῷ, p. 218 et seq.

its nature. Christians will be "in Christ" only till the Second
Coming; then "being in Christ" will come to an end, and we
shall be "with Christ". Moreover, our state after the Second
Coming will not be simply a supreme form of being in Christ
in a final and complete manner. It is an utterly different kind of
fellowship. The mystical union bestows many supernatural
benefits, but it does not give us in advance the glory of
the next life. It is merely a pledge of future glory. Paul's mysticism is complemented and consummated by eschatology. This
eschatology, which derives from Judaism, teaches that the present
world will come to an end, and looks forward to a new world,
where a life of glory with God awaits the elect in the kingdom of
God. Such a doctrine must necessarily stamp a special character
on Paul's mysticism.

Hellenistic mysticism presents a quite different picture, for it
possessed nothing corresponding to the eschatology of late Judaism and early Christianity. As A. Schweitzer points out,[77]
eschatology means the expectation of an end of the world which
may take place at any moment, with the accompanying events,
hopes and distress. Hellenistic mysticism had no doctrine of a
divine intervention in human history with an eschatological
consummation as its goal. Paul's eschatology does not deal with
what may be called individual eschatology, namely the death,
judgement, and life after death of individual men. On this matter
there is an irreconcilable gulf between Paul and Hellenistic
mysticism, which necessarily gives Paul's mysticism a stamp of
its own.

The numerous points on which the two agree should not

[77] *Geschichte der paulin. Forschung* (1913), p. 178.

lead us astray. It is true that Hellenistic mysticism also distinguishes between union with God before and after death; complete and final union with the divinity takes place only after death, for then the divine powers which constitute man's essence can return to the divinity and ascend into it (*Poimandres,* § 26). But even in this life man can leave his body in ecstasy and attain divinization and union with God. Indeed, this is the special aim of such mysticism. The facts are aptly summed up by Dibelius when he says: "The mystic experiences the supreme consummation in the present life when he attains divinization, whereas Paul, and the whole primitive Church, hope for the consummation in the future at the Second Coming of the Lord, when the world shall be transfigured."[78] This describes the doctrine of Tract XIII, of the final prayer of Asclepius in the Mimaut papyrus, and of the *Liturgy of Mithras.* In the first named, Tat asks Hermes whether the transcendental body which is composed of divine powers can be dissolved, and receives the answer: "Do you not know that you have become god, and the son of a god, just like me?" (XIII, 4).

According to Reitzenstein, Hellenistic mysticism does draw a distinction between this life and the next, and there are reasons for doubting whether the complete vision of God and divinization were conside possible in this life.[79] It is certainly truered that there is some inconsistency in the picture which the Hermetic writings present. Tract X, 4–6 seems to teach that divinization can take place only after death, and that the full vision of God causes the death of the body. There is a passage in the final prayer of *Poimandres* (§ 32), where Reitzenstein claims that the vision in

[78] *Deutsche Lit.-Ztg.* (1921), p. 725.
[79] *Hellenist. Mysterienreligionen,* p. 290 et seq.

this life is distinguished from the vision hereafter: "I pray not to be deprived of thy vision (gnosis) in so far as our nature is capable of it (τῆς γνώσεως τῆς κατ᾽ οὐσίαν ἡμῶν); grant thou this prayer".[80]

But even here Hellenistic mysticism is far from Paul, and Reitzenstein is guilty of exaggeration when he says: "On this point the experience of the pagan is exactly the same as that of the Christian. In both cases it is the intensity of the experience which is changed; the idea remains the same. This is true of Paul also. He is dead to the world, but sometimes this fact has a greater reality for him than at others."[81] This is not correct. There is a resemblance, but it fades when compared to the difference. Our present gifts appear perfect or imperfect to Paul according to the angle from which he regards them: when he thinks of the time before Christ, these gifts are perfect; but when he looks forward to their consummation in the next life, they appear imperfect. This is not to deny that he is sometimes, as in 1 Cor. 4:9 et seq., influenced by his prevailing disposition.

Greater importance attaches to the fact that Hellenistic mysticism looked forward only to individual immortality. Its goal was complete divinization when the individual ascends fully and finally into the divinity (*Poimandres*, §§ 21, 26). Some texts deny the possibility of complete divinization while living in the body; but this imperfect form leads straight to full divinization after death. The state which is reached in ecstasy is perfected and made eternal after death. In other words, ecstasy is an anticipation of complete divinization.

---

[80] *Studien*, p. 29.   [81] *Hellenist. Mysterienreligionen*, p. 291.

Eschatology is an integral part of Paul's piety. Like all early Christians, he awaited the great intervention of God which shall bring this world to an end and fulfil and perfect our salvation. But this perfection does not consist in making the mystical relation with Christ eternal and more intimate. This relationship is replaced by something much more perfect: we shall be *with* Christ in the eternal kingdom, with a spiritual glorified body formed in the image of Christ (see e.g., 1 Cor. 15:49; Rom. 8:29; Phil. 3:21; Col. 3:4).

The Comparative Religion school, particularly Bousset, deny the importance of eschatology in Paul's thought: they say that its place is taken by the doctrine of union with Christ, and that whatever eschatology the Epistles contain is merely a survival from his Jewish past. Under criticism Bousset modified his view somewhat, but he still maintains that the Jewish eschatology which we find in Paul's teaching is merely the remnant of an old doctrine which is gradually losing its grip on the Apostle.[82] This theory does not correspond to the facts. Paul held the same views on eschatology as the rest of the primitive Church, and, moreover, he personally was full of the same deep desire for the Coming of the Lord. There is abundant evidence of this in the Epistles: here are only a few instances: "We ourselves groan within ourselves, waiting for the adoption of the sons of God, the redemption of our bodies" (Rom. 8:23). "We have a good will to be absent rather from the body and to be present with the Lord" (2 Cor. 5:8). He adopts in 1 Cor. 16:22 the Aramaic prayer for the Coming of the Lord: "Maran–atha" ("Come Lord"). He considers that the fervent desire for the Coming

[82] Bousset, *Jesus der Herr*, p. 29.

of God's Son from Heaven is an essential part of Christianity (1 Thess. 1:10). Christians are men who await the revelation of the Lord (1 Cor. 1:7; Rom. 8:25; Phil. 3:20), while non-Christians are those "who have no hope" (1 Thess. 4:12) in the Second Coming of Christ and the resurrection of the body. This hope and expectation is the source of his repeated warnings to be prepared for the day of Christ (see 1 Thess. 5:23; Rom. 13:11 et seq.). He implores his children to be without blame on the day of the Lord (1 Thess. 3:13; Phil. 1:10), and he is confident that he himself will experience this joy (1 Cor. 1:8; Phil. 1:6).

To appreciate this deep desire for the Coming of Christ we must recall the belief of the entire early Church, including Paul, that only the Coming of Christ will bring this world to an end and thereby give us full possession of salvation. We already possess something great and glorious, but it pales in comparison with the brilliance of what the future will bring us. What we possess now is the pledge of the Spirit (2 Cor. 1:22; 5:5; Rom. 8:23). In the present life the old man is destroyed and a new life is given to us in the mystery of Baptism. But this reality is of the sacramental and mystical order (Rom. 6:4 et seq.): it gives us a pledge of future gifts, but it does not yet confer the gifts themselves upon us. We do not yet possess the rights of sons or the glorified body: in brief, we are not yet the image of Christ in Heaven. The motto of our life is still "we are saved by hope" (Rom. 8:24). What is best and finest is still to come: "Ourselves also who have the first fruits of the Spirit: even we ourselves groan within ourselves, waiting for the adoption of the sons of God, the redemption of our body" (Rom. 8:23). We are still bound by our earthly bodies (Rom. 6:12; 2 Cor.

5:6), we still live in the flesh (Gal. 2:20), our earthly habitation has not yet been dissolved (2 Cor. 5:1, 4). But we bear our treasure in vessels of clay, and therefore we are beset by all kinds of sufferings, hardships and struggles, and we must constantly fight against the flesh which struggles for mastery with the spirit in us (Gal. 5:17). "Your life is hid with Christ in God" (Col. 3:3), and this life will be revealed only in the future (Rom. 8:18), when the longed-for day "of the revelation of the sons of God" dawns (Rom. 8:19).

It is only at Christ's Second Coming that our Redemption will be complete, and we shall actually have undiminished possession of salvation. Paul praises it without ever growing weary; it comprises such glorious things: complete freedom from the earthly body, and clothing with the heavenly body (Phil. 3:21; 1 Cor. 15:24), possession of the rights of sons (Rom. 8:23), and entry upon our heavenly inheritance (Gal. 3:29; Col. 3:24). So the distress of this life fades before the glory of the future: "I reckon that the sufferings of this time are not worthy to be compared with the glory to come" (Rom. 8:18; see 2 Cor. 4:17). That is why Paul argues with such intensity against those who deny the resurrection of the dead. It is the gate which leads to God's eternal kingdom, and without it the entire work of Redemption is valueless: "If Christ be not risen again, your faith is vain: for you are yet in your sins. Then they also that are fallen asleep in Christ are perished. If in this life only we have hope in Christ, we are of all men most miserable" (1 Cor. 15:17 et seq.). This chapter is devoted to proving the reality of the resurrection of the dead, which stands or falls with the resurrection of Christ; it concludes with the stirring call: "Therefore, my beloved brethren, be ye steadfast and unmoveable: always abounding in the work of the Lord, knowing that your labour is not in vain in the Lord" (1 Cor. 15:58; see Phil. 1:23 et seq.; 1 Thess. 4:17). When the full force of these words sinks in, we realize how low a value Paul puts on the things of this world, including our mystical union with Christ, when compared with our future glory.

It is significant that Paul uses different phrases to denote the heavenly gifts in this life and those in the next. The phrase "in Christ" refers to this life, while the next life is denoted by "with (σύν) Christ". The phrases are not equivalents. "With Christ" is a higher good than "in Christ", and it is a relationship of a different order. When he uses the phrase "with Christ" he is adopting an expression dealing with space to describe association with Christ in the transcendental world.[83] The same idea appears in 1 Thess. 4:16: "We . . . shall be taken up together with them (the dead) in the clouds to meet Christ, into the air: and so shall we be always with the Lord." In the last sentence Paul is thinking of the association of Christians in the heavenly kingdom of God with their Lord, the first born of the dead, whose co-heirs and brothers they have become (Rom. 8:23, 17; Gal. 3:29); the Christians, being risen from the dead and clothed in the glorified body, are transformed thoroughly into the image of Christ (Phil. 3:21; 1 Cor. 15:49; 2 Cor. 3:18), and gaze upon him face to face. Mystical fellowship gives place to personal association.

This polarity is characteristic of Paul's piety, and it is due to the fact that his mysticism is complemented by his eschatology, which has nothing in common with Hellenistic eschatology; it cannot be equated to "the change of the momentary ex-

---

[83] Lohmeyer, Σύν Χριστῷ, p. 222 et seq.

perience". There are passages in the Epistles where there appears to be an inconsistency between what Paul says of our state in this life and his description of our future hope; but such differences are not due to any weakness in the Apostle's judgement. They arise because of his different points of view. In this connection we can make the same observation as in III, 3, as may be seen from the following comparison:

Present	*Future*
The body of sin is destroyed (Rom. 6:6; 8:10; Gal. 5:24), the body of the flesh is despoiled (Col. 2:11).	We await the redemption of our body (Rom. 8:23).
You are justified (1 Cor. 6:11; Rom. 5:1).	We hope to be justified (Gal. 5:5; Rom. 3:30).
We are children of God (Rom. 8:14; et seq.; Gal. 4:6).	We wait for the adoption of the sons of God (Rom. 8:23).
We are (shall soon be) glorified (Rom. 8:30; 2 Cor. 3:18).	We shall be glorified (Col. 3:4; Rom. 8:18).
The kingdom of God is present (1 Cor. 4:20; Rom. 14:17; Col. 1:13 et seq.).	We shall inherit the kingdom of God (1 Cor. 6:9; 15:50; Gal. 5:21).
You are risen again (Col. 2:12 et seq.; 3:1; Eph. 2:6).	God will raise us up (Rom. 8:11; 1 Cor. 6:14; 2 Cor. 4:14).
We are in Heaven (Eph. 2:6; cf. Phil. 3:20).	We shall enter Heaven (2 Cor. 5:8; 1 Thess. 4:17).

There is a contradiction in form between these statements, which can be explained in exactly the same way as the contradictions in III, 3 above. It is easy to show that there is no inconsistency in thought. For example, he speaks in Rom. 8:19 of the desire for the revelation of the children of God, and in 8:18 of the glory which shall be revealed; in Phil. 3:20 he describes Heaven as our home, and in Col. 3:1 he says "If you be risen with Christ". In all these cases the context shows that he is referring to the sacramental mystical experience.

3. Paul has also an utterly different doctrine of the vision of God from that which the Hellenistic mystics held.

The vision of God in ecstasy plays a major role in Hellenistic mysticism;[84] it is usually described as γνῶσις, γνῶναι Θεόν, or Θέα (μεγίστη). The vision of God is the goal to which all the longing and activity of the mystic is directed, for it transforms his entire being, makes him god, and withdraws him from the force of fate. The Hermetic writings divide mankind into two groups: the great mass of non-Gnostics (who are held in ἀγνωσία, X, 8), and the small remnant of Gnostics ("those who are in Gnosis", IX, 4). Gnosis is the same thing as virtue, while the lack of it is vice (X, 8; XI, 21). "He who possesses Gnosis, is good and pious and already divine" (X, 8). "He who has known him (God) has been filled with all good things and has divine thoughts different from the thoughts of the many" (IX, 4). On the other hand, it is "utter vice not to know the Divine" (XI, 21).

The object which is known in Gnosis is God, the All, one's

---

[84] See Reitzenstein, *Hellenist. Mysterienreligionen*, pp. 66 et seq., 262 et seq., 284 et seq.; J. Kroll, *Lehren des Hermes,* p. 360 et seq.; Deissner, *Paulus und die Mystik*, p. 101 et seq. (see on this, Posselt in *PhilolWschr* [1918], p. 884 et seq.). R. Bultmann in *ThWb*, i (1933), 692–6 (Gnosis); ii (1935), 843; Pascher, *Der Königsweg zu Wiedergeburt und Vergottung bei Philon v. A.* (Paderborn, 1931), pp. 134 et seq., 194 et seq.

own self as an immortal being; in brief, the transcendental world. "The oriental thinks that he grasps the world when he sees the god in his true form; but the god is also his own self, and it is in the god that man sees the world; indeed it is only through the god himself that man can see the god, and through this vision the god enters into us completely."[85]

When Poimandres asked Hermes what he wished for, the reply was: "I wish to learn what exists, to understand its nature, to know God" (I, 2). When the creation was ended God said: "Let the spiritual man (ἔννους) realize that he is immortal and that love is the cause of his death and let him know all being" (I, 18). "He who knows himself attains a wonderful salvation" (I, 20). "If you recognize that God consists of light and life, and that you also consist of these, you will return again to life" (I, 21). "My (Nous) presence is a help to them, and they immediately know everything" (I, 22). In Tract XIII Hermes sings the hymn which the divine powers sing according to I, 26; Tat, who has received further illumination through Nous, then begins a similar hymn of praise; he is able to do so because, as Hermes tells him, "through Nous thou hast learnt thyself and our Father" (§ 22). To see God means to see the All and one's own immortal essence; and the sight of these is the vision of God.

So far as we can judge, the Mysteries also had as their goal the vision of God, or of the gods, or of the All. In Apuleius' *Mystery of Isis,* Lucius comes into the presence of the lower and upper gods, and prays to them from near at hand (11, 23). In the *Liturgy of Mithras,* the initiate wishes to "see all" (verse

[85] Reitzenstein, *Studien,* p. 141.

485). He is given a promise that he will be raised on high, and
he believes that he is in the midst of the air. "And in that hour
you will hear nothing, neither man nor being, and you will see
nothing of the perishable things of the earth. You will see pure
immortality. For in that day and that hour you will see a con-
stellation of gods: the gods who go round the Pole as they
ascend to Heaven, and others descending" etc. (verses 541–7,
Preisendanz, i, 90).

The vision of God has glorious effects. It gives man salvation,
and means for him the ascent to Olympus (X, 15); it transforms him into something transcendental, and makes him
divine (X 4–6; XIII, 14). The prayer of Asclepius says: "We
rejoice that thou hast shown thyself to us, we rejoice that while
we are still held in the body thou hast made us divine by the
knowledge of thyself" (verses 599–601, *Preisendanz*, i, 58).
Hermes tells Tat: "Thou hast become god" (XIII, 14). The
mystic undergoes an essential transformation, a change of his
substance; he gains an immaterial form of life, a divine form;
he is reborn, and feels that he is transferred into a heavenly
body.[86]

The sources use numerous expressions to describe the effect
of the vision of God. In the *Mystery of Isis,* Lucius says that he
"is like one reborn *(renatus)*" (11, 16); we are told that he has
been transformed *(reformatus)* (11, 27), and he explains that he
has been changed into Osiris (*Osiris non in alienam quampiam
personam reformatus,* 11, 30). Hermes tells Tat that by God's
mercy he has been transported "into an immortal body", and
is no longer the same person as before (XIII, 3). Tat himself

---

[86] See also J. Behm in *ThWb,* iv, 764 et seq.

gains a body composed of divine powers, and now sees the Transcendental (XIII, 11–14). This heavenly body, which is acquired at the "essential birth", is indissoluble and immortal (XIII, 14). And so, having the vision of God, he attains perfection in this world, a divine being exists in him, and he already possesses the heavenly form of being. There is no further essential change possible for him in the next life.[87] There can only be a difference of degree, as we see from X, 4–6: "Those who have succeeded in gaining much of this vision, often fall asleep because of the life of the body, until they reach the glorious vision which our predecessors Uranus and Kronus have shared."

The vision of God in this life takes place during ecstasy. Man can attain the vision only if he has produced or at least prepared for the ecstasy. There are passages in the Hermetic writings which teach that God wishes men to know (see) him (I, 31; X, 15; VII, 2), and others which declare that Nous, the instrument of Gnosis (X, 10), is granted only to the pious (I, 22; IV, 4). But one point which is frequently stressed is that only one who is free from the senses can see God: I, 22; VI, 2 et seq.; X, 5 ("The vision is profound silence and the subjection of all the sense"); XI, 20 et seq.; XIII, 1, 7 ("Subdue the bodily senses and the birth of the god will take place"). Tract XIII gives reason for thinking that the vision of God brings about rebirth; and in the *Liturgy of Mithras* the mystic is taught how to produce the ecstasy in which the journey to Heaven takes place.

What is Paul's attitude to this Hellenistic idea of the vision

---

[87] See above p. 176 et seq.

of God? He is familiar with the concept of Gnosis as a transcendental vision which is not based on intellectual knowledge, but is of an ecstatic or charismatic nature. But he does not share the doctrine of the Mysteries.

According to Paul, it is only after death that we can first have the vision of God and of Christ who is with God. In 2 Cor. 5:6[88] he teaches that while we remain in the body we are far from God: "For we walk by faith and not by sight" (verse 7). He means that we do not now enjoy the vision: our present life is a bodily life, and it is led in the sphere of faith, which cannot grasp the knowledge of supernatural things. "To walk by sight" is the same as being "with God" (verse 6); it means seeing him face to face, and having personal contact with him. Paul's thought about the supernatural world which he longs for is not the thought of a pantheistic mystic; it is the theology of a former Jew. The vision of God is for him the same thing as being with God; and such a vision is impossible as long as we dwell in our earthly home. As Windisch says, "The statement in verse 7 rules out mystical-ecstatic piety."[89]

Paul does not deny absolutely the possibility of such a vision of God during this life. But he differs from the Hellenistic Gnostics in his concept of its nature and importance. This is made clear in 1 Cor. 13:12:[90]

"We see *now* through a glass in a dark manner: but *then* face to face.

Now I know in part: but *then* I shall know even as I am known."

[88] See Windisch, *2. Korintherbrief*, p. 167.   [89] Ibid.

[90] See J. Behm, "Das Bildwort vom Spiegel 1 Kor. 13:12" in *Reinbold-Seeberg-Festschrift*, i (1929), pp. 314–42; Dupont, *Gnosis*, pp. 106–48.

212

Here, as in verses 2 and 8 et seq., Paul admits that there is a Gnosis. But he immediately describes it as to "know in part", and as seeing "through a glass [that is, only indirectly] in a dark manner", and he insists in verses 8 and 10 that it will be destroyed at the Second Coming of Christ. It is noteworthy that he does not say that it will be perfected. Evidently he considers this gnosis utterly different from the vision in the next life, which is a part of glory (Phil. 3:21).

Even these few texts are sufficient to demonstrate that Paul does not share the theory of the Hellenistic mystics. Indeed he could not have taken over their theory in its entirety, for that would have entailed a denial of his concept of God. The Greeks thought that the vision of God makes man divine, an idea which would have been utterly repugnant to the former Jew. Even at the Second Coming of Christ Christians do not become divine.

In this connection it is significant that Paul attaches relatively little value to Gnosis. Charity is far superior to it and to all other charisms. No Greek mystic could have written statements like: "If I should know all mysteries and all knowledge . . . and have not charity, it profiteth me nothing" (1 Cor. 13:2), or "If any man love God, the same is known by him" (1 Cor. 8:3), for Gnosis is the very core of Hellenistic piety. Tract X, 9 says: "He who has Gnosis, the vision of God, is good and pious and already divine", which is almost a direct contradiction of 1 Cor. 8:3. Unlike the Hermetic mystics Paul never urges the Christians to "strive for Gnosis" (VII, 2), but he says "the greatest of these is charity" (1 Cor. 13:3). In 1 Cor. 12:8; 13:2, 8 Paul explains that gnosis is one of many charisms, which may be given to one man and not to another; it will come to an end like prophecy, speaking in tongues and the other charisms. The indispensible things for Christians, even for an exemplary Christian, is not knowledge, but charity. In Greek mysticism, on the other hand, it is knowledge, the vision of God, which creates the new supernatural man. On this point Paul's doctrine and Greek mysticism are utterly irreconcilable.

It is objected that Paul does speak of a real vision of God in this life; the exponents of this view refer particularly to 1 Cor. 9:1; 2 Cor. 3:18; 12:1 et seq.; 1 Cor. 2:10 et seq. Reitzenstein insists that this is the conclusion to be drawn from the vision at Damascus. He holds that the two epistles to the Corinthians drive us to the conclusion that Paul and his communities believed that this vision of God in the past enables man permanently to know all by himself, and is connected with the possession of the Spirit in the highest sense;[91] he claims that Paul had in full measure the knowledge of self which the Hermetic writings, the magical papyri and other texts attribute to the Hellenistic mystic.

Paul's own account of the vision at Damascus[92] is that Christ was seen by him (1 Cor. 9:1), and that he saw Christ (1 Cor. 15:8). But Paul had done nothing to cause this vision; he had not longed for it, nor prepared himself by asceticism, as the Hellenistic mystics did. Indeed, until that moment, he was a violent persecutor of Christ Crucified.

When considered from the standpoint of Comparative Religion, this vision falls into a quite different category from the vision of God which the Hermetic writings describe. Paul did

---

[91] *Hellenist. Mysterienreligionen,* p. 379.
[92] See also Deissner, *Paulus und die Mystik,* p. 138 et seq.

not see God or the All; he saw Christ, an historical Person, who now has a spiritual existence.

Moreover, the vision at Damascus had a different purpose from the visions of Hellenistic mysticism. Christ Triumphant without any forewarning intervened in the life of Saul, his passionate persecutor, took possession of his inmost soul, and made him a disciple. The effect of the vision was the conversion and the calling of an enemy. Paul saw the glory of God shining in the countenance of Christ whom he had detested, and he realized that Christ really was the Messias who had risen from the dead. That was the content of the vision.

Paul says that this was the moment when he was called as Apostle of the Gentiles (Gal. 1:16; 1 Cor. 9:16; 2 Cor. 2:14), and received the charism of the Apostolate. This call was the foundation of the freedom and independence which he so often asserted. He was highly conscious of his standing as an apostle, and he refers to the Spirit which dwells in him (1 Cor. 2:10 et seq.; 7:40). There is a superficial resemblance between this and the knowledge of self to which the Hellenistic Gnostics laid claim. But the similarity does not extend as far as Reitzenstein would have us believe.[93]

It is not correct to say that Paul's consciousness of his apostolic office led him to reject all tradition. In Paul's eyes the sources of revelation were the words of Jesus and the Old Testament (see 1 Cor. 7:10; 11:23), and he also holds in respect the original apostles and the Jerusalem community (see Gal. 1:18 et seq.; 2:1 et seq.). He knows that he has received the highest gifts of grace, but he feels the most profound humility and modesty

[93] Op. cit., pp. 78, 91.

215

(see 1 Cor. 4:9 et seq.; 9:16 et seq.; 15:9 et seq.; Phil. 2:10 et seq.). The Hellenistic mystics show no trace of such humility; it reminds us rather of the Old Testament prophets. Paul did not study Greek mysticism and thereby become an apostle conscious of his own freedom and independence; it was Christ's call which produced these effects: "Jesus Christ by whom we have received grace and Apostleship" (Rom. 1:5).

1 Cor. 2:6–16 has been adduced in an endeavour to show that Paul taught some kind of a vision of God in this life. Dibelius[94] describes this passage as "the famous passage, with its strong Gnostic flavour, concerning the secret wisdom which is revealed only to the spiritual man". It is alleged that Paul refers here to two kinds of preaching in which he engaged: the simple preaching of the Cross for "little children", and a more profound preaching to spiritual men; this "preaching of wisdom" is supposed to be described in verse 10 where he says: "The Spirit of God searcheth all things, yea, the deep things of God." The expression "the deep things of God" is said to be a technical term for something "profoundly mysterious", a wisdom which is reserved for a few who are "perfect", just as was done in Greek mysticism and mystery religions.

The only correct point in this theory is that Paul does speak of two kinds of preaching,[95] and that the preaching of wisdom is not identical with the preaching of the Cross which he describes in 1 Cor. 1:17 et seq. But he himself explains perfectly clearly that the mysterious wisdom concerns God's plans for salvation,

[94] *Deutsche Lit.-Ztg.* (1921), p. 726.

[95] See Deissner, op. cit., p. 39 et seq.; Reitzenstein, op. cit., p. 333 et seq.; Dibelius, op. cit., p. 725 et seq.; Bultmann in *Deutsche Lit.-Ztg.* (1922), p. 194.

including eschatology: "We speak wisdom among the perfect: yet not the wisdom of this world, neither of the princes of this world that come to nought. But we speak the wisdom of God in a mystery, a wisdom which is hidden, which God ordained before the world, unto our glory: which none of the princes of this world knew. For if they had known it they would never have crucified the Lord of glory . . . But to us God hath revealed them, by his Spirit. For the Spirit (that is, the Holy Ghost who dwells in us) searcheth all things, yea the deep things of God" (verses 6–10).[96] Through the Spirit we know "the things that are given us from God" (verse 12). The same idea appears in two other passages: 1 Cor. 15:51: "Behold I tell you a mystery. We shall all indeed rise again, but we shall not all be changed", and Rom. 11:25: "I would not have you ignorant, brethren, of this mystery . . . that blindness in part has happened in Israel, until the fullness of the Gentiles should come in." Again he says in 1 Thess. 4:14: "This we say unto you in the word of the Lord"; the preceding verse 13a is repeated in Rom. 11:25a.

Paul did have a deeper insight into the mysteries of God than ordinary Christians. But these insights concerned the plan of salvation. Paul had no interest in anything else, for he was a deeply spiritual man, and religion, particularly salvation, was his entire preoccupation. The source of this wisdom was not a vision of God. He learned it through the inspiration of the Holy Spirit who dwelt in him, or from the infallible revelation of God. This mysterious wisdom is available to all Christians (1 Cor. 3:1 et seq.), and it does not elevate Paul's nature or make him divine.

[96] Kümmel, ad loc., correctly says that the "wisdom" which is now revealed for the first time deals with the heights and depths of God's eschatological plan of salvation.

Posselt and others[97] have rightly rejected Reitzenstein's[98] attempt to deduce such a doctrine from 1 Cor. 3:3: "Are you not carnal and walk you not according to man?"

Another matter which calls for consideration at this point is the rapture to Paradise which Paul reports in 2 Cor. 12:1–4.[99] This passage might be taken to prove that Paul actually did have a vision of God, and that such a vision is therefore possible in this life. But the Jews consistently reserved the name Paradise for the abode of the just after death. It is not possible to be certain whether Paul's rapture into the "third Heaven" was the same experience as transport into Paradise; we cannot tell whether or not he considered that Paradise was in the third Heaven. When he was transported he heard "secret words which it is not given to man to utter"; he makes no mention of seeing anyone or anything. The "visions and revelations of the Lord" of verse 1 were those which he had received from the Lord. He speaks of a vision of Christ only when he is dealing with the vision at Damascus. From the standpoint of Comparative Religion this mysterious transport into the third Heaven falls into an entirely different category from the "journey to Heaven" or "vision of God" of the mysteries. In Paul's case the experience had no connection with salvation.

Paul's account of this experience is given in the third person.

[97] *PhilolWschr* (1918), p. 873 et seq.

[98] *Hellenist. Mysterienreligionen*, p. 341.

[99] See Deissner, op. cit., pp. 83 et seq., 90 et seq., 139; Windisch, *2. Kor.-Br.*, p. 369 et seq.; Reitzenstein, op. cit., pp. 369, 415; E. Käse; mann in *ZntW*, xli (1941), pp. 63–71; H. Bietenhard, *Die himmlische Welt im Urchristentum und Spätjudentum* (Tübingen, 1951), pp. 163, 247, 251; H. Traub in *ThWb*, v, 535.

He speaks of himself as a man in Christ, and attempts have been made to construe this expression as embodying a distinction between the higher and lower man, as if Paul meant that the lower man remained on earth while the higher man, the bearer of revelation, was transported. The wording of the passage (2 Cor. 12:1–4) does not favour this assumption. Paul declares twice that he does not know whether this man was in his body or without it, so he must have considered that it was possible to be transported in the body.

The Hellenistic mystics, on the other hand, taught that the vision of God is reached without the body. Tract XIII tells us explicitly that Hermes and Tat shed their earthly bodies and entered heavenly bodies. And in the *Liturgy of Mithras* the initiate leaves his earthly body and goes to Heaven in his heavenly body ("Since, being born mortal, I cannot ascend on high with the golden rays of the imperishable light, stand still, O perishable human nature, and [receive] me [again] safe and sound after the inexorable and painful distress." Verses 529–535, *Preisendanz*, i, 90).

Windisch claims that Paul's transport into the third Heaven is paralleled most closely by a rabbinical story in the Babylonian Talmud (*Chagiga* 14b–16a). The story is that according to the teaching of Rabbanan four men entered Heaven: "the first looked and died; the second looked and came to grief (became mad), the third lost his merits, but the fourth, Rabbi Aqiba, went up in peace and returned in peace." Windisch conjectures that this legend preserves a very ancient tradition, and that Paul clothed his experience in the form of Jewish teaching about Heaven: "a journey to Heaven without evil consequences is a lofty and rare occurrence, which only Paul and

Aqiba achieved."[100] Be that as it may, it is absolutely certain that the transport of Paul into the third Heaven is not to be equated with the "journey to Heaven" or the "vision of God" of the Hellenistic mystics.

The most important divergence between Paul and the Greeks appears in connection with the Greek doctrine that the vision of God produced an essential change in the mystic, who gains a transcendental body. There is not a word about this in Paul. The Apostle is convinced that he will be clothed in a heavenly body when Christ returns, and then he will be with Christ entirely and for ever. This certainty does not derive from a vision of God or of Christ, for it applies to all Christians indiscriminately. Its basis is not a vision in this life, but the fact that Christ rose again, and that through Baptism we have fellowship with the death and life of Christ. This explains why Paul shows no anxiety for ecstatic visions in this life; he does not desire them himself, and he does not encourage others to do so. It is a different matter when he is thinking of the aftermath of Christ's Second Coming. He does not set a very high value on the charisms which do not contribute to the building up of the Church (see 1 Cor. chap. 14).

When writing to the Corinthians he merely alludes to the rapture which he had experienced. He regarded it simply as an anticipation of the final ascent into Paradise. It was not a rebirth which elevated him into a higher, spiritual being, for he was already a new creature (2 Cor. 5:17). In other words, Paul did

[100] Op. cit., p. 375 et seq. The entry into Paradise here is usually interpreted as referring to being engaged in metaphysical speculation. According to Bietenhard (op. cit., pp. 91–5), who is followed by W. Bousset and others, the four Rabbis were in ecstasy.

not consider that this experience was anything more than a high mark of God's favour, and it apparently happened only once. He never claims that it is the title on which his authority is based; it is mentioned only when he is enumerating his privileges. As Deissner[101] says, it did not have the importance for Paul's spirituality which similar experiences had in Greek mysticism, and Paul himself attached no such significance to it.

E. Käsemann says that this rapture into the third Heaven was a unique experience which befell Paul alone, and which had nothing to do with his service of the community as an apostle. It was a purely personal event, which concerned his relationship to God and to Christ. That is why he says so little about it, and simply puts it on the same footing as his speaking in tongues (1 Cor. 14:18 et seq.) and his ecstasy (2 Cor. 5:13). The transport raised him above the surroundings of the Body of Christ and set him beside the great figures of the Old Testament like Henoch, Moses and Elias, and in the New Testament, beside Christ the Lord. "While still living in this world Paul was permitted to anticipate the eschatological event which previously had happened only to Christ Triumphant." As A. Stolz has recognized, the rapture raised Paul into Paradise, that is, the original home of Adam, and at the same time into the situation where the eschatological mysteries await their revelation.[102] It elevated him above the world of sin and "placed him in Paradise in anticipation of the joy and consummation which await the Christian life after it is freed from the body of sin", it gave him "a share in the familiarity with God which Adam enjoyed in Paradise, and which shall be enjoyed at the end of time".[103]

[101] Op. cit., p. 90.
[102] *Theologie der Mystik* (1936).   [103] Pp. 44, 63, 64.

221

But it must be borne in mind that Paul makes no mention of a revelation of God or of Christ; what he did experience were heavenly places and unutterable words, that is, words which he neither could nor was allowed to utter.

The theory that Paul knew of a vision of God similar to that after which the Greek mystics strove, is founded above all on 2 Cor. 3:18: "We all, beholding the glory [δόξα] of the Lord with open face, are [thereby] transformed into the same image [of the Lord] from glory to glory, as [is done] by the Spirit of the Lord."[104] Bousset considers that these words, shot through with mysticism, clearly expound the great theme: "The vision of God makes us divine."[105] Reitzenstein thinks that 2 Cor. 5:1 et seq. teaches that there is a material change, and he claims that this text describes this change which Christians must undergo here upon earth to fit them for receiving the heavenly body.[106]

[104] See Reitzenstein, *Hellenist. Mysterienreligionen,* pp. 77, 357 et seq.; Deissner, op. cit., p. 111 et seq.; Windisch, *2. Korintherbrief,* p. 127 et seq.; Weiss, *Urchristentum,* p. 406 et seq.; Nisius in *Zeitschr. f. kath. Theol.* (1916), pp. 617–75; Göttsberger in *Bibl. Zeitschr.,* xvi (1924), pp. 1–17; Kurfess in *Katholik* (1918), p. 257 et seq.; Corssen in *ZntW,* xix (1920), p. 2 et seq.; Posselt in *PhilolWschr* (1918), p. 886 et seq.; Dibelius, *Paulus und die Mystik,* pp. 62 et seq., 73; G. Kittel in *ThWb,* ii, 395, 693 et seq.; J. Behm in *ThWb,* iv, 762–5; J. Dupont, "Le chrétien, miroir de la gloire de Dieu, d'après 2 Cor. 3:18" in *Rev. biblique,* lvi (1949), pp. 392–411; Kümmel in Lietzmann, *2. Kor.* (4th ed.), ad loc.; Schlier, *Beiträge zur evangel. Theologie,* i (Munich), p. 65 et seq.

[105] *Kyrios Christos,* p. 168, note 3.

[106] Op. cit., p. 357. According to Reitzenstein we have here the metaphor of a miraculous or Spirit mirror which makes the looker resemble the divine form which he sees. This complex theory is not sufficiently worked out, and it cannot be examined here. It is discussed by E. Käsemann, *Leib und Leib Christi* (Tübingen, 1933), p. 167. Schlier paraphrases it thus: "Paul recognizes even in this life a miraculous transformation of

The exegesis of this verse is extremely difficult. The English word "seeing" renders the Greek word κατοπτριζόμενοι. This word could mean "reflecting" or "seeing in a mirror". There is no doubt that it has the latter meaning, for there is a decisive parallel in Philo (*Allegorical exposition of the Law* 3, 101): "Of such a kind was Moses who said 'Show me thy face that I may know thee' (Exod. 33:13), that is, reveal thyself to me, but not through heaven, earth, water, air, or anything created; I wish to see thy appearance, not reflected in something else, but in thee, the Godhead; for appearances in created things dissolve, but those in the uncreated remain perpetually firm and eternal." Similarly here Paul says in verse 18a that we have no covering over our hearts as the people of Israel had (verse 15), but with uncovered face we see in the mirror the glory of the Lord. This reference to a mirror does not convey the idea of obscurity which appears in 1 Cor. 13:12; it denotes a clear and definite knowledge, as in a good mirror.

Nevertheless there is probably the idea that our sight of the glory of the Lord is indirect and not immediate. If he were thinking of an immediate vision of Christ in glory (as in 1 Cor. 9:1; 15:8), he would not have said "we all", for it is only at the Second Coming that all men shall see Christ in glory (Col. 3:4). The vision to which Paul here refers takes place when we hear with faith the preaching of the Gospel which testifies to the exaltation of Christ to heavenly glory. The prologue to St. John's Gospel says of the Word who appeared in the flesh, "we saw his (divine) glory" (1:14; cf. 2:11), but when Paul speaks of Christ's life on earth he refers to him as being humbled and in the form of a

man which through the power of the Holy Ghost takes place by steady gazing on the Lord Jesus."

servant (Phil. 2:7); he does not speak of Christ's glory (δόξα) unless he is thinking of the Risen Christ who sits at the right hand of the Father (Rom. 1:4; Phil. 2:9 et seq.; 3:21; 1 Tim. 3:16).

But what is the meaning of the sentence: "We are transformed into the same image (or form, 1 Cor. 15:49; Rom. 8:29) from glory to glory"? It clearly describes the effect which the vision of the glory of the Lord has upon us. The vision transforms us into the same image, and this transformation does not take place all at once, but is a gradual process. The problem is to decide the nature of the transformation. Is it something spiritual, or is it a mysterious process such as the Hellenistic mystics believed in, namely the beginning of the glorification of the body and the production of the spiritual body? The majority of exegetes consider that it is a spiritual process, but the Comparative Religion school favours the second alternative.

Windisch[107] holds that the glory (δόξα, actually brilliance) is the light of glory *(lumen gloriae)* which the Lord of glory (1 Cor. 2:8) shines upon us. He says that what Paul and those like him see is the real glory of the Lord (2 Cor. 4:6). He contends that whereas Phil. 3:21 and 1 Cor. 15:49 et seq., teach that the transformation will not take place until the next life, the present passage implies that the transformation begins in this life through a gradual process. He alleges this passage as evidence that Paul was deeply versed in the experiences of the mysteries, on the ground that the Apostle here recognizes that there is a vision by which the initiate is transformed into the image of the divine Person whom he is permitted to see. He adds that this does not happen only in the material sphere;

[107] Op. cit., p. 129.

parallel with it there is a spiritual transformation such as is described in Rom. 12:2 ("be reformed in the newness of your mind"), a spiritual *transfigurari,* to borrow Seneca's term (*Ep.* 6, 1; 94, 48). He says that unless this were the case, the process could not be said to affect all Christians.

There are two serious difficulties against this view. Windisch himself recognizes them.

The first difficulty is that elsewhere Paul always says that we shall suddenly be transformed into the likeness of Christ in his heavenly glory, and that this will take place at the Second Coming (Phil. 3:21; 1 Cor. 15:49, 51 et seq.). He nowhere says that the possession of the Spirit carries with it a super-physical transformation of man. The possession of the Spirit is only a guarantee of our future resurrection, and it is also the motive from which God effects the resurrection according to Rom. 8:11, if we accept the reading "because of his Spirit that dwelleth in you".

The second difficulty is connected with this. Paul teaches that all will be transformed. But, if we understand the process of transformation as the Greek mystics did, it can happen only to the very small number who have actually seen Christ. Moreover, the process of "beholding in the mirror" must be as progressive as the transformation. Where does this vision of the glory of the Lord take place? Bousset[108] thinks that it happens in the liturgy, while Windisch[109] considers that it also occurs elsewhere. But these are merely conjectures with no support from the text.

So it can safely be said that the "mystery" interpretation of this passage is by no means certain. Büchsel, among others,

---

[108] *Kyrios Christos,* p. 109.   [109] Op. cit., p. 131.

rejects it entirely; he writes: "2 Cor. 3:18 does not say that Christians undergo a bodily change in this life. . . A new body is the final result, not the efficient cause of the Christians' possession of the Spirit."[110] Furthermore, it should be borne in mind that Paul believes in the resurrection of the body, while in Greek mysticism the earthly body of the mystic plays no role whatever, least of all after death. A Greek mystic could never have said: God "shall quicken also your mortal bodies" (Rom. 8:11; cf. 2 Cor. 4:14; 1 Cor. 6:14; 15:52; 1 Thess. 4:16).

There is often close kinship in language between Paul and Greek mysticism, and there is no reason to deny this kinship, at least in the case of 2 Cor. 3:18. Nevertheless it must not be forgotten that Paul was a converted Jew, and his views about human destiny were utterly different from those of the Greeks. His words must be interpreted in the light of his theology as a whole.

The meaning of 2 Cor. 3:18 must therefore be that through the operation of the Spirit Christians constantly receive the glory of the Lord, and in the religious and ethical sense are transformed gradually into his nature. In other words, this text expresses the same idea as Gal. 4:19: "until Christ be formed in you".

There is no doubt that the Greek word for "are transformed" can be used in this spiritual sense. Paul himself does so in Rom. 12:2: "Be reformed in the newness of your mind"; and the corresponding Latin word *(transfigurari)* is employed by Seneca in the same way: "I know that I shall not merely be improved: I shall also be transformed" *(Ep.* 6, 1).

The only remaining problem is whether the word δόξα can de-

---

[110] *Geist Gottes,* p. 397, note.

note a (progressive) expression of the spiritual image of the glorified Christ. This is certainly not its usual meaning. But it is noteworthy that earlier in this chapter Paul had used the word of the apostolic office and of the New Testament, where it must have a spiritual meaning. There is a parallel in verse 9: "If the ministration of condemnation be glory, much more the ministration of justice aboundeth in glory."

Undoubtedly we are dealing with a mystical idea when we meet the concept that in this life the Christian is transformed into the image of Christ by seeing his glory. Dibelius considers that this is the closest Paul ever came to the divinization mysticism of the Greeks. This is the only place in the Epistles where the idea appears. The closest parallel would be Rom. 8:30: "Whom he justified, them he also glorified", and this has little in common with the text from Corinthians.

But a number of points must be kept in mind. To begin with, in Greek mysticism the transformation was effected by the subject's actions. Here, however, it is wrought by Christ, who gives the faithful the pledge of the Spirit, and thereby gives them a share in his glory. Secondly, in Greek mysticism the transformation makes the mystic divine. There is nothing similar here; the mystic does not become Christ. Thirdly, all the faithful may be transformed; it is not the prerogative of a small group. Fourthly, in spite of this transformation, the present life and the next remain utterly distinct. It is still true that "we walk by faith and not by sight" (2 Cor. 5:7; Rom. 8:24 et seq.). Finally besides the indicative of 2 Cor. 3:18, we also find the imperative: "Be reformed" (Rom. 12:2).

4. The importance which Paul attaches to ethics and conduct gives his mysticism a special character.

As has been shown in II, 4, the antipathy of many Protestant theologians to mysticism is principally due to their idea that mysticism means sentimental religion without moral obligation. They speak of the "ethical irresponsibility of the mystic", and insist that, in the eyes of a mystic, union with God in ecstasy is more important than doing good; indeed, they claim that since the mystic is divine he is beyond good and evil. They contrast this mystical piety with what they call prophetic piety. The characteristics of prophetic piety are a profound awareness of the absolute sanctity of God, humble subjection to him, a deep appreciation of one's own unworthiness and sinfulness, and an active endeavour to lead a moral life.

Paul's piety was of this prophetic type. He was not a mystic in the sense described above.[111]

On the other hand, that description of mystical piety fits Hellenistic mysticism perfectly.[112] Conduct was of little importance in it, as is to be expected in view of its Dualist basis and its religious goal of divinization. In the ecstatic vision of God man is thoroughly transformed; he becomes divine, either because a being composed of pure divine powers enters him, or because he becomes aware of the divine element in himself, the element

---

[111] So Deissner, *Paulus und die Mystik,* p. 136.

[112] See Deissner, ibid., pp. 36 et seq., 63 et seq., 120 et seq., 140 et seq.; Reitzenstein, *Poimandres,* p. 180, note 1; *Hellenist. Mysterien-religionen,* pp. 67, 195, 292 et seq.; Kroll, *Lehren des Hermes,* pp. 300, 383 et seq.; Bousset in *Gött. Gel. Anz.* (1914), p. 745 et seq.; Posselt in *PhilolWschr* (1918), pp. 871 et seq., 887 et seq.; Bräuninger, op. cit., p. 33 et seq.; Leipoldt, *Sterbende und auferstehende Götter,* p. 64 et seq.; Idem, "Der Sieg des Christentums über die Religionen der alten Welt" in *Theol. Abh., L. Ihmels dargebracht* (Leipzig, 1928), pp. 49–83; G. von Randenborgh, *Vergottung und Erlösung* (1927).

from the upper world which is in him from the beginning like a spark which is sunk in matter – both theories occur. The physical man of the senses who belongs to the evil lower world, sinks into insignificance; indeed, there is no intrinsic relationship between him and the higher essential self of the man who has become divine or been reborn. So when the mystics and the mysteries speak of salvation (σωτηρία, salus), as they often do, they refer to something affecting the subject's nature rather than to an ethical process. This salvation is attained, either by undergoing all kinds of dedication ceremonies, or else by pure speculation in the vision of God. The goal of mysticism is liberation from the compulsion of destiny, protection from punishment after death, and the attaining of immortal life in the next world. So the purpose of the blessings or of the ecstatic vision of God is freedom from the domination of fate and the assurance of a happy life hereafter. They are not designed to free men from the bonds of sin, and to make them ethically good.

In Apuleius' *Mystery of Isis* it is emphasized that pitiless fate *(fortuna nefaria)* has no further power over the initiate, for the mighty Isis who governs fate (11,6 25) has taken him under her protection (11,25). The Eleusinian mysteries had promised the initiate security from an evil lot in the next life. As early as the Homeric Hymn to Demeter we find praise of the fortune of the initiate and stress upon the woeful destiny of those who are not initiated:

Happy is he of men upon the earth who has seen this. But he who is not initiate and who has no share, has not a like destiny, for when he dies he is under dank darkness (verses 480–482).

O. Kern calls this the "most ancient beatitude of antiquity".

It is repeated time and again by the poets. A fragment of Pindar declares:

Happy is he who goes under the earth having seen these things. He knows the end of life, and he knows the beginning which Zeus gives (Fr. 137a).

In Sophocles, Fragment 753 (Nauck²) we read:

Happy, thrice happy, are those mortals, who have once seen such rites and then go down to Hades. For them alone there is life there. For the others there is only distress and bitter suffering.

And Plato speaks thus of Orphism in *Phaedo* 69c:

The men who introduced the mystery ceremonies amongst us must have been people of great quality. They preach in mysterious form the doctrine that one who comes to Hades without the blessing and without being received into the ranks of the pure, must lie in the pool of Hell, while the pure and just may dwell with the gods in the next life.

Nevertheless the mysteries were frequently the subject of vigorous criticism, at least in Hellenistic times. A number of sources report a saying of Diogenes that Pataecion the robber would have a better life after death than Epaminondas, as he has been initiated into the mysteries.[113] Philo repeatedly complains that morally disreputable people were initiated into the mysteries: "It frequently happens that no upright men are initiated, but many thieves, pirates, and loose women, because they give money to the initiator and to the hierophant."[114] This judgement of Philo's is confirmed by Roman poets;

---

[113] E.g., Plutarch, *De aud. poet.*, iv (see Rohde, *Psyche,* i [1921], p. 295).
[114] *De vict. off.*, xii, 261 M, and *Concerning the single laws,* i, § 223.

Juvenal, for example, calls the priestess of Isis, or Isis herself, a bawd (6, 488 et seq.). Josephus tells us (*Antiquities* 18, 3, 4 §§ 65 et seq.) that in the year A.D. 19, a reputable and outstanding lady was handed over to a rake at the temple of Isis in Rome. Writers of the Imperial age constantly complain about the wantonness of the priestesses of Isis.[115] Livy (39, 8–19) tells us of the reaction when the Bacchanalians had entered Rome and were discovered there at their secret practices. The initiates were accused of every possible offence: unchastity, false witness, poisoning, and even stealing corpses.[116] Even allowing for exaggeration, we cannot gainsay the evidence of the monuments, which show that these accusations were not entirely feats of imagination.

However, it is only fair to point out that the mystery communities cannot be simply written off as gatherings of scoundrels. The mystery religions had other characteristics in addition to those we have mentioned. Like any elevated religion, Greek religion did endeavour to lead its adherents to a better pattern of conduct. This was particularly true of the Mysteries of Eleusis and Samothrace, which were still active in the Hellenistic era. The philosophers criticized these mysteries, but they never accused them of undermining morals. Moreover, there are sources which emphasize their good moral effect. In the *Frogs* of Aristophanes (886 et seq.), Aeschylus prays: "O Demeter, thou who nourisheth my spirit, grant that I may be worthy of thy initiation." Epictetus (3, 21) defended the Eleusinian Mysteries against a lampooner, and said that their practices were established

---

[115] Leipoldt, op. cit., p. 64 et seq.
[116] See Reitzenstein, *Hellenist. Mysterienreligionen,* p. 100 et seq.

by the ancients "for edification and for the improvement of life". Diodorus of Sicily, who lived in the time of Augustus, wrote that the people of Samothrace regarded the initiate as holier, juster, and in every respect better than themselves (5, 49).

In regard to the Oriental-Hellenistic mysteries, certain moral influences can be attributed at least to the Mysteries of Mithras and of Isis. The prayer of thanksgiving of Lucius (in Apuleius 11, 25) gives evidence about the Mysteries of Isis:

> Thou holy and eternal saviour of mankind, always gener-
> ous to the weak, thou sendest sweet mother-love to the
> forlorn who are in distress. But I am of too small a spirit to
> thank thee as thou dost deserve, and I am too poor to bring
> thee the right sacrifice . . .
>
> So I will gratefully perform what a pious poor man can:
> I will conceal in the most secret depth of my breast thy di-
> vine countenance and thy most holy form, and I will ever
> preserve it there and keep it before my soul.

An inscription from the island of Ios of the second or third century A.D. contains a prose hymn where Isis says:

> I gave the commandment that children should love their
> parents, and imposed punishment on those who did not love
> their parents. With my brother Osiris I put an end to cann-
> ibalism . . . I taught men to honour the images of the gods . . .
> I destroyed the domination of tyrants, I ensured that justice
> is stronger than gold and silver, I gave the commandment
> that the truth should be considered honourable, I devised
> the contract of marriage . . .

Mithraism also imposed certain ethical obligations on its followers, as we would expect from a religion of Iranian origin.

For Iran was the homeland of Dualism, which taught that there is a constant struggle between the two principles of light and darkness, good and evil. "The expansion of Mithraism and of the worship of Isis was certainly due in no small measure to their moral content which made a strong impression on an amoral world."[117] Nevertheless it is true "that even here it is difficult to find moral effects in the proper sense. The worship of Adonis, Attis, Cybele, and other Oriental deities which surrounded early Christianity had no moral element at all."[118] Leipoldt does not exaggerate when he says: "It is true only to a very limited extent that the pagan cults deliberately connected religion with morality."[119]

The Hermetic writings seem to adopt a higher moral tone. They equate ignorance of God (ἀγνωσία) with vice, and knowledge of God with virtue (X, 8; XI, 21). The only real sin is godlessness, that is, not knowing God, and the only virtue is the knowledge of God (XVI, 11). "Neither evil spirit nor fate has any power over the pious man, for God saves the pious man from all evil. The one and only good in man is piety." Lactantius, *Inst.* 2, 15, 6 quotes this as a saying of Hermes. In *Poimandres* §§ 22 et seq., Nous says: "I come only to the holy, and good, and pure, and merciful and pious, and my coming is a help to them and they immediately know everything and please God by love . . . And before they give their body to its

---

[117] G. Kittel, *Religionsgeschichte und Urchristentum*, p. 115. Origen, *Contra Celsum*, 3, 59 quotes Celsus as saying that the invitation to a pagan mystery festival contained the words: "[Let him come] who is free from all malice, and who is conscious of no wicked deed, and who has lived well and justly."

[118] G. Kittel, op. cit.   [119] Op. cit., p. 65.

death, they feel repugnance at the experiences of the senses, for they know what kind of effects they produce." I extirpate their wicked desires so that they may no longer perform evil deeds. "I am far from the ignorant and wicked and evil, from the envious and avaricious, from murderers and unholy men, and I deliver them to the avenging demon." The demon increases their evil passions further. At the end of *Poimandres,* Hermes relates how, after instruction about the nature of the All and the highest vision, he began to preach to men the beauty of piety and knowledge (§§ 27 et seq.): "O you people, O earth-born men, who have yielded to drunkenness and sleep, be prudent . . . Why have you earth-born men surrendered to death, when you have the power to attain immortality? Repent, you associates of error and companions of ignorance; break free from the dark light, leave the things which pass, and grasp immortality. Some mocked at me and surrendered themselves to the way of death, but others asked me for instruction. And I taught them how and in what manner they could be saved." In Tract VII a sermon entitled, *That ignorance of God is the greatest evil among men,* contains the passage: "O men, you who are inebriated, who have drunk the intoxicating drink of godlessness, whither are you being led? Stop, be sober . . . and if you cannot all do so, let those do it who are able. For the evil of ignorance binds the soul which is imprisoned in the body, by preventing it from anchoring in the harbours of salvation (σωτηρία) . . . Seek for a guide who can lead you to the gates of knowledge, where there is shining light, where no one is drunk, where all are temperate, for they look with their hearts upon him who lets himself be seen" (§§ 1–2).

But this piety does not contain the kind of ethic which we

find in the New Testament. Essentially it equates piety with knowledge of God or with the endeavour to attain the vision of God, and godlessness with the contrary. In other words, it does not call for moral endeavour, but for the effort to attain mystical knowledge of God.[120] The matter of which our bodies are composed is the same thing as evil (VII, 2; IV, 6).[121] And therefore the renunciation of vice is identical with the laying aside of the body in the vision of God. Man does not attain true life until he has availed himself of Nous to free himself from his lower nature. Each man has a free choice: he may devote himself to this knowledge, or he may remain in ignorance. Piety means that he turns to the knowledge of God. There are scarcely any moral injunctions in the Hermetic writings. As Reitzenstein points out,[122] Hellenistic piety is lacking completely in any feeling of guilt, or any desire to be reconciled with the God who has been offended. It is at this point that we meet the fundamental cleavage between Hellenism and Christianity.

A man who possesses the knowledge of God is holy and free from vices. Strictly speaking he can still sin, for his body is still subject for the time being to material things and to sin. Yet in the last analysis it is not his real self which commits the sin. God has withdrawn the mystic from the domination of fate and of evil, and has transferred him to the next life, and so the power of sin over the body now has no meaning for the Gnostic. His body is not involved any more, for the body in question is no longer his. His body can sin, but his real self

[120] E. Schwartz, *Charakterköpfe,* ii (1919), p. 114: They seek "to become divine magically, while leaving their consciences untouched or undisturbed".

[121] See Kroll, op. cit., p. 341 et seq.   [122] *Poimandres,* p. 180, note 1.

cannot do so, it only seems to sin. This is said explicitly in Tract XII, 7,[123] where Hermes explains: "All men must suffer what is laid down for them by fate. But those who have received the Logos, over whom, as we have said, Nous is master, do not suffer it in the same way as the others, for they are free from vice. They suffer, but they are not wicked." Tat then asks: "What do you mean, Father? Are not the murderer and the adulterer and all the others wicked?" Hermes answers: "No, my son. The man who has received the Logos must suffer (what fate has decreed) like an adulterer and a murderer, but not because he is an adulterer or a murderer. It is impossible to escape death, just as it is impossible to escape birth. But if a man possesses Nous, it is possible for him to escape wickedness."

What is Paul's attitude to ethics? We are not concerned here with the general question of Paul's moral teaching; the problem is to discover the attitude of Paul as a mystic. It is unnecessary to explain that morality plays a great part in Paul's theology, and that he could not have conceived of Christian life without morality. But are morality and mysticism simply juxtaposed in Paul's theology, or is there an organic bond between them? Do Paul's ethics derive from his mysticism, as the flower develops from the bud? Do mystical statements provide the reason for his moral injunctions? Does Paul base his call for good conduct on the fact that we are mystically united with Christ?[124]

[123] See Reitzenstein, op. cit., p. 67; Deissner, op. cit., p. 81.

[124] See Bartmann, *Paulus,* p. 113 et seq.; Bultmann, "Das Problem der Ethik bei Paulus" in *ZntW* (1924), p. 123 et seq.; Windisch, "Das Problem des paulinischen Imperativs": ibid., p. 265 et seq.; Mundle, "Religion und Sittlichkeit bei Paulus in ihrem inneren Zusammenhang" in *ZsystTh,* iv

The answer to this question is clear and unchallenged: Paul connects morality with mysticism. Our fellowship with Christ is not simply something natural, like the mystical union of the Greeks. It is a sacramental and moral relationship, and therefore is the source of moral obligations (see III, 3). This fellowship with Christ is not the only moral motive which Paul proposes; he also takes motives from eschatology (see 1 Thess. 2:12; 5:4 et seq.; 2 Thess. 1:5 et seq.; 1 Cor. 7:29 et seq.), from the example of Christ (Phil. 2:5 et seq.), and from our possession of the Spirit (Gal. 5:25; 1 Cor. 6:11).

But in a number of passages he explicitly insists that our obligation to lead a moral life derives from our union with Christ. An examination of the texts in question will supplement what has already been said in III, 3 about the ethical element in Paul's mysticism.

The most important exposition of the moral obligations which derive from our fellowship with Christ appears in the Epistle to the Romans, chapters 6 and 7. What Paul had said in 5:20 et seq., might have been misinterpreted to mean that it is better for a Christian to remain in sin, so that the grace of Christ may abound still more. In these two chapters Paul puts himself out to dispel the possibility of any such misunderstanding of his words. He lays down the principle: The Christian must not sin; and he supports this statement with three arguments, each introduced by the question: "Know you not?" The three proofs are contained in 6:2–14; 6:15–23; and 7:1–6.

(1926–7), p. 456 et seq.; G. Staffelbach, *Die Vereinigung mit Christus als Prinzip der Moral bei Paulus* (Freiburg i. Br., 1932); L. Nieder, *Die Motive der religiös-sittlichen Paränese in den paulinischen Gemeindebriefen* (Dissertation, Munich, 1952, unpublished).

The first proof opens with the sentence: "We that are dead to sin, how shall we live any longer therein?" (verse 2). He explains that we become dead to sin by Baptism, through which the Christian enters upon a mystical fellowship with the death and life of Christ. In Baptism the old man is crucified and the body of sin is destroyed, so that the Christians are dead to sin and have risen to a new life for God in Christ. From this fact it follows inescapably that Christians are bound to lead a sinless life: "Let not sin therefore [οὖν] reign in your mortal body, so as to obey the lusts thereof. Neither yield ye your members as instruments of iniquity unto sin . . . but present your members as instruments of justice unto God" (verses 12–14). In this passage the statement and the injunction are related as gift and duty. The gift which you have received imposes on you a duty and an obligation. The new sphere of life into which you have been transferred demands from you that you lead your lives accordingly. This close connection whereby moral obligation has its roots in Baptism, is expressed in verse 4 by a purpose clause: "We are buried together with him by Baptism . . . that . . . so we may also walk in newness of life".

The whole line of argument may be summed up by saying that our life is so closely united with the death and resurrection of Christ that it must fully correspond to his life. Strictly speaking we ought also to share in his resurrection, and we shall do so at the Second Coming. At present we cannot share in it, and so we must develop the only similarity that is possible for us, namely similarity of conduct.

The second argument is based on the relation of master and servant. It may be expounded as follows: We owe obedience to him in whose service we are. You have been freed from the service of sin and thereby have become servants of God. Therefore you must serve God, and this is incompatible with sinning. The connection with Baptism is not so clear here as in the previous argument. Nevertheless, Baptism enters into this argument also, for it is Baptism which is responsible for our change of allegiance. According to verse 6b liberation from slave-service to sin is a consequence of our mystical death in Baptism (verse 6a), and he says explicitly in verses 18 and 22 that the Christians have been freed from sin.

The third argument is akin to the second. It is a comparison of our union with Christ to the relationship which exists in marriage.[125] The marriage and the marriage bond last only as long as both parties are alive. If either party dies, the other is free and can contract a new union. The same applies to the bond with the Mosaic Law. Through the body of Christ Christians have been made dead to the Law, so that they can now belong to another, namely to him who has risen from the dead. They are now bound to him, and must therefore bring forth fruit for God. Paul's meaning is that Christ satisfied the demand of the Law by dying on the Cross, and thereby he became free from the servitude which he voluntarily undertook for the sake of men. By Baptism Christians have shared in the suffering of Christ's death and have also shared in its consequence, namely freedom from the Law. As a result of this they belong to Christ.

The argument may be summed up thus: When they were bound to the Law which awakened sin, naturally they sinned

---

[125] Difficulties could be raised about the development of the comparison, but the meaning is clear.

and brought forth fruit to death. Now, when they are bound to Christ, it is equally natural that they should no longer sin, but should bring forth fruit to Christ.

In 1 Cor. 5:7 et seq., Paul argues that since the Christians are "unleavened", they are obliged not only to expel the incestuous man (verse 7), but also to avoid all evil themselves (verse 8). It is clear that he is thinking of Baptism, as we see from 6 : 11: "You have been washed".

In 1 Cor. 6:15 et seq., he argues that because they belong to the Body of Christ they have a duty to avoid unchastity. Finally, in Col. 3:1 et seq., he supports his moral injunctions by referring to the death which they have undergone in Baptism (2:12, 20; 3:3), and to the resurrection which they have experienced (2:12 et seq.). "If you be risen with Christ, seek the things that are above (3:1) . . . mortify your members which are upon the earth (3:5) . . . stripping yourselves of the old man (3:9) . . . and putting on the new [man]" (3:10).

In addition to our mystical union with Christ, Paul also argues from our possession of the Spirit that we are bound to lead a sinless life. There is a close connection between Paul's mysticism and his doctrine concerning the Spirit (cf. Rom. 8:10 et seq.), as has been demonstrated in II, 3. So a brief exposition of his teaching on this point will supplement what has already been said.

The principal passage is Gal. 5:16–25, where the Apostle instructs them to walk in the Spirit (verse 16) and to be led by the Spirit (verse 18), for sin no longer has power over them (verse 16). He means that they must let their new vital principle, the Spirit, work in them, by co-operating with the Spirit, for the flesh is powerless. Since they have died with Christ (verse 24) the flesh has been deprived of its superiority over them, and it cannot dominate them any more if they surrender totally to the Spirit. In verse 25 he declares: "If we live in the Spirit, let us also walk in the Spirit." In other words, their actions must correspond to their nature, the conduct of their lives must be in harmony with their new vital principle (cf. Col. 3:7).

In Rom. 8:9–11 he says that Christians are not in the flesh but in the Spirit. So far as sin is concerned, their body is dead. Their moral obligation arises from this: "Therefore, brethren, we are debtors, not to the flesh, to live according to the flesh . . . but if by the Spirit you mortify the deeds of the flesh, you shall live" (verse 12 et seq.). He declares that they are obliged to mortify – that is, to kill – deeds of the flesh.

In 1 Cor. 6:19 et seq. (as in 3:16 and 2 Cor. 6:14), he calls Christians temples of the Holy Ghost. He then draws the conclusion from this fact: "Glorify God in your body."

What has been said here, and also the examination of the moral aspect of Paul's mysticism in chapter 3, demonstrates clearly that even the objective and divine side, the sacramental side of this mystical union, is not to be thought of as something natural or magical.

It is true that Baptism is an objective act of God's, which is attached to certain rites. It is also correct that by Baptism God withdraws men from the sphere of the flesh and of sin, and transfers them to a new sphere. Moreover, the new "life", the "new creation", is a work of God's. But this does not relieve men of their moral obligations; on the contrary, it is precisely because of these objective facts that men have moral duties.

And the resurrection, which is the final and supreme result of Baptism, depends on the fulfilment of these duties.[126]

1 Cor. 10:1 et seq., is perhaps the place where Paul expresses this doctrine most emphatically. He uses the history of the generation which wandered in the desert to show the Corinthians that the sacraments by themselves give no guarantee of attaining the goal of salvation. The Israelites also received a kind of baptism and ate heavenly food, yet God rejected them: "But with most of them God was not well pleased: for they were overthrown in the desert", and they did not succeed in reaching the Promised Land. Their failure was a punishment for their sin. This is an example for us, and it is contained in the Scripture in order to warn us. "Wherefore, he that thinketh himself to stand, let him take care lest he fall" (verse 12). Even a Christian can be lost (see also Rom. 8:13; 1 Cor. 6:9 et seq.; Gal. 5:19 et seq.).

---

[126] Only Christianity has such a union of an objective divine action with moral obligations. The majority of Protestants misunderstand this double element. The Comparative Religion school does recognize the sacramental character of Baptism and of the Eucharist, but they generally make the mistake of thinking that sacramental means the same as magical. The others deny the sacramental character of these actions, and regard them as mere symbols. Thus, for example, Deissner, *Paulus und die Mystik,* p. 224 et seq.; Clemen, *Religionsgeschichtliche Erklärung des N.T.* (1924), p. 160 et seq. Sommerlath's assessment is very good in *Ursprung des neuen Lebens,* p. 100 et seq.

Bibliography

Bartmann, B. | *Paulus. Die Grundzüge seiner Lehre und die moderne Religionsgeschichte* (Paderborn, 1914).

Bertrams, H. | *Das Wesen des Geistes nach der Anschauung des Apostels Paulus* (Münster i. W., 1913).

Bousset, W. | *Kyrios Christos. Geschichte des Christusglaubens von den Anfängen des Christentums bis Irenäus* (Göttingen, ²1921).
Jesus der Herr (Göttingen, 1916).

Bover, J. | "De mystica unione 'in Christo Iesu' secundum b. Paulum" in *Biblica*, i (1920), pp. 209–26.

Bräuninger, F. | *Untersuchungen zu den Schriften des Hermes Trismegistos*, Phil. Diss. (Berlin, 1926).

Brun, Lyder | "Zur Formel 'in Christus Jesus' in dem Brief des Paulus an die Philipper" in *Symbolae Arctoae,* i (1922), pp. 19–37.

Büchsel, F. | *Der Geist Gottes im Neuen Testament* (Gütersloh, 1926).

Cerfaux, L. | *Christ in the Theology of St. Paul* (New York, 1959).

Colon, J.-B. | "A propos de la 'mystique' de S. Paul" in *Revue des sciences relig.,* xv (1935), pp. 157–83, 325–55.

Deissmann, A. | *Die neutestamentliche Formel "in Christo Jesu"* (Marburg, 1892).
Paulus, Eine kultur- und religionsgeschichtliche Skizze (Tübingen, ²1925).

Deissner, K. | *Paulus und die Mystik seiner Zeit* (Leipzig, ²1921).

Dey, J. | *Palingenesia. Ein Beitrag zur Klärung der religionsgeschichtlichen Bedeutung von Tit. 3:5* (Münster i. W., 1937).

Dibelius, M. | *Die Isisweihe bei Apuleius und verwandte Initiationsriten* (Heidelberg, 1917).
"Erklärung von 1 und 2 Thess., Phil." (³1937), "Kol., Eph." (²1927), in Lietzmann's *Handbuch zum N.T.*
"Glaube und Mystik bei Paulus" in *Neue Jahr-*

bücher für Wissenschaft und Jugendbildung, vii (1931), pp. 683–99.

"Paulus und die Mystik: Eine heilige Kirche" in *Zeitschrift für Kirchenkunde und Religionswissenschaft,* ed. by F. Heiler, xxii (1941), pp. 57–67.

Dieterich, A.   *Eine Mithrasliturgie* (Leipzig, ³1923).

Dodd, C. H.   *The Bible and the Greeks* (London, 1935).

Dupont, J.   *Gnosis. La connaissance religieuse dans les épîtres de S. Paul* (Louvain, 1949); reviewed by R. Bultmann, "Gnosis": *Journal of Theol. Studies,* N. S. iii (1952), pp. 10–26.

Feine, P.   *Der Apostel Paulus. Das Ringen um das geschichtliche Verständnis des Paulus* (Gütersloh, 1927).

Festugière, A. J.   *L'idéal religieux des Grecs et l'évangile* (Paris, 1932).

Geffcken, J.   *Religiöse Strömungen im 1. Jahrh. n. Chr.* (Gütersloh, 1927).

Gressmann, H.   *Die orientalischen Religionen im hellenistisch-römischen Zeitalter* (Berlin, 1930).

Heigl, B.   "Antike Mysterienreligionen und Urchristentum" in *Biblische Zeitfragen,* xiii, pp. 11–12 (Münster i. W., 1932).

Hertling, L. v.   "Zur Mystik des hl. Paulus" in *Zeitschrift für Aszese und Mystik,* iii (1928), pp. 146–51.

Hopfner, Th.   "Die orientalisch-hellenistischen Mysterien" in Pauly-Wissowa, *Realenzyklopädie der klass. Altertumswissenschaft,* xvi (1935), 1315–1350.

Huby, J.   *Mystiques paulinienne et johannique* (Paris, 1946).

Jonas, H.   *Gnosis und spätantiker Geist,* pt. 1: *Die mythologische Gnosis* (Göttingen, 1934); pt. 2,1: *Von der Mythologie zur mystischen Philosophie* (ibid., 1954).

Juncker, A.   *Die Ethik des Apostels Paulus,* i (Halle, 1904), ii (1919).

Kittel, G.   *Die Religionsgeschichte und das Urchristentum* (Gütersloh, 1932).

Kroll, J.   *Die Lehren des Hermes Trismegistos* (Münster i. W., 1914).

Lietzmann, H.   "Erklärung von Röm." (²1919), "1 u. 2 Kor." (⁴1949; mit Ergänzungen von W. G. Kümmel), "Gal." (²1923), in his *Handbuch zum N. T.*

Lohmeyer, E.   "Σὺν Χριστῷ" in *Festgabe für Deissmann* (Tübingen, 1927), pp. 218–57.

Meinertz, M.   *Theologie des N.T.,* 2 vols. (Bonn, 1950).

Michaelis, W.   *Der Brief des Paulus an die Philipper* (Leipzig, 1935).

Mittring, K.   *Heilswirklichkeit bei Paulus. Ein Beitrag zum Verständnis der unio cum Christo in den paulinischen Briefen* (Gütersloh, 1929).

Mocsy, E.   "De unione mystica cum Christo" in *Verbum Domini,* xxv (1947), pp. 270–9, 328–39.

Mundle, W.   *Das religiöse Leben des Apostels Paulus* (Leipzig, 1923).
Der Glaubensbegriff des Paulus (Leipzig, 1932).

Nilsson, M. P.   *Geschichte der griechischen Religion,* ii (Munich, 1950).

Oepke, A.   *Der Galaterbrief* (Leipzig, 1937).

Percy, E.   *Der Leib Christi in den paulinischen Homologumena und Antilegomena* (Lund, 1942).

Posselt, E.   Besprechung von Deissner, "Paulus und die Mystik" ([1]1918), in *Philologische Wochenschrift,* xxxviii (1918), pp. 865–893.

Prat, F.   *The Theology of St. Paul,* trans. J. L. Stoddard, 5th impression (London, 1945).

Preisendanz, K.   *Papyri graecae magicae. Die griechischen Zauberpapyri,* edited and translated, i (Leipzig, 1928), ii (1931).

Randenborgh, G. van   "Vergottung und Erlösung. Ein religionsgeschichtlicher Vergleich zwischen der hermetischen Gnosis und den Paulusbriefen" in *Vom Dienst an Theologie und Kirche, Festgabe für A. Schlatter* (Berlin, 1937), pp. 97–115.

Reitzenstein, R.   *Poimandres* (Leipzig, 1904).
Die hellenistischen Mysterienreligionen nach ihren Grundgedanken und Wirkungen (Leipzig, [3]1927).

Reitzenstein, R. and Schaeder, H.   *Studien zum antiken Synkretismus. Aus Iran und Griechenland* (Studien der Bibliothek Warburg 7) (Leipzig, 1926).

Schauf, W.   *Sarx. Der Begriff Fleisch beim Apostel Paulus* (Münster i. W., 1924).

Schlier, H.   *Der Brief an die Galater* (Göttingen, 1949).

Schmidt, T.   *Der Leib Christi. Eine Untersuchung zum urchristlichen Gemeindegedanken* (Leipzig, 1919).

Schmitz, O.   *Das Lebensgefühl des Paulus* (Munich, 1922). *Die Christusgemeinschaft des Paulus im Lichte seines Genitivsgebrauchs* (Gütersloh, 1924).

Schnackenburg, R.   *Das Heilsgeschehen bei der Taufe nach dem Apostel Paulus* (Munich, 1950).

Schneider, J.   *Die Passionsmystik des Paulus. Ihr Wesen, ihr Hintergrund und ihre Nachwirkungen* (Leipzig, 1929). "Eschatologie und Mystik im N.T." in *Zeitschrift für Theologie und Kirche,* xiii (1932), pp. 111–29.

Schweitzer, A.   *Mysticism of Paul the Apostle* (London, 1953).

Sommerlath, E.   *Der Ursprung des neuen Lebens nach Paulus* (Leipzig, ²1927).

Weber, H. E.   "Die Formel 'in Christo' und die paulinische Christusmystik" in *Neue kirchliche Zeitschrift* xxxi (1920), pp. 213–60. *"Eschatologie" und "Mystik" im N.T. Ein Versuch zum Verständnis des Glaubens* (Gütersloh, 1930).

Weber, W.   *Christusmystik. Eine religionspsychologische Darstellung der paulinischen Christusfrömmigkeit* (Leipzig, 1924).

Weijers, M.-R.   "In Christo Jesu" in *Revue Thomiste,* xlvii (1947), pp. 499–516.

Weiss, J.   *Das Urchristentum* (Göttingen, 1917).

Wendland, H. D.   "Das Wirken des Heiligen Geistes in den Gläubigen nach Paulus" in *Theologische Literaturzeitung,* lxxvii (1952), pp. 457–70.

Wiencke, G.   *Paulus über Jesu Tod. Die Deutung des Todes Jesu bei Paulus und ihre Herkunft* (Gütersloh, 1939).

Windisch, H.   *Der 2. Korintherbrief* (Göttingen, 1924). *Paulus und Christus. Ein biblisch-religionsgeschichtlicher Vergleich* (Leipzig, 1934).

Wissmann, E.   *Das Verhältnis von Πίστις und Christusfrömmigkeit bei Paulus* (Göttingen, 1926).

Index of Passages

1. New Testament

Only the more important texts are listed

2. Other Sources

Index of Persons

Index of Subjects